Return to the Scene of the Crime

Return to the Scene of the Crime
The Returnee Detective and Postcolonial Crime Fiction

Kamil Naicker

UNIVERSITY OF KWAZULU-NATAL PRESS

Published in 2021 by University of KwaZulu-Natal Press
Private Bag X01
Scottsville, 3209
Pietermaritzburg
South Africa
Email: books@ukzn.ac.za
Website: www.ukznpress.co.za

© 2021 Kamil Naicker

All rights reserved. No part of this publication may be reproduced or transmitted in any form or by any means, electronic or mechanical, including photocopying, recording, or any information storage and retrieval system, without prior permission in writing from University of KwaZulu-Natal Press.

ISBN: 978 1 86914 480 7
e-ISBN: 978 1 86914 481 4

Managing editor: Sally Hines
Editor: Alison Lockhart
Layout: Patricia Comrie
Indexer: Christopher Merrett
Cover design: Marise Bauer, MDesign
Cover photograph: George Prentzas, Unsplash

NATIONAL INSTITUTE FOR THE HUMANITIES AND SOCIAL SCIENCES

The financial assistance of the National Institute of Humanities and Social Sciences (NIHSS) towards this publication is hereby acknowledged. Opinions expressed and conclusions arrived at are those of the author and are not necessarily to be attributed to the NIHSS.

Printed and bound in South Africa by Creda Communications, Cape Town

For my grandmothers,
Joan Rabkin and Panjerathnam Naicker

Galip had once told Rüya that the only detective book he'd ever want to read would be one in which not even the author knew the murderer's identity. Instead of decorating the story with clues and red herrings, the author would be forced to come to grips with his characters and his subject, and his characters would have a chance to become people in a book instead of just figments of their author's imagination.
— Orhan Pamuk, *The Black Book*

The splinter in one's eye is the best magnifying glass.
— Theodor Adorno, *Minima Moralia*

Contents

Acknowledgements	xi
Introduction	1
1 A Case of Arrested Development: Kazuo Ishiguro's *When We Were Orphans*	14
2 Investigating the Pathologist: Michael Ondaatje's *Anil's Ghost*	40
3 Death of an Idea: Francisco Goldman's *The Long Night of White Chickens*	68
4 A Foreign Country: Gillian Slovo's *Red Dust*	98
5 Hijacked Narrative: Nuruddin Farah's *Crossbones*	129
Conclusion	152
Select Bibliography	173
Index	181

Acknowledgements

My thanks go to the National Institute for the Humanities and Social Sciences for their generous support over the years. Thank you also to my supervisors, Professor Meg Samuelson and Professor Sandra Young and to my PhD examiners, Professor Kerry Bystrom, Professor Annie Gagiano and Professor Upamanyu Pablo Mukherjee, for all their encouragement and suggestions. Further thanks to my editor Alison Lockhart, to Katherine, Chantelle and Alexandre D., and to my family.

Introduction

This book investigates the ways in which the crime novel genre has been taken up and adapted in order to depict and grapple with ideas of justice in selected postcolonial contexts. It approaches this investigation through the figure of the 'returnee detective' – an investigator who has returned to their country of origin from abroad and is faced with decoding violence – and determines how this recurring figure is used to mediate readers' understanding of civil conflict in the postcolonial world.

Crime fiction has long had the reputation of being a guilty pleasure genre. In 'The Guilty Vicarage: Notes on Detective Stories, by an Addict', first published in 1948, W.H. Auden writes:

> For me, as for many others, the reading of detective stories is an addiction like tobacco or alcohol. The symptoms of this are: Firstly, the intensity of the craving - if I have any work to do, I must be careful not to get hold of a detective story for, once I begin one, I cannot work or sleep till I have finished it. Secondly, its specificity - the story must conform to certain formulas (I find it very difficult, for example, to read one that is not set in rural England). And, thirdly, its immediacy. I forget the story as soon as I have finished it, and have no wish to read it again. If, as sometimes happens, I start reading one and find after a few pages that I have read it before, I cannot go on (2016).

The canon, as depicted here, is a distraction: light, forgettable and, paradoxically, relaxing. This somewhat frivolous reputation endures to this day. Browse any airport bookshop and you will likely find an abundance of murder stories arrayed for the pleasure of those taking a holiday or a long-haul flight. The subject matter may be grim, but something about the genre holds out the promise of comfort and relaxation.

Gill Plain says: 'Crime fiction in general, and detective fiction in particular, is about confronting and taming the monstrous. It is a literature of containment, a narrative that "makes safe"' (2001: 3). Although the traditional crime novel may be rife with narrative violence, the form promises 'containment' of the horrors it depicts. Even in cases where the literary criminal evades the reach of the law, they are seldom permitted to slip the bonds of narrative authority. The generic formula is predicated on an ethos of isolation and naming: the perpetrator is identified amid a group of other characters and clearly marked as the guilty party. This act of separation 'makes safe', as Plain would have it, by suggesting evil as something anomalous, which may be extracted and labelled as beyond the bounds of social acceptability.

Auden describes the central dynamic of the mystery story as 'the ethical and eristic conflict between good and evil' (2016). The doubleness of the struggle Auden describes is a staple of early crime fiction, but even the more anarchic later forms tend to maintain the 'eristic' triumph implicit in identifying a criminal. This may be true even in cases where the meting out of ethical punishment proves beyond the investigator's power. Where the justice system is portrayed as being too flawed or inadequate to deal with aberrant individuals, the texts still hew to the principles of the whodunit by naming their perpetrators, setting them apart.

Many of these later forms, particularly those that employ the thriller aesthetic, tend to evoke suspense through the depiction of a potentially deadly investigation and the uncertainty of justice, rather than solely holding out the promise of a solution to the initial crime. The perpetrators are ultimately 'pinned down' by the narrative and made guilty in the eyes of readers, even if they evade arrest and even if the primary interest lies in the detective's response to their crime. While the criminal's eventual fate may be less than morally satisfying, the 'monstrous' is nonetheless tamed by the novel's formal qualities, which insist on revelation and unmasking. Thus, contemporary crime novels often deliver wish fulfilment through the provision of narrative cohesion and certainty, although the ethical battle at the heart of the novel may not always be resolved in a similarly conclusive manner.

The very familiarity of crime genre conventions means that crime fiction formulae are ripe for subversion. In his discussion of genre, Tzvetan Todorov says: 'For there to be a transgression, the norm must be apparent . . . Genres are precisely those relay-points by which the work assumes a relation with the universe of literature' (1975: 8). In order to portray something untamable, inexplicable or unprovable, a writer may present a mystery in the time-honoured way, but then decline to meet readers' expectations of resolution and explanation, emphasising the limitations of the form. As Eyal Segal states:

> Familiarity with a generic plot convention may influence the reader's expectations with regard to future story developments as much as explicit proleptic commentary by the narrator, whereas the breaking of such a convention may produce a surprise as powerful as that stemming from the abrupt revelation of a gap in the mimetic sequence of previously narrated events (2010: 161).

By evoking and then transgressing from the well-known norms of the crime genre – a genre commonly thought of as formulaic and simplistic – a writer may call attention to the challenging complexity of the subject matter they present. The power of these representations is aided by the use of contrast, which evokes surprise by throwing any deviations into stark relief. In this book, I explore the use of such generic surprise as a distinct form of postcolonial world-making. Instead of following the generic path to form a narrative of 'containment', the novels I discuss here breach or explode the form in order to render a morally complicated or chaotic world.

The history of the crime genre renders it uniquely suited to this kind of political intervention. Auden's formulation of 'the ethical and eristic conflict between good and evil' (2016) suggests a universal theme, but this apparently timeless struggle is inevitably woven through with the cultural mores and prejudices of its particular era. Early examples of crime fiction often seamlessly and explicitly align good and evil with orientalist binaries and the containment of crime with exclusionary nationalist imperatives.

Emerging during the period of the British Empire, English mystery stories from the early twentieth century frequently use the binary of good versus evil as an essentialist catch-all for citizen/foreigner, West/East and white/black oppositions. For example, Agatha Christie's *The Lost Mine* (2013) is set in a London opium den and the British villain at the heart of the story has been corrupted by drug-dealing Chinese immigrants, brought low by his contact with the other. Although the expression of these themes has become somewhat more subtle with the maturation of the crime genre, formulations of good and evil in crime fiction are inevitably infused with contemporary ideas of legitimacy, deviance and social threat. Of the thriller form, for example, Philip Simpson argues:

> The thriller plot typically proceeds in linear fashion, from one danger to the next, until the ultimate defining confrontation between good and evil. However, the conflict usually addresses at some subliminal level a contemporary anxiety (or more than one) facing the thriller's audience: the fear of a foreign enemy, the fear of inner-city crime, the fear of the disenfranchised drifter and so forth (2010: 188).

In the course of this book I demonstrate that, in addition to informing the crime genre, the idea of the binary conflict 'between good and evil' (Auden 2016) underlies both colonial ideologies and essentialist resistances to those ideologies – those which, in Kwame Anthony Appiah's words, preserve the 'imaginary identities' assigned by colonial discourse (1991: 150). Therefore, a genre underpinned by insider/outsider oppositions, and traditionally ending in denunciation and isolation, can be effectively reworked to show the complexity and frustrations of societies in which notions of 'self' and 'other' are no longer so clearly delineated. Abdul R. JanMohamed describes colonial ideology as 'a Manichean allegory of white and black, good and evil, salvation and damnation, civilization and savagery, superiority and inferiority, intelligence and emotion, self and other, subject and object' (1983: 4). By breaking down these oppositions through the resistance of generic fulfilment, authors are able to render the complexity of a world that defies these categories.

This breakdown of binaries is particularly evident in the context of postcolonial civil conflict. The end of colonialism means there is no longer a clear 'Manichean' distinction between self and other. Moreover, the intimacy of civil war means that perpetrators are neither anomalies nor outsiders: they may know their victims well and their behaviour is part of a society-wide collapse, rather than a personal or rogue aberration. There is no hope here of extracting criminality and returning to the status quo – in part because the very social fabric has been ruptured and in part because civil atrocities may involve more intimate betrayals than those perpetrated in the context of foreign invasion.

In many cases, the arbiters of the law may themselves be engaged in brutality. Nancy Scheper-Hughes asserts that when violence is endorsed by the state, murder becomes a 'cruel but usual' (2010: 153) expectation for targeted groups. Because one form of violence is centralised and legitimised, social mores are forced into mutation, changing what is meant by appropriate, moral or justified behaviour. In this atmosphere of collaboration and ambivalence, innocence and guilt may become fruitless designations. South African crime writer Margie Orford describes her original turn to the genre as 'a way to contain my own fear and to make sense of the obliterating chaos of violence' (2013: 220). However, following the atrocity of the Marikana massacre of 2012, during which South African police opened fire on protesting mineworkers, Orford notes a change in her imperative to write. Of the massacre, she poses the rhetorical question, 'How does one fit a crime, an ethical failure of that magnitude, into a fictional work?' (221). The novels I explore here take on similar questions, exploding the very notion of crime by rewriting the genre in a fractured or overloaded form, eschewing ideas of 'fit' and closure in order to depict a world in which in which violence cannot be corralled or controlled within a binary of law and deviance, and where there is no expectation of closure or consolation.

In this book, I explore five different portrayals of postcolonial violence. In each, I argue, the 'world-making' project of the novel eclipses the original mystery that the narrative presents. The five novels I explore are *When We Were Orphans* by Kazuo Ishiguro, *Anil's Ghost* by Michael Ondaatje (both first published in 2000), *The Long Night of White Chickens* by Francisco Goldman (first published in 1992), *Red Dust* by Gillian Slovo (originally published in 2000) and *Crossbones* by Nuruddin Farah (originally published in 2011). The novels are set in China, Sri Lanka, Guatemala, South Africa and Somalia, respectively. Each is an English-language novel set in a postcolonial nation during a period of civil war or violent transition, and each features a protagonist who has returned from abroad in order to assume the role of detective. A 'detective' is broadly defined here as a moral observer who is intent upon clearing up a mystery, although some of the returnees operate in their professional capacity as lawyers, journalists or forensic pathologists. Each text has a different geographical and temporal setting, but engages with a similar historical moment – the eruption of civil violence in the years following decolonisation.

What unites each of the countries portrayed in these novels is the way in which guilt and innocence (and their attendant associations of self and other) have been forced into realignment by the end of colonial rule and the rise of civil conflict. In *The Foreign in International Crime Fiction: Transcultural Representations*, Jean Anderson, Carolina Miranda and Barbara Pezzotti state:

> The exotic and the foreign are the quintessence of mystery. The 'Other' – and the 'Unknown' – arouse feelings of curiosity and fear. They demand to be encountered, investigated, decoded and, possibly, rejected. It comes as no surprise then, that foreign characters and foreign settings have had a privileged space in crime fiction since its origins (2012: 13).

In the context of civil war, these oppositions are broken down and 'crime' becomes more insidious and intimate than the traditional mystery motif allows. The returnee detective furthers the breakdown of conventional categories by performing the role of hybrid mediator within the text. The returnee figure is at once strange and familiar, lacking both the strong sense of identity that is necessary in order to maintain the mystery of the 'other' and the objectivity to comfortably apportion blame to either side. Postcolonial crime fiction set in the context of civil conflict therefore emerges as a distinct category requiring a distinct critical approach.

In this book I explore the kinds of pressures the sociopolitical settings of these novels exert on the formal qualities of the texts and the ways in which the rendering of the complex dynamics of postcolonial civil war impacts on characterisation, resolution and narrative cohesion.

Michael Holquist's article 'Whodunit and Other Questions: Metaphysical Detective Stories in Post-War Fiction' (1971) is an important point of departure here. He defines the metaphysical detective story as one that subverts crime fiction conventions in order to provoke existential and cognitive disquiet through defamiliarisation. However, I argue that these postcolonial crime stories present a challenge that is more politically invested than that of the stories he describes. Of metaphysical detective stories, Holquist argues:

> Instead of reassuring, they disturb. They are not an escape, but an attack ... That is the lesson of the metaphysical detective story in our own time. It sees the potential for *real* violence – violence to our flabby habits of perception – in the *phoney* violence of the detective story (1971: 155-6).

The novels discussed in this book certainly depart from the idea of 'reassurance' and the tidily solved crime. A background of civil unrest lends an insidious and intimate cast to the question of culpability, as does the figure of the returnee detective, who in addition to seeking to solve the crime must also face survivor's guilt and his/her past incarnations as villain, victim, collaborator and witness. However, although the narratives are often open-ended, the 'metaphysical detective' label does not adequately describe them. The novels' 'jumbled' quality reflects the limited scope for closure in the contexts they are depicting: thus, the innovations in form can be seen as providing a commentary on the difficulties of reconciliation after civil war and of identifying a single villain in a hopelessly entangled postcolonial world. By contrast, Holquist's description of the metaphysical detective story is of a philosophical puzzle. Even when the puzzle becomes existential, it is seldom sociopolitical: the violence is 'phoney', part of an exercise in defamiliarisation, rather than a deep engagement with the idea of crime and its implications.

Patricia Merivale and Susan Elizabeth Sweeney expand on Holquist's formulation in their book *Detecting Texts: The Metaphysical Detective Story from Poe to Postmodernism*. Although their book engages with more recent scholarship, it maintains the terms of Holquist's study by discussing stories that 'self-consciously question the very notion of reality' (1999: 4) and not those whose jumbled form reflects the confusion and turmoil of conditions of social breakdown and the complexity of transnational identity.

This book takes up some of Holquist's theories on structure, particularly his contention that the open-ended form of the metaphysical detective story functions to 'disturb' the reader. The same can be said of the postcolonial genre, but this disturbance often has what Edward Said's *Reflections on Exile* might term 'worldlier' implications (2013). At times, the texts' lack of closure does speak to a kind of hopelessness, but in each case it is a feeling that is closely tied to historical context and not existential ennui. My argument in this book makes use of Holquist's theories on structural breakdown, as well as periodically referring to Merivale and Sweeney, but I suggest a political dimension to what has largely been a philosophical contention.

Another point to consider is what the crime genre offers to writers who choose to depict postcolonial violence and what kind of ideologies emerge from the subversion of the genre's conventions. In discussing the historical relationship between crime fiction norms and political - and particularly, colonial - ideology, I refer to Upamanyu Pablo Mukherjee's book, *Crime and Empire: The Colony in Nineteenth-Century Fictions of Crime* (2003). Mukherjee's work focuses on early crime fiction and how many of its conventions grew out of the beliefs and anxieties attending the growth of the British Empire. It therefore provides invaluable commentary on the underlying political ideologies of many of the generic formulae from which the novels under discussion here depart. Mukherjee's discussion of the prevalence of criminal terms ('order, deviance and punishment' [2003: 1]) in rhetorical justifications of international intervention is also pertinent to my discussion of how my chosen texts abandon or complicate these ideas of social aberrance. Stephen Knight's *Form and Ideology in Crime Fiction* (1980) stresses the relationship between belief systems and the formal qualities of the crime genre and is therefore also useful in my discussion.

The next strand of the research focuses on the texts' portrayal of return. The returnee detective figures operate both as contextual mediators for the reader (literary devices) and as players within the worlds of the novels. They provide a way of framing (representing, but also necessarily delimiting) postcolonial conflict for foreign readers. It is vital here to examine representation - how the returnees are depicted in comparison to their local counterparts and the way in which they are used to translate and filter the local context. An important question is whether the use of an intermediary figure makes the settings more relatable to foreign readers, or whether it creates distance between the protagonist and the other characters in the texts. A key source in this regard is Judith Butler's *Frames of War: When Is Life Grievable?* (2010). The focus here is on objective and subjective depictions of pain, and the difference between violence that evokes empathy and the sensationalisation of violence for scopic enjoyment. Are some deaths depicted as being more 'grievable' than others? How does 'personhood' come to be attributed to or withheld from certain characters in the texts?

My discussion of the characterisation of the returnee detectives (their role within the worlds of the novels) draws on a range of theory. I refer to Said's *Reflections on Exile* and his formulation of 'contrapuntal thinking' (2013) as an antidote to the rigid binary opposition of home and away. As a comparison to this formulation, I discuss Theodor Adorno's idea of morality becoming detached from sectarian and nationalistic thought ('not being at home in one's own home' [2005: 112]). This discussion is instrumental in determining what the symbolically homeless detective figures bring to the investigations they undertake and how they balance universal and local conceptions of truth and morality. I further explore the figure in the light of Marianne Hirsch and Nancy K. Miller's assertion that 'to some extent, the desire for return always arises from a need to redress an injustice, one often inflicted upon an entire group of people caused by displacement or dispossession, the loss of home or of family autonomy, the conditions of expulsion, colonization and migration' (2011: 7). In doing so, I examine the relationship between redress and return in the personal and professional journeys the detectives undertake.

Chapter outline

Each of the five chapters discusses a different novel and each has a unique focus, rather than providing variations on a single theme. The intention is to note the commonalities between the countries portrayed (and correspondingly, the texts as a whole) without flattening the unique pressures that each postcolonial context exerts on the generic conventions of crime fiction. As Ania Loomba points out: 'Because they produced comparable (and sometimes uncannily similar) relations of inequity and domination the world over, it is sometimes overlooked that colonial methods and images varied hugely over time and place' (2015: 36). To avoid generalisation, I dedicate a chapter to each novel and discussion of its sociopolitical setting, while devoting the conclusion to a discussion of the novels' commonalities and diversions.

In some cases the focus of an individual chapter is directed by the subgenre of crime fiction upon which each author has decided to build. For example, Ishiguro's *When We Were Orphans* subverts the formula of the Golden Age mystery,[1] thereby facilitating a discussion of nostalgia, restoration and empire. Contrastingly, Ondaatje's *Anil's Ghost* imitates

---

1. I define 'Golden Age' novels primarily as those written in interwar England, which present the detective as successfully exerting rationality against the threat of chaos and which offer the reader closure by providing watertight solutions to the mysteries they present. However, I follow Julian Symons in including Arthur Conan Doyle's Sherlock Holmes stories among them, even though the term is more commonly applied to texts from the 1920s and 1930s. Where a distinction is required between the pre-First World War Sherlock Holmes stories and interwar fiction, I refer to the early Golden Age and the late Golden Age, respectively.

the thriller genre in its depiction of extreme violence and is therefore more productively read in terms of the detective figure's move from the forensic to the affective gaze. At other times, the focus is directed by historical context – for example, the subject of South Africa's Truth and Reconciliation Commission (TRC) exerts unique pressures on the crime fiction genre, as the proceedings intended to separate culpability from retribution. In novels such as Slovo's *Red Dust*, the result is an unstable and ambivalent narrative arc that does not tend towards closure.

In discussing the novels' departure from historic forms of crime fiction, I focus strongly on generic expectation. In his discussion of genre theory, Daniel Chandler contends:

> Assigning a text to a genre sets up initial expectations. Some of these may be challenged within individual texts (e.g. a detective film in which the murderer is revealed at the outset). Competent readers of a genre are not generally confused when some of their initial expectations are not met – the framework of the genre can be seen as offering 'default' expectations which act as a starting point for interpretation rather than a straitjacket. However, challenging too many conventional expectations for the genre could threaten the integrity of the text. Familiarity with a genre enables readers to generate feasible predictions about events in a narrative. Drawing on their knowledge of other texts within the same genre helps readers to sort salient from nonsalient narrative information in an individual text (1997: 8).

For the most part, I evaluate these novels in terms of their relationship to the 'default expectations' Chandler describes. In other words, I refer to the genre in terms of norms and assumptions, rather than to the canon in all its multiplicity, except when the primary texts evoke a specific comparison. For example, Ishiguro's *When We Were Orphans* explicitly conjures up images of Sherlock Holmes, who is idolised by its protagonist. Rather than employing an in-depth comparison between specific, conventional examples and their postcolonial counterparts, I focus on the formal qualities of the postcolonial novels and the way in which they both rely on and depart from the 'reputational' norm. The formal qualities of the crime novel – for example, suspense, characterisation and narrative closure – have strong ideological implications and can constitute the affirmation of a particular world view. Thus, an author's departure from these norms may not simply 'threaten the integrity of the text', but also represent a resistance to the ideology these qualities affirm.

The first chapter uses Ishiguro's novel to set the terms of the analysis and outline its psychological investments. Ishiguro's novel differs from the other novels in several ways: for one thing, the other novels have more contemporary settings, whereas *When We Were Orphans* is primarily set in the period between the two world wars. For another, *When We Were Orphans* engages with the neocolonial exploitation of China and the resultant war between China and Japan, rather than depicting civil violence. However, the novel engages with many of the issues raised by civil war scenarios by depicting violence within the International Settlement in Shanghai and the outbreak of an East/East conflict during the last years of the British Empire, meaning that the lines of identity become similarly blurred.

I have chosen *When We Were Orphans* because it provides the most salient and self-conscious subversion of the mystery format. Ishiguro's novel plays with the form of the Golden Age novel and, by changing its structure, he showcases the many limitations of the world view it presents (Machinal 2009: 87). Nostalgia and restoration are key themes in this chapter and I explore the ways in which the increasingly disturbed protagonist adopts the expectations of the Golden Age genre in the course of his quest for emotional and temporal restitution.

While Chapter 1 focuses on innovations in form, the second chapter pays closer attention to style and characterisation. The narrative arc in *Anil's Ghost* follows the title character's journey through re-citizenship, as she locates herself as part of Sri Lanka, rather than as an impartial bystander. The protagonist undergoes an evolution during the novel, which leads up to a public denunciation of the Sri Lankan government. This chapter investigates the influences that inform Anil's transformation and Ondaatje's decision to locate it outside of a sociopolitical framework. This will be particularly important in introducing the question of how the returnees' complex identities are depicted as influencing their ethical and deductive processes.

Anil's Ghost has been the object of much critical contention. R. Wijesinha decried it as an 'orientalist' (2003) text that exploits the Sri Lankan Civil War for the sake of sensationalism. Although my focus is led by Anil's role as returnee detective, I engage with these debates as they relate to the character's re-citizenship. I discuss whether the novel's refusal to 'citizen' Anil through ethnic or linguistic initiations represents a humanist resistance to the divisive sectarian discourses that have riven the country apart, or whether it becomes an exotic oversimplification in the service of a suspenseful narrative. I further evaluate Anil's journey in relation to the forensic thriller, which privileges the scientific gaze and a linear progression towards truth, and in which 'the forensic pathologist engaged in reconstructing the victim's suffering and identity must (for the narrative to move towards closure) bring the abject back within the symbolic order' (Horsley and Horsley 2006: 20).

Chapter 3 explores the idea of the crime story as a social or national allegory and discusses whether this extends the genre or limits it in a different way. Like the other writers considered in this book, Goldman shows the difficulty of assigning blame in the context of civil conflict – in this case, the Guatemalan Civil War, which is fuelled and abetted by the neocolonial interventions of the United States. Guatemala is represented by the figure of Flor de Mayo, whose murder catalyses the narrative. Although the novel initially appears to be building towards the identification of Flor's murderer, it ultimately reneges on this promise. This chapter raises questions about agency and gender when the female body is used as metaphor for conquest and colonialism, particularly in a context where femicide and gendered violence has been rife. It builds on the questions in Chapter 2, by asking what happens when transnational identity is made analogous to an unsolvable investigation.

Slovo's *Red Dust* is set during the TRC hearings in South Africa and focuses on the complexities and trauma that apartheid has left in its wake. In a 2011 interview with the *Sydney Morning Herald*, Slovo, echoing Plain and Orford, references the sense of security provided by the crime genre. She states:

> I think there was something about the constraint of plot [in crime novels] that made me feel safe as a novelist . . . But the safety of crime, which is what drove me to it, also drove me away from it. I wanted to be more daring. I wanted to explore other things, namely feelings (Christopher 2011).

In Chapter 4, I examine *Red Dust*, in which Slovo moves beyond generic expectation to depict a more complex emotional and political landscape.

I argue that Slovo alters the form in order to explore the promises held out by different forms of justice. I examine how the novel's protagonist, who works as a prosecutor in New York, is used to suggest the disparities between the restorative and retributive approach, and the novel's juxtaposition of social spectacle and intimate trauma. The chapter also explores how the depiction of the state-sanctioned violence of apartheid pressurises a generic form that is traditionally predicated on the idea of crime as an aberration. Because Slovo's novel juxtaposes South Africa and New York, the chapter includes a discussion of the implications of Slovo's rendering of South Africa in relation to its protagonist's sending country, the United States.

The fifth novel under discussion is Farah's *Crossbones*, which operates both as a stand-alone novel and as the conclusion to the author's Past Imperfect trilogy. The novel is set in 2006, in the midst of the civil war that began after the 1991 collapse of the national government in Somalia, and focuses on Al-Shabaab activity and piracy in the country. The pirates in the text refer to themselves as 'privateers' and 'coastguards', and much of the narrative is devoted to exploring why the label of 'piracy' has been applied and whether piracy constitutes criminal activity in a country wracked by years of dictatorship and civil war. In this chapter, I discuss Farah's decision to render post-collapse Somalia through a narrative that withholds answers, rather than establishing a firm narrative line, exploring the idea of this technique as a resistance to the stereotyping discourses that have been generated in relation to the region.

In the concluding chapter I compare the ways in which each author embarks on portraying their respective protagonists' journeys of return and also examine the different ways in which the writers render their particular postcolonial contexts and the varying effectiveness with which they use and subvert the conventions of crime fiction in order to project these worlds.

1

A Case of Arrested Development
Kazuo Ishiguro's *When We Were Orphans*

First published in 2000, Kazuo Ishiguro's *When We Were Orphans* spans 28 years and moves between London and Shanghai. Although the protagonist is a detective by profession, his mission is an unusually personal one: he wishes to solve the case of his parents, who disappeared during his childhood in China. As he searches for the truth, Christopher Banks realises that what he has perceived as a personal tragedy is, in fact, inextricably entangled with the legacy of British colonialism. In the course of his investigation, he is not only witness to the outbreak of the Second Sino-Japanese War (1937-1945), but is also forced to confront the atrocities of the opium trade and his own family's role in it.

At first glance, *When We Were Orphans* reads as a heavily stylised tribute to the Golden Age of early twentieth-century detective stories. It is only gradually that the book's global and political themes become apparent and the formulaic narrative arc is broken down. There is not, at this point, a comprehensive term to describe this kind of deliberate subversion of the mystery format. The closest is perhaps Michael Holquist's formulation of the 'metaphysical detective story':

> The metaphysical detective story does not have the narcotizing effect of its progenitor; instead of familiarity, it gives strangeness, a strangeness which more often than not is the result of jumbling the well-known patterns of classical detective stories. Instead of reassuring, they disturb. They are not an escape, but an attack . . .
>
> That is the lesson of the metaphysical detective story in our own time. It sees the potential for *real* violence – violence to our flabby habits of perception – in the *phoney* violence of the detective story (1971: 153-6).

When We Were Orphans subverts the idea of the detective story as an 'escape' by disrupting or 'jumbling' the expected progress of the narrative. However, Ishiguro's structural innovations are not simply in the service of defamiliarisation. Rather, by engaging with the genre and adapting its traditional formula, Ishiguro showcases the many limitations of the world view it presents. *When We Were Orphans* reveals much of what the traditional form suppresses: ambiguity, marginalised peoples and the difficulty of assigning guilt and innocence in an interconnected, postcolonial world (Machinal 2009: 87). The text is therefore better interpreted in the light of what Edward Said calls 'worldliness': 'a knowing and unafraid attitude towards exploring the world we live in' (Said 2013). Holquist's definition suggests a highly intellectual, abstract game, but the violence depicted in novels like *When We Were Orphans* is given gravitas by its engagement with world history. As a result, the challenge it offers is not merely aesthetic, but deeply political as well.

Although Ishiguro's novel demolishes Golden Age conventions (and it is a thorough demolition: he breaks almost every imperative listed in S.S. van Dine's famous 'Twenty Rules for Writing Detective Stories'), it nonetheless demonstrates the emotional appeal of the genre. The protagonist initially finds refuge and solace within its bifurcated, parochial world view. Through his eyes, we begin to understand the unlikely idea of the murder mystery as a vehicle for comfort and escapism. In her article 'Who Killed the Golden Age of Crime?' P.D. James explains this apparently contradictory appeal:

> The detective stories of the interwar years were paradoxical. They might deal with violent death, sometimes in its most horrible manifestation, but essentially they were and remain novels of escape . . . Reading these novels today they produce the same comfort as they did when they were written. We enter a world of recognised morality, where evil is sanitised and we can settle down in a familiar English world where all problems will be solved and peace and normality restored in that imaginary postlapsarian Eden (2013: 1).

Ishiguro initially places the reader in the 'familiar English world' to which James refers, but gradually widens the lens to expose this 'Eden' as facile and altogether unsustainable. The protagonist's belief in the rules of genre stem from a reluctance to admit that the world's evil cannot so easily be uprooted or 'sanitised' and that the trappings of his profession do nothing to guarantee his own innocence.

Genre and delusion

Hélène Machinal argues: 'Economically and effectively, Ishiguro establishes this recognizable terrain [of the Golden Age canon] by setting up the generic expectation that our rational and dispassionate detective will solve whatever mystery is laid before him' (2009: 80). Indeed, Ishiguro evokes Sherlock Holmes on the first page, when his protagonist, Christopher Banks, says: 'I decided my future lay in the capital and took up a small flat at Number 14b Bedford Gardens in Kensington' (2000: 1). His description of the apartment, as Machinal notes, evokes Holmes's lodgings on Baker Street. The 'generic expectation' established here is soon undermined, however, as it becomes clear that Christopher is projecting the conventions of the Golden Age genre onto his own, altogether more complex life. We are first made aware of this through a derisive remark made by one of Christopher's schoolmates, who sneers: 'But surely he's rather too short to be a Sherlock' (8). This lets us know that Christopher's role is self-consciously mimetic – that the imitation of Holmes is his own undertaking, rather than one Ishiguro has imposed from outside the world of the book. When Christopher describes his life in Holmesian terms, he is not speaking from within the genre, but as a reader himself.

Even though the novel is set in the period between the two world wars (contemporaneous with the late Golden Age), we are made aware early on that Christopher is somehow out of step with his society. Counterpoints to his perspective are embedded in the apparently casual remarks of his peers and his interactions with others often hint that the world is not quite as he sees it. In Chapter 1, an acquaintance offhandedly refers to him as having been 'an odd bird' (Ishiguro 2000: 3) at school, a charge Christopher denies so assiduously that we can only suspect that he protests too much. He gives the reader several examples of his 'bold spirit' and social achievements at boarding school, but his argument is unconvincing, the more so because he rounds off the litany by saying 'I do not wish to imply that this remark of his, about my being "an odd bird", preoccupied me for more than a few moments' (9).

Soon afterwards, an older man Christopher meets at a society party offers another counterpoint to his perspective, albeit in a more tactful way, when he questions Christopher's hopes of becoming a detective:

> 'Not interested in museums, by any chance? Chap over there, known him for years. Museums. Skulls, relics, that kind of thing. Not interested? Didn't think so.' He went on gazing around the room, sometimes craning his neck to see someone. 'Of course,' he said eventually, 'a lot of young men dream of becoming detectives. I dare say I did once, in my more fanciful moments. One feels so idealistic at your age. Longs to be the great detective of the day. To root out single-handedly all the evil in the world. Commendable. But really, my boy, it's just as well to have, let us say, a few other strings to your bow. Because a year or two from now – I don't mean to be offensive – but pretty soon you'll feel quite differently about things' (Ishiguro 2000: 14).

Tobias Döring interprets this exchange as evidence that Christopher's choice of career is 'little more than a Museum piece, a "relic" of the times gone by, henceforth an object of historical study like the old "skulls" that promise a more adequate career' (2006: 68). Although Döring's article is excellent in many respects, this seems to me a fundamental mischaracterisation of what drives Christopher's ambition. His interest is not in history, but in fantasy. He is not, after all, charged with being old-fashioned. Instead, he is termed 'young' and 'idealistic'. The speaker's mention of his own youth indicates that such idealism is a function of immaturity, rather than of a particular era. In effect, Christopher wishes to apprentice himself to a tradition that has never existed. His icon is the improbable literary detective, who is able to act, as James would have it, 'rather like an avenging deity' (2013: 1). This does not strike his contemporaries as being anachronistic, but rather as 'fanciful' and unrealistic. Christopher is perceived as eccentric because he persists in taking detective literature seriously well into adulthood, rather than because Holmes's reign as a cultural icon has ended.

It is evident that one driving force behind Christopher's ambitions is his pursuit of the power to set things right, or to 'root out single-handedly all the evil in the world' (Ishiguro 2000: 14). However, his choice of Holmes as a particular idol is equally significant. In comparing Christopher's narration to Watson's chronicling of Holmes, Machinal says:

> This shift from a narrator who can never quite grasp the reasoning process of the great detective, to a detective-narrator whose subjectivity, whose emotion, often overwhelms the scientific and rational aspects of the detective function reveals at the level of the form itself a tension at the heart of this novel (2009: 84).

Ishiguro's introduction of such an emotionally burdened detective suggests that the usual form is too simplistic to provide the reader with more than an affectless '*deus ex machina*' (Van Dine 1928) for a protagonist. Christopher's humanity and fallibility are used to highlight the implausibility of a genre that characterises the detective as a supreme rational authority. However, while Ishiguro's characterisation exposes the artificiality of the traditional thinly drawn sleuth, it also reveals a lot about Christopher's motives.

Ishiguro adds depth to Christopher's delusions by acknowledging that the appeal of the Holmes character lies, not just in his prowess, but in his many deficiencies as well. Of Holmes, Christopher Clausen writes: 'He is ... the sort of isolated intellectual who today would be called alienated: introverted, frighteningly analytical, and often cynical' (1984: 105). Indeed, Watson says that Sherlock 'loathed every form of society with his whole Bohemian soul' (Doyle 2013: 1). Nevertheless, Holmes remains admirable because his deficits (his brusqueness, his drug use and his relative friendlessness) are also his virtues, enabling him to perform his astonishing social function.

As Machinal notes, Watson's position as narrator means that we have no choice but to take Holmes at his word. The form of the Holmes stories does not facilitate any soul-searching on Holmes's part: his 'melancholia' (Auden 2016: 2) is sketched for the reader, but we are never asked to inhabit it. His intermittent cocaine binges allow his consciousness to go temporarily dark between mysteries (Holquist 1971: 142). This makes him the perfect role model for someone who, like Christopher, wishes to excuse his monomania and social awkwardness. For example, when Christopher is awkwardly trying to negotiate a fashionable party, he consoles himself with the thought that detectives 'tend to be earnest, often reclusive individuals who are dedicated to their work and have little inclination to mingle with one another, let alone with society at large' (Ishiguro 2000: 10). In this way, he subsumes his own insecurities into the detective role, presenting his inadequacies as evidence that his mind is fixed on loftier things. In the same way, he is able to explain away his bizarre leaps of logic by casting himself as an eccentric genius and hinting at specialist knowledge that he never actually reveals.

Christopher's determination to 'solve the case' has evolved from a childhood coping mechanism. Following the disappearance of his expatriate parents in Shanghai, the young boy is sent 'home' to England, where he is encouraged to 'look forward' (Ishiguro 2000: 9) and not to mope, advice he understandably finds difficult to follow. Instead, he acts out his parents' rescue again and again. The first hint we are given of this behaviour comes in Chapter 1, in which Christopher states: 'I certainly realised quickly enough that it would not do for me to indulge openly - as I had been doing routinely in Shanghai - my ideas on crime and its detection' (5). His 'ideas on crime' are really just fantasies of turning back the clock. He is unable to contemplate the idea that his parents may be beyond his help and dismisses any evidence that suggests this. If, as Döring argues, the frequent references to museums are indeed symbolic, it is more probable that they symbolise Christopher's curatorial attitude to his own past. His commitment to the 'investigation' is hampered by his desire to keep both hope and history safely behind glass. Indeed, it takes him decades to return to Shanghai, suggesting that he is afraid of reality intruding upon his fantasy of reclamation.

The idea of the past as a single, harmonious picture informs both Golden Age fiction and the myths that often attend emigration and exile. In 'Nostalgia and Its Discontents', Svetlana Boym asserts:

> Nostalgia is a sentiment of loss and displacement, but it is also a romance with one's own fantasy. Nostalgic love can only survive in a long-distance relationship. A cinematic image of nostalgia is a double exposure, or a superimposition of two images - of home and abroad, of past and present, of dream and everyday life. The moment we try to force it into a single image, it breaks the frame or burns the surface (2007: 7).

The second half of the novel depicts Christopher's return to China, where he finally begins to investigate his parents' disappearance. On arriving in Shanghai, he struggles to reconcile what he finds with the 'long-distance' image he has cherished for so long. The blurring of the two cities lends a frantic, hallucinatory quality to the text. This is compounded by the violence he witnesses: he arrives at the outbreak of the Sino-Japanese conflict to find that his old home in the International Settlement has become a war zone.

The Second Sino-Japanese War broke out in 1937 and was to continue for the duration of the Second World War. Prior to this, China had been a 'semi-colonized victim of global imperialism' (Mitter 2014: 279), with the United States, Britain and France all claiming extra-territorial rights within the country. Christopher's childhood in the International Settlement, in which he is surrounded by 'Chinese, French, Germans, [and] Americans' (Ishiguro 2000: 77) reflects this period, but he returns to China just as the imperial order is being thrown into disarray, threatening to take his world view with it.

Zuzana Foniokóva applies a surrealist analysis to Christopher's return to the city:

> One can interpret Banks's story in Shanghai as a dream that amounts to a fulfilment of his childhood wish. The character dreams about putting into practice the impotent daydreams of a child. As the dream merges with reality into 'Surreality', the Shanghai story is not presented as something unreal, but as a part of Banks's life, connected to both his past and his future (2007: 119).

While Shanghai does bend to reflect Christopher's mental state, it is arguably in a more complex way than Foniokóva suggests. Her reference to surrealism is astute and valid; however, the Freudian approach is rather too equivocal to describe what occurs in Shanghai. Reality is still visible, if only dimly, and the logic is more volatile than the idea of wish-fulfilment implies. By this stage, as Döring notes (2006: 79), most people Christopher encounters seem to buy into his bizarre beliefs. Even as gunfire thunders outside, one of the international set exclaims: 'I tell you, Mr Banks, when news of your impending arrival reached us, that was the first good news we'd had here in months' (Ishiguro 2000: 167). But the threat of a contradictory revelation is present as well, even when Christopher does semantic backflips to avoid it. For example, the Japanese soldier he meets is always on the verge of asserting the truth – the fact that he is a stranger and not the childhood friend Christopher so desperately wishes him to be:

> He nodded. 'I fight here, many weeks. Here, I know just like' – he suddenly grinned – 'like my home village.' I smiled too, but the remark had puzzled me. 'Which home village is this?' I asked.
> 'Home village. Where I born.'
> 'You mean the Settlement?' Akira was quiet for a moment, then said: 'Okay. Yes. Settlement. International Settlement. My home village.'
> 'Yes,' I said. 'I suppose it's my home village too' (Ishiguro 2000: 272).

In this sense, the Shanghai scenes conform more closely to Carl Jung's subjective theory of dreaming, in which each player represents an aspect of the dreamer himself (1954: 509). Although Christopher professes the same beliefs and intentions as before, other characters, notably 'Akira', begin to voice his unspoken doubts on his behalf. The further he ventures into the war zone, the more this unwelcome polyphony intrudes. As Christopher shuns these alternative voices it becomes clear that he needs to shut out the truth if he is to maintain his fantasy of rescue. His attempts to limit his world to that which can be solved leads him further and further into a wilful refusal to listen. By portraying his detective's literal inability to process what is being said to him, Ishiguro suggests that the rules of the genre can only stand if certain complexities and voices are silenced and excluded.

Christopher has promised himself (and, by extension, the reader) an unequivocal solution to the mystery. The narrative arc has been tending towards this 'single image', but breaks under pressure. He experiences an emotional and mental breakdown as he tries to fit everything into the 'frame' of his fantasy (Boym 2007: 7). In attempting to subsume everything into his generic outlook, he at once minimises the scale of what is occurring and exaggerates his own powers and failings. The Sino-Japanese War is 'my fault' (Ishiguro 2000: 260); a couple killed in the crossfire might be his parents; the anonymous Japanese soldier can only be the friend he lost long ago.

Describing the war zone, Christopher says: 'I often had the impression we were moving through not a slum district, but some vast, ruined mansion with endless rooms' (Ishiguro 2000: 256). The reference to the ruined mansion can be read as symbolising the collapse of the Golden Age ideal. In the Golden Age, Stephen Knight says: 'The archetypal setting of the English novels . . . was a more or less secluded country house' (2003: 78). When Christopher is confronted with real violence, poverty and political upheaval, it proves too much for his narrow world view and the parochial idyll comes tumbling down.

Finally, he collapses into delirium and wakes up in state of grim acceptance. When a soldier remarks to him that childhood is a 'foreign land', he replies: 'Well, Colonel, it's hardly a foreign land to me. In many ways, it's where I've continued to live all my life. It's only now I've started to make my journey from it' (Ishiguro 2000: 295). Part of this 'journey' will involve acknowledging the less savoury aspects of his childhood and it is these long-suppressed memories, rather than any further 'investigation', which will lead him to the truth. This is another way in which Ishiguro departs from Golden Age conventions: Knight notes that in the Golden Age novel, 'the reader is challenged to match the detective's process of identifying the murderer and there should therefore be "fair play": the reader should be informed of every clue the detective sees' (1980: 7). However, Christopher frequently hides clues from both the reader and himself. Indeed, just before his mother's disappearance, he is lured from the house by a supposed family friend and left in a crowded part of town. He describes his refusal to process what has happened in active terms, saying: 'For the next few moments I remained standing there in the crowd, trying not to pursue the logic of what had just occurred' (Ishiguro 2000: 127). Christopher avoids interpreting this incident until the very end of the novel, but it proves to be of critical importance.

The narrators of many of Ishiguro's novels have been somewhat 'unreliable' (Machinal 2009: 80), but their unreliability is nearly always rooted in self-deception. Because their evasions are attempts to ignore uncomfortable truths, rather than to conceal them from others, these narrators lead one to question the very idea of memory as a reliable source. *When We Were Orphans* takes this subversion further by suggesting that even the most rational of inquiries is by nature subjective because the deductive gaze is always under the direction of a fallible human being. Christopher's 'clues' end up being the very memories he has banished from his mind. He avoids pursuing them until after his hopes of restoration have vanished, sensing that they may well add up to an unrecoverable loss.

The Golden Age story generally ends with a firm denouement that resolves what W.H. Auden describes as 'the ethical and eristic conflict between good and evil' (2016: 1). Of *When We Were Orphans*, Machinal says: 'Our anticipation of, in Auden's terms, the restoration of the state of grace has been frustrated because the conditions that allow for such fine predictability and neat closure have altogether unravelled' (2009: 84). However, Christopher does discover the truth about his family and although the 'state of grace' is withheld, the conclusion of the novel provides something richer and more complex. Brian Finney takes note of 'the tone of muted contentment in the final chapter that supersedes the angst that drove Banks to outperform himself in his chosen profession all his adult life' (2002). Indeed, Christopher abandons his hopes of restoration, but gains something else in the process. His awakening can be read as a move from one form of nostalgia to another. Boym argues:

> Two kinds of nostalgia are not absolute types, but rather tendencies, ways of giving shape and meaning to longing. Restorative nostalgia puts emphasis on *nostos* and proposes to rebuild the lost home and patch up the memory gaps. Reflective nostalgia dwells in *algia*, in longing and loss, the imperfect process of remembrance. The first category of nostalgics do not think of themselves as nostalgic; they believe that their project is about truth (2001: 61).

Boym's definition of reflective nostalgia involves accepting the fallibility of one's own memories, rather than regarding one's image of the past as the absolute truth. When Christopher first returns to Shanghai, he embodies restorative nostalgia in that he literally wishes to 'rebuild the lost home': he visits his childhood house, now occupied by another family, and announces his intention to move back in once he has found his parents. By the end of the book, however, he has accepted that he can revisit his past only through 'longing and loss, the imperfect process of remembrance' (Boym 2001: 61). The novel's 'imperfect' ending speaks to this kind of ambivalence. Christopher describes finding his mother in a care home in Hong Kong. She is suffering from dementia and does not recognise him. Years later, he says: 'After she died, I thought about having her reburied here [in England]. But there again, when I thought it over, I decided against it. She'd lived all her life in the East. I think she'd prefer to rest out there' (322). Christopher accepts the cumulative facts of his mother's life, rather than trying to cling to the image of her he has salvaged from childhood. He no longer believes in the absolute temporal and emotional restitution that is offered by the Golden Age genre, but his return to Shanghai has not been in vain. The final chapters suggest that his character has developed through the dissolution of his expectations, rather than the achievement of an absolute 'solution'.

When We Were Orphans conforms to a new motif that sets the postcolonial crime genre apart from its progenitors – that of the detective who must grapple with their exilic identity in order to gain more nuanced powers of observation. That Christopher is prepared to let his mother 'rest' in her complexities shows a new disregard for rigid ideas of home and abroad, as well as for established social rituals. Said describes this kind of perception as 'contrapuntal thinking', which he characterises as one of the advantages of the 'unhealable rift' of displacement:

> We take home and language for granted; they become nature, and their underlying assumptions recede into dogma and orthodoxy. The exile knows that in a secular and contingent world, homes are always provisional. Borders and barriers, which enclose us within the safety of familiar territory, can also become prisons, and are often defended beyond reason or necessity. Exiles cross borders, break barriers of thought and experience (2013).

This resonates strongly with the change Christopher Banks undergoes in the course of the narrative. It is no coincidence that he becomes a reliable narrator only once he has abandoned his myopic obsession with 'Englishness'. At the close of the novel he is able to see the nuances and contradictions implicit in his mother's life. He accepts that repatriating her body would be an empty ritual, a mere concession to the established 'dogma' and 'orthodoxy' of nationality. For himself, it is cosmopolitan London, rather than an image of England, which Christopher claims as having 'become my home' (Ishiguro 2000: 334). Here, 'home' does not suggest something preordained, but rather something 'provisional' and ambivalent, won by experience rather than heritage.

Christopher is also able to arrive at a less literal interpretation of family, instead of rigidly defining it by what he has lost. The last line in the book is given to an ageing Christopher, who lists his various pastimes and concludes: 'Nevertheless, there are those times when a sort of emptiness fills my hours, and I shall continue to give Jennifer's invitation serious thought' (Ishiguro 2000: 334). Jennifer is Christopher's adopted daughter, who has suggested that he move to the countryside to be closer to her. This is the first time that we see Christopher planning for a future that is not just a reconstituted version of his past. Moreover, it is the first time that Christopher describes Jennifer in any emotional detail. Her centrality to this concluding scene suggests that Christopher's adult life in England, along with the family he has created, has belatedly become as real to him as the childhood he lost in Shanghai.

Identity and empire
While subverting its narrative conventions, *When We Were Orphans* also challenges the Golden Age genre's Eurocentrism and its connotations of British exceptionalism. On his return to Shanghai, Christopher is gradually awakened to the complexity of the opium trade in China. Initially, he is in pursuit of a textbook villain, but he finds that all the adult figures from his childhood are culpable, to a greater or lesser extent. What has befallen the country, and swept away Christopher's childhood, is the result of years of collusion and colonial exploitation. His father worked for a company that imported Indian opium into China, bringing 'untold misery and degradation to a whole nation' (Ishiguro 2000: 60). His mother, whom he remembers as an ardent anti-opium campaigner, has been forced to negotiate with a warlord. In yet another bitter twist, the police inspector he idolised and relied upon as a child is revealed to have succumbed to opium addiction. In *Opium: A History*, Martin Booth writes that as early as 1893, 'opium controlled not only its millions of addicts, but it also orchestrated British expansion into China, other nations quickly following the vanguard' (1996: 140). *When We Were Orphans* emphasises the far-reaching effects of Britain's weapon-isation of the drug and the co-dependent international relationships that ensued.

Given the collaborative nature of the opium trade, it becomes impossible for Christopher to assign guilt and innocence in the matter of his parents' disappearance. There can be no victory for the detective in such a situation because, as William O. Walker III writes: 'Opium politics, in the first half of the twentieth century, proved to be a game that nobody won' (1991: 200). Boundaries are further blurred and complicated by the outbreak of the Second Sino-Japanese War. As an 'East/East' conflict, it realigned power relations, with Japan's aggressive invasion and attempted colonisation of China coinciding with England's decline as an imperial power. As an adult, Christopher finds his position as an Englishman in Shanghai uncertain and mutable: when he is apprehended by Japanese soldiers, both parties are uncertain as to whether he is a 'prisoner or a guest' (Ishiguro 2000: 292).

However, at the beginning of the novel, Christopher sees himself as an unequivocal protagonist and unquestioningly conforms to the Golden Age genre's often facile and essentialist view of morality. The narrative entails a progressive breakdown of this view. As Finney argues:

> In Ishiguro's fiction to be orphaned, to be deprived of parental security, becomes a trope for transnational identity, for doing without a fatherland or motherland. The protagonist comes to realize that the feared other is actually located within the self that has discursively created that other out of its own fears. Like the protagonist, the privileged few have peopled the world beyond their safe borders with monsters of their own imagination. In the course of the novel Ishiguro forces the reader to recognize that the representatives of colonialism, while attempting to foist onto the colonized the stigma of eternal childishness, are in fact themselves childlike, having evaded maturation by projecting the unacceptable within themselves onto the subjects of their colonial discourse (2002).

However, Finney does not allow for the fluidity of Ishiguro's metaphors: the idea of orphanhood is without doubt linked to transnational identity, but this is by no means the only manner in which orphanhood is used in the text. For example, Döring discusses the motif as one of Ishiguro's many allusions to *Great Expectations* (2006: 84). In many of Dickens's novels, orphanhood heralds the beginning of a journey in which the protagonist's strength and resourcefulness is tested. The question of whether one can turn out to be the 'hero of one's own life' (Dickens 2005: 3) pervades Ishiguro's text as well. In addition to symbolising displacement and rootlessness, the motif of orphanhood is also used to challenge the idea of the individual's potential for self-determination in society (a theme discussed later in this chapter). However, much of Finney's analysis is pertinent, particularly his identification of the self/other opposition, which bolsters Christopher's beliefs, and the idea of Christopher's essential puerility as mirroring the narrowness of the imperial world view.

As Finney notes, Christopher's upbringing in the International Settlement in Shanghai reinforces the idea of the centre under siege. In his remembrances, the International Settlement is depicted as an outpost of 'home', surrounded by the otherness of 'abroad'. He says:

> I for one was absolutely forbidden to ender the Chinese areas of the city, and as far as I knew, Akira's parents were no less strict on the matter. Out there, we were told, lay all manner of ghastly diseases, filth and evil men. The closest I had come to going out of the Settlement was once when a carriage carrying my mother and me took an unexpected route along that part of the Soochow creek bordering the Chapei district; I could see the huddled low rooftops across the canal, and had held my breath for as long as I could for fear the pestilence would come airborne across the narrow strip of water (Ishiguro 2000: 54).

The reference to the conspiratorially 'huddled' rooftops shows a young boy's mental personification of the district: it is not merely depicted as a venue for unsavoury doings, but takes on a sinister character of its own. Even in Christopher's adult perception, Chapei retains its almost mythical significance as the unknown 'out there' beyond British control. When he returns to Shanghai, he panics when he realises where his driver has taken him, even though there is no discernable difference between the two areas:

> 'Fighting very near. Not safe here.'
> 'What do you mean, the fighting's near?' Then an idea dawned on me. 'Are we anywhere near Chapei?'
> 'Sir. We in Chapei. We in Chapei some time.'
> 'What? You mean we've left the Settlement?'
> 'We in Chapei now.'

'But... Good God! We're actually outside the Settlement? In Chapei? Look here, you're a fool, you know that? A fool! You told me the house was very near. Now we're lost. We're possibly dangerously close to the war zone. *And we've left the Settlement*' (Ishiguro 2000: 240).

That Christopher does not immediately notice the change in districts emphasises the fact that the line they have crossed is metaphorical, rather than actual. His absolute faith in the Settlement as a secure bastion is an integral part of his delusion. As Finney states: 'Banks' memories of his childhood and the International Settlement cloud his perception of the actuality when he returns, undermining his principal adult skill of detecting the truth from what visual evidence is available' (2002).

Christopher's reaction to leaving the Settlement is exaggerated and borderline histrionic, but it has its basis in the attitudes he absorbed as a child. These attitudes, in turn, have a basis in historical fact. During the Second Sino-Japanese War, the International Settlement of Shanghai would prove of major symbolic and strategic importance, as Rana Mitter points out:

> Shanghai's status as an enclave of foreign privilege rested on its connection to a growing and prosperous China outside the Settlement borders, whether a weak imperial China or a Nationalist China growing in strength. But the 'moonscape' of the battered Chinese city, the refugee flight that destroyed the region's marketing and transport networks, and the collapsing Nationalist government spelled doom for the huge financial – and emotional – investment that Westerners had made in Shanghai (2014: 186).

In 1943, the Settlement would be returned to Chinese control as part of a diplomatic treaty. However, this occurred only after the influx of thousands of refugees into the Settlement had dramatically heralded the loss of imperial control (Mitter 2014: 303). Within the novel, the 'doomed' island of extra-territoriality is used to represent Christopher's perception of himself as a protagonist fending off external forces. At the same time, it foreshadows the impending worldwide breakdown of colonial complacency that accompanied the Second World War. As Machinal makes clear: 'The obsolescence of the myth of Britain as an imperialist power is exposed not only in the light of the historical emergence of the new colonial powers such as Japan, but – still more tellingly – through the collapse of the confident organization of [Christopher's] world' (2009: 90). The image of the Settlement as an emotionally loaded, false bastion of security is one of the strongest ways in which Ishiguro links Christopher's personal curatorship (or the 'confident organization of his world' [Machinal 2009: 90]) to the exclusions and denials necessary to maintain the imperial myth.

The fear of 'out there' resides at the very heart of the Golden Age genre. The idea of crime as deviant and peripheral presupposes a moral (and sometimes national) core upon which outside influences must not be allowed to encroach. When Christopher, describing Chapei, says, ' [I] held my breath for as long as I could for fear the pestilence would come airborne across the narrow strip of water' (Ishiguro 2000: 54), his anxiety is both historical (as demonstrated by Mitter's assertion above) and generic. In '"Out-of-the-Way Asiatic Disease": Contagion, Malingering, and Sherlock's England'. Upamanyu Pablo Mukherjee argues: 'In the fiction of Conan Doyle and other late-Victorian authors, [the] pathology of imperial intimacy was often expressed in the drastically altered physiology of English men and women returning from their imperial outposts' (2013: 79). Evil is thus shown to be an 'alien contagion' spreading inwards from the Empire and threatening British identity (Harris 2003: 447).

In 'The Speckled Band', for example, Watson describes the sinister Dr Roylott:

> A large face, seared with a thousand wrinkles, burned yellow with the sun, and marked with every evil passion, was turned from one to the other of us, while his deep-set, bile-shot eyes, and his high, thin, fleshless nose gave him somewhat the resemblance to a fierce old bird of prey (Doyle 2013: 110).

We learn that Roylott has been 'burned yellow' after a long stay in 'the tropics' (Doyle 2013: 109) and that the climate has also ignited his hereditary predisposition to 'violence of temper approaching to mania'.

The opium trade adds another dimension to the idea of contagion by suggesting addiction as a gateway to deracination. In Agatha Christie's *The*

Lost Mine, a short story of the late Golden Age, the criminal is revealed to be a businessman named Mr Pearson, who has had a Chinese man killed in order to seize documents that reveal the location of a profitable mine in Burma. Although his crime is eventually revealed, Christie mitigates his responsibility by depicting him as having been morally degraded by his visits to a Chinese-run opium den in London. Even as he is proving Pearson guilty of abduction and theft, the detective says:

> I fancy Mr. Pearson smoked the opium fairly often down there and had some peculiar friends in consequence. I do not think he meant murder. His idea was that one of the Chinamen should impersonate Wu Ling and receive the money for the sale of the document. So far, so good! But, to the Oriental mind, it was infinitely simpler to kill Wu Ling and throw his body into the river, and Pearson's Chinese accomplices followed their own methods without consulting him (Christie 2013: 149).

As in the case of Doyle's depiction of Dr Roylott, this story suggests the 'pathology of imperial intimacy' (Mukherjee 2013: 79), with opium specifically marked as a gateway to becoming the 'other'. Mr Pearson's contact with the drug has brought him into close contact with 'Orientals', but Christie implies that these 'Chinamen' are more prone to expedient violence than Pearson could have hoped to understand, and his own character is ruined as a result.

Early on in *When We Were Orphans*, we hear Christopher's mother denounce the opium trade in essentialist terms, calling it 'un-Christian and un-British' (Ishiguro 2000: 62), a judgement that positions British Christianity as an essentialist moral centre. This was an argument commonly put forward by anti-opium campaigners of the time, as Booth points out:

> A missionary, Revd James Johnstone, although accepting the opium trade had a beneficial side, admitted: 'I shall have to present such an array of dark facts on the other side that you shall pronounce the whole trade to be a foul blot on the fair name of England, as well as a curse to India, and a deadly wound in the heart of China (1996: 152).

Rather than being rooted in a universalistic humanitarianism, the protests were based in the very nationalistic oppositions that had precipitated the trade in the first place. They relied on the fear that opium could destroy British exceptionalism by 'lowering' its traders to the level of their colonised subjects, sullying 'the fair name of England'. As in Christie's short story, this implies an essential English character that was at risk of being tarnished. At the end of Ishiguro's novel, the anti-opium campaigners are revealed as having been 'very naïve' (Ishiguro 2000: 306) in their failure to recognise the opium trade as a foundational element of Britain's colonial strategy, rather than a rogue deviation from British greatness. In underlining this shift in thought, Ishiguro breaks down the Golden Age association between evil and the other, furthered by the revelation of what really happened to Christopher's parents.

The job of the classic literary detective is to ensure that the centre continues to hold: Christopher compares his role to that of twine binding together the slats of a blind (Ishiguro 2000: 142). He is so accustomed to perceiving evil as a kind of mutation or foreign 'pestilence' (54) that he misses the clues in plain sight. For example, it takes him until the end of his trip to Shanghai to realise that the person he should be looking for is his 'Uncle' Philip, an Englishman and a regular fixture of his childhood home in the Settlement. Philip, it emerges, has been complicit in selling Christopher's mother (his 'fellow-Christian' [307]) to the warlord Wang Ku. He has been implicated in some of Christopher's flashbacks, but for a long time Christopher prefers to pursue an imaginary band of kidnappers, stating early on that 'it may be a foolish way to think, but it has always been my feeling that Uncle Philip will remain a less tangible entity while he exists only in my memory' (64). This diffidence implies that the grotesque caricatures that dog Holmes frighten Christopher less than the treachery of a close family friend.

Philip is a disturbing character precisely because of his complexity: his motive is revealed to have been an unsettling combination of greed, altruism and sexual entitlement. By contrast, the warlord Wang Ku is scarcely depicted at all and remains remote. His role in the deception underlines the collaborative nature of the opium trade, which allowed Britain to run China 'virtually like a colony, but with none of the usual obligations' (Ishiguro 2000: 307). However, Wang Ku is never brought into sharp focus, perhaps because Ishiguro trusts that we have already encountered this villain too many times before. His role in the book is important, however: by stressing the complicity between various nations and organisations, Ishiguro is able to dismantle orientalist binaries, rather than simply reversing them. Instead of polarising East and West, he underlines the collaborative mechanics of both colonialism and the opium epidemic, undermining the idea of national character.

This is reflected in one of the early Shanghai scenes, in which a young Christopher asks whether he might 'copy' Philip's behaviour in order to become a more convincing Englishman. Their conversation foreshadows Christopher's later attempts to construct his adult identity. After Christopher expresses his concerns about not being English enough, he and Philip have the following exchange:

> 'Well, it's true, out here, you're growing up with a lot of different sorts around you. Chinese, French, Germans, Americans, what have you. It'd be no wonder if you grew up a bit of a mongrel.' He gave a short laugh. Then he went on: 'But that's no bad thing. You know what I think, Puffin? I think it would be no bad thing if boys like you all grew up with a bit of everything. We might all treat each other a good deal better then. Be less of these wars for one thing. Oh yes. Perhaps one day, all these conflicts will end, and it won't be because of great statesmen or churches or organisations like this one. It'll be because people have changed. They'll be like you, Puffin. More a mixture. So why not become a mongrel? It's healthy.'
> 'But if I did, everything might . . .' I stopped.
> 'Everything might what, Puffin?'
> 'Like that blind there' – I pointed – 'if the twine broke. Everything might scatter' (Ishiguro 2000: 77–8).

The image of the blind is a recurring one in the novel. It originates with the young Akira, who informs Christopher that 'it was we children who bound not only a family, but the whole world together. If we did not do our part, the slats would fall and scatter over the floor' (Ishiguro 2000: 75). This is the origin of some of Christopher's grandiosity, as well as his preoccupation with embodying Englishness: as a child, he accepts Akira's assertion that he needs to be 'enough Englishman' (74) if he is to maintain the peace between his parents. Even when he is exposed to the wider adult world, he persists in trying to 'bind' it together, this time using the adhesive twine to symbolise the role of the detective, or 'those of us whose duty it is to combat evil' (142). Machinal comments on the performative aspects of Christopher's identity:

> Indeed, it becomes clear that Banks's role as a detective is, precisely, a performance, the adoption of an identity derived from a fictional source. Just as in his description of his lodgings he commented on the potential approval of a visitor, attention to the form of his narrative reveals a consistent preoccupation with how he is being perceived, a preoccupation that borders on a requirement that he is perceived – that he become a celebrity, a figure on the public stage (2009: 85).

Christopher's performative identity is not limited to his aspirations as a private detective, however. His 'Englishness' is also a somewhat stilted act. By twinning Christopher's ambitions towards Englishness with his longing to be a detective, Ishiguro suggests that both roles are 'derived from a fictional source' (Machinal 2009: 84). This is made evident when Uncle Philip, his proto-Englishman, is unmasked as the 'Yellow Snake', a communist informer. Unlike Dr Roylott, he is not depicted as a deracinated traitor, his face 'burned yellow' and 'marked by every evil passion' (Doyle 2013). In fact, despite his sinister title, Philip remains his bumbling, unnervingly avuncular self. Far from being addled by opium addiction, he has been lauded by European missionaries as 'that admirable beacon of rectitude' (Ishiguro 2000: 64) in recognition of his campaigns against the drug.

Through breaking down Christopher's generic assumptions, Ishiguro ultimately suggests that 'Englishness' is a construct, rather than an essence (Döring 2006: 84). Rather than being a distinct identity, it is inseparable from, and reliant on, the very others it professes to reject. In *Orientalism*, Said argues:

> The Orient is not only adjacent to Europe; it is also the place of Europe's greatest and richest and oldest colonies, the source of its civilizations and languages, its cultural contestant, and one of its deepest and most recurring images of the Other. In addition, the Orient has helped to define Europe (or the West) as its contrasting image, idea, personality, experience (1978: 9–10).

When We Were Orphans supports this idea. The perversely dependent relationship between China and Britain is underlined by the eventual revelation that it is Wang Ku, and not Christopher's anodyne 'aunt in Shropshire' (Ishiguro 2000: 4), who has been funding his life in England. Döring argues:

> His ultimate devastation . . . comes with the destruction of what Uncle Philip calls his 'enchanted world', the painful realization that he owes his rise in English society to the fortune and benevolence of a Chinese warlord, i.e. the kind of person his professional duty would have been to fight. Thus, Christopher Banks comes into his true inheritance by losing all his cultural capital and former functions: the knowledge that is here restored to him robs him of his rationale (2006: 80).

Indeed, the revelation of Wang Ku's role in Christopher's life casts a new light on everything that has been narrated thus far. He realises he is not his mother's saviour, but a direct beneficiary of her sexual slavery. At the same time, his identity as an Englishman is shattered. All his acquisitiveness has thus far been in the service of appearing more English: on the very first pages, he recounts buying 'a Queen Anne tea service, several packets of fine teas, and a large tin of biscuits' (Ishiguro 2000: 1–2) in order to impress his first visitor. Like the tea, that supposed arbiter of Englishness, Christopher's lifestyle is nominally English, but actually has its origins elsewhere. His dinners at the Dorchester, and his London house, which overlooks a 'moderately prestigious' square (133), take on the weight of colonial abuse and obligation, which is epitomised by, but not limited to, his debt to Wang Ku. Like Britain itself, Christopher's comfortable existence is revealed as having been built on distant atrocities.

The Second World War

When We Were Orphans grapples with the question of personal power by taking on the idea of the detective as a solitary arbiter of law and order. In his introduction to *The Cambridge Companion to Crime Fiction*, Martin Priestman makes the point: 'The traditional interest in the charismatic detective has tended to focus attention on the (British) eccentric amateur and (American) embittered private eye, to the near-exclusion of the many fictional police detectives whose strength lies in teamwork rather than solitary brilliance' (2003: 5).

Christopher initially styles himself as one of these solitary heroes, but as Ishiguro widens the historical lens, the individual's significance declines to the point of absurdity. Ishiguro suggests the Second World War as a catalyst of a profound change in global ideas of power and responsibility. Ishiguro's novels tend to focus on the moments before and after cataclysmic events: in *A Pale View of Hills* (2005), we witness the quiet devastation following the Nagasaki bombing, and *The Remains of the Day* (2009) focuses primarily on the build-up to the Second World War. *When We Were Orphans* can also be considered as occupying this kind of space: although Christopher is only witness to the outbreak of fighting in Shanghai, Ishiguro depicts the Second Sino-Japanese War as an early spark in a global conflict. Christopher, for whom Shanghai has always meant the International Settlement, initially perceives it as an isolated incident of violence. Eventually, however, he comes to understand the national and international ramifications of what he has seen. This is reflected in the words of one of the Japanese captors/hosts who apprehend Christopher and escort him out of the war zone:

> Suddenly he let out a strange laugh, which made me start. 'Mr Banks,' he said, 'do you realise, do you have any idea, of the unpleasantness yet to come?'
>
> 'If you continue to invade China, I am sure . . .'
>
> 'Excuse me, sir' – he was now quite animated – 'I am not talking merely of China. *The entire globe*, Mr Banks, the entire globe will before long be engaged in war. What you just saw in Chapei, it is but a small speck of dust compared to what the world must soon witness!' He said this in a triumphant tone, but then he shook his head sadly. 'It will be terrible,' he said quietly.
>
> 'Terrible. You have no idea, sir' (Ishiguro 2000: 295).

The trope of the individual out of his depth in historical tides is a common one in Ishiguro's work (Machinal 2009: 79). Frequently, his narrators overestimate their importance in the greater scheme of things. In *An Artist of the Floating World* (Ishiguro 1986), Masuji Ono is wracked with guilt and paranoia over Japan's involvement in the Second World

War, believing himself to be nationally reviled. In the end, he is revealed to have been a minor and little-remembered player in the conflict. As one of his compatriots says: 'It was simply our misfortune to have been ordinary men during such times' (193). Similarly, Stevens in *The Remains of the Day* lives vicariously through the supposed 'greatness' of his master, Lord Darlington, at a terrible cost to his own life (Ishiguro 2009: 258). In *When We Were Orphans*, the looming presence of the conflict adds a historical dimension to the breakdown of the narrative's initial premise. Christopher's Golden Age delusion is gradually stripped away, but the threat of war suggests that he is not the only one who is due an awakening. In his mind, 'solving the case' becomes synonymous with saving the world. In this sense he is deluded, but his aspirations are not so far from the self-belief expressed by some of the other characters.

Christopher's love interest, Sarah Hemmings, is initially determined to marry a 'distinguished man' who will contribute to 'a better world' (Ishiguro 2000: 47), a project she pursues so single-mindedly that he describes her as a 'zealot'. She eventually settles on Sir Cecil Medhurst, who has helped to establish the League of Nations, and who complacently dismisses the idea of another world war as an impossibility. When they meet in London, Cecil affirms his belief in personal power, suggesting that he and Christopher are both instrumental in 'hold[ing] the line' against those who are 'conspiring to put civilisation to the torch' (42).

However, by the time the Sino-Japanese conflict begins, Cecil is depicted as a hopeless, abusive alcoholic who is taking out his powerlessness on his new wife. Shocked by his sudden loss of colonial privilege, he describes Shanghai as 'too deep for me, my boy. Too deep by far' (Ishiguro 2000: 179). Even though diplomacy initially seems like a more feasible avenue for maintaining peace than 'detection', both Cecil and Christopher are effectively trying to stem centuries of historical resentment with a single-handed coup and both are nearly destroyed in the process. In *Crime and Empire: The Colony in Nineteenth-Century Fictions of Crime*, Mukherjee discusses Britain's colonisation of India, stating that 'the East India company tried to invest its colonialist regime with the moral justification of bringing law to what was shown to be an essentially anarchic and criminal country' (2003: vi). In the light of its resemblance to this 'moral justification' of colonialism, Christopher's resolution to take on 'the growing turmoil all over world' (Ishiguro 2000: 153) is revealed as somewhat less egregious than it initially appears.

Sarah is given her own sad awakening. Initially, Christopher and Sarah engage in the same kind of games as Holmes and Irene Adler in 'A Scandal in Bohemia' (Doyle 2013: 17), taking turns to sabotage each other's attempts at social climbing. As they enact their antagonistic attraction, we are led to believe that Sarah is Christopher's 'match', the only woman 'clever', 'fascinating' and 'complicated' enough to outwit him. However, the consequences of their relationship end up being much graver than their first encounters suggest. Once she is in Shanghai, Sarah realises that, far from empowering her, her long-awaited marriage has turned her into a victim. She has even less power than the diminished Cecil, who at least retains his patriarchal hold over her.

The flaw in her romance with Christopher is the fact that she comes to terms with her lack of power before he has been able to fully comprehend his own. Of Shanghai, she says, 'I can't stay here anymore. I tried my best, and I'm so tired now. I'm going away' (Ishiguro 2000: 223). Christopher is offered the chance to escape to Macao with Sarah, but finds that he cannot yet give up on 'solving the case' in Shanghai. At the last minute, he changes his mind and sets out to find the house where he believes his parents are being held. By the time he comes to his senses, he realises that Sarah will now be long gone. In turning his back on her, Christopher sacrifices the possibility of future happiness in order to chase the shadow of his past. Sarah has suggested sending for Christopher's adopted daughter so that they can be 'a little family' (226), but Christopher prefers to try to retrieve the frozen familial ideal he has been clinging to all his life.

Sarah leaves Shanghai alone and eventually ends up in an internment camp, an ordeal that will permanently destroy her health. This underscores the relative triviality of everything that has gone before: Sarah is originally presented as a fixture of fashionable London, on her way up the social ladder. Her social aspirations (which Christopher shares) become meaningless as Ishiguro transplants her and assigns her a serious, protracted fate elsewhere. Like Cecil's drunken attempts at roulette, the idea of gaming the system and emerging victorious is made ridiculous. However, Christopher does not realise this until he is confronted by the great leveller of the Second World War.

All the major players in *When We Were Orphans* are similarly revealed to be much less powerful than they first appear. Much of the power discussed in the parts of the book that showcase fashionable London is shown to be illusory. Icons of strength are used to instil a false sense of security, much as Christopher's early fantasies of rescue relied on the figure of Inspector Kung, the officer in charge of his father's case. Indeed, Kung makes an appearance during Christopher's second stint in Shanghai. He is now destitute and addicted to opium, but he is neither the hero of Christopher's imaginings nor the 'worthless ragamuffin' (Ishiguro 2000: 209) of local rumour. Instead, the old man foreshadows Christopher's eventual incarnation as a retired investigator himself. He admits that Shanghai has 'defeated' him, but can still look back on his investigative triumphs with some pride (217). In spite of his expulsion from polite society, and his fondness for 'the pipe', Kung is a kind, quietly dignified old man who has managed to do a modest amount of good. These are qualities that Christopher will eventually come to value, and even adopt himself, but he has to give up his childish understanding of personal power before he can do so.

The theme of individual powerlessness is at odds with the Golden Age's depiction of authority. The Golden Age detective's strongest feature is the ability to restore harmony in the aftermath of a crime. The detective subdues his antagonists through the power of articulation, or by 'naming names'. As Ronald R. Thomas points out, protagonists like the prototypical Holmes use identification and coerced confessions to 'author' others and their narrative authority often becomes a means of stereotyping and pacifying foreign bodies (1994: 659). Although characters like Holmes are seldom noted for their physical prowess, they perform a disarming function by co-opting the voice of the 'criminal' who is being apprehended.

Contrastingly, Christopher's powers of articulation become more and more degraded during the novel, as he clutches for any explanation that will allow him to claim the status of hero. He is so unreliable that the reader is increasingly unable to trust his version of events. By the time he encounters Philip, Christopher no longer trusts himself. He says: 'I was until recently under the impression both my parents were being held captive in Chapei. So you see, I have not been so clever' (Ishiguro 2000: 306). His side of the interview consists mainly of blunt questions and shocked silences.

His attempts at labelling his story's players also prove futile: when he first meets the false 'Akira', Christopher tries to assert his own version of history: '"Now look," I stood up and cried at the crowd. "You've made a mistake. This is a good man. My friend. Friend"' (Ishiguro 2000: 266). He blithely relies on his detective persona and his word as an Englishman to lend him an authority he does not possess. When he waves a revolver at a group of Chinese civilians, he credits his own 'strident tone' (267) and 'demeanour' (268) with causing them to scatter, rather than the fact that he is brandishing a loaded gun. Childishly, Christopher believes that his own determinations of 'friend' and 'foe' are enough to supersede the enmities that have torn Shanghai apart.

Conclusion

In Ishiguro's *When We Were Orphans*, the Golden Age structure is subjected to the stresses of worldly engagement, resulting in the breakdown of both narrative and protagonist. By thwarting all of Christopher's attempts to explain and demarcate the world, Ishiguro questions the founding myths upon which colonialism, detective fiction and narrative are based. As Christopher loses his bearings in the midst of a conflict with multiple players, the reader is invited to look beyond the binaries of East and West; friend or foe. The novel thus provides a vantage point on the complexities of the decline of empire in the twentieth century. Paradoxically, the book's power lies in its renunciation of narrative authority, its many loose ends suggesting the value of acknowledging history as a story that is complex, subjective and always incomplete.

2

Investigating the Pathologist
Michael Ondaatje's *Anil's Ghost*

First published in 2000, *Anil's Ghost* is set in the 1990s, at the height of the Sri Lankan Civil War. Unlike the protagonist of *When We Were Orphans*, the main character is not a traditional detective, but a forensic pathologist, who has been tasked with investigating human rights violations that have occurred during the conflict.

The novel contains many of the tropes seen in Michael Ondaatje's earlier work – for example, the conflict setting, the use of vignettes and a limited cast of characters. However, in other ways it can be regarded as a distinct departure from type. For one thing, it includes many elements of the thriller genre. The main character, Anil Tissera, engages in a risky investigation that sets the narrative's suspenseful pace. The novel also represents a departure in the sense that it is Ondaatje's first novelistic foray into Sri Lanka, the country of his birth.[1] This act of return is mirrored by the book's protagonist, who travels back to Sri Lanka as a representative of an international human rights organisation.

Much of the novel is preoccupied with Anil's struggle to reclaim a Sri Lankan identity and to reconcile her prolonged absence from the country with her mandate as a moral observer. Accompanied by Sarath, a local archaeologist, Anil sets about reconstructing and identifying a skeleton found in an area that can only be accessed by government officials. Anil is the instigator of the investigation, which she justifies as follows: 'Some people let their ghosts die, some don't. Sarath, we can do something' (Ondaatje 2011a: 49). In Anil's world, 'doing something' entails reconstructing the circumstances around a death, giving weight to a crime by removing the anonymity of both victim and perpetrators. In

---
1. Ondaatje explores Sri Lanka in his poetry (1999) and in his memoir, *Running in the Family* (1982).

the process of identifying the skeleton, she hopes to shine a light on 'a certain kind of crime' (272) that has become an open secret in Sri Lanka – in other words, the government's killing of its own citizens. She says of the skeleton: 'To give him a name would name the rest' (52). From the outset, the reader is aware of the victim's likely cause of death. Therefore, the suspense of the narrative does not rely so much on the identification of a perpetrator, but on whether Anil can gather conclusive evidence, and what will happen if she does. The potential consequences loom increasingly large as the narrative progresses and more characters find themselves drawn into the investigation.

While it conforms to many of the conventions of the forensic thriller, the novel ultimately critiques the idea that mass trauma can be explained or quantified by scientific means. Anil gradually realises that 'there could never be any logic to the human violence without the distance of time. For now it would be reported, filed in Geneva, but no one could ever give meaning to it' (Ondaatje 2011a: 51). The narrative resists all logical attempts to decode the Sri Lankan war from above and the forensic discovery ultimately rings hollow and anti-climactic. Instead, the novel asserts the need for empathy and receptivity on the part of those attempting to understand the conflict. In the novel, Anil's gradual loss of objectivity is depicted as a positive and more rewarding form of social engagement, even as it clouds her scientific judgement.

Anil's personal journey often overshadows the official inquiry and the climax of the narrative is not the revelation of Sailor's identity (Davis 2009: 23), but Anil's moment of self-identification as a Sri Lankan:

> Sarath in the back row, unseen by her, listened to her quiet explanations, her surefootedness, her absolute calm and refusal to be emotional. It was a lawyer's argument and, more important, a citizen's evidence; she was no longer just a foreign authority. Then he heard her say, 'I think you murdered hundreds of us.' Hundreds of *us*. Sarath thought to himself. *Fifteen years away and she is finally us* (Ondaatje 2011a: 269).

Although the narrative takes place from multiple points of view, Anil's reconciliation of her 'citizenship' with her role as 'a foreign authority' emerges as a major theme. Her move away from impartiality is exemplified by Ondaatje's use of setting: while Anil and Sarath are in Colombo, their 'laboratory' is located on board the *Oronsay*, a now-docked passenger liner. The ship, which 'had once travelled between Asia and England, from Colombo to Port Said, sliding through the narrow-gauge waters of the Suez canal and journeying on to Tilbury Docks' (Ondaatje 2011a: 14) is being used as extension of the local hospital, which is overflowing with war casualties. On one level, the 'gutted' hulk of the luxury liner works as a fairly obvious symbol of the state of the nation – the sectarian violence in Sri Lanka as part of the wreckage of empire. As John D. Rogers explains:

> Before British rule, identities were often constructed and reconstructed, both by power holders and aspirants to power. Despite many exclusivist and some essentialist identities, there was no fully developed essentialist sociology. After British rule was established, identities continued to be constructed and reconstructed, but this process took place within a more rigid intellectual framework. It was within this framework that the twentieth-century centralization of state power and extension of the franchise led to the rise of ethnonationalism and the Sinhalese-Ceylon Tamil polarization that now dominates Sri Lankan politics (1994: 19-20).

While the image of the ship hints at this history, the theme of colonial damage is not clearly surfaced in the rest of the novel. Although the text refers periodically to Sri Lanka's colonial era, particularly with relation to the theft of Sri Lankan artefacts and the archaeologist Palipana's attempts to wrestle 'archaeological authority in Sri Lanka away from the Europeans' (Ondaatje 2011a: 75), it does not explicitly address the idea of the colonial system of divide and rule as a catalyst for the current conflict. For this reason, the image of the ship has a stronger resonance with Anil's (and perhaps Ondaatje's) individual project of return. The *Oronsay* also appears in *The Cat's Table*, Ondaatje's fictionalised account of his childhood immigration to England, where it is described, in all its former glory, as a 'castle that was to cross the sea' (Ondaatje 2011b: 1).

From a scientific point of view, the ship is a poor place for Anil to work: the lighting is bad and the space below deck is bristling with rats, 'scurrying perhaps over the instruments when she and Sarath were not there' (2011a: 33). However, the ship's association with motion and migration means that the idea of separation and return is constantly evoked, even as Anil pieces together Sailor's forensic history. Thus, the two inquiries (rational and emotional) become interdependent and interlinked. Anil's investment in the case becomes 'contaminated' by emotion and identification as she seeks to reconstruct her own identity alongside that of the skeleton.

The duality of the investigation, in which Anil's project of return often eclipses the story of Sailor's life and death, may be one reason for some of the criticism that has surrounded the text. It can be argued that her experience as an expatriate is privileged above local experience in the novel. In a brief, dismissive review, R. Wijesinha (2003) states: 'Despite some merits, *Anil's Ghost* is basically a highly wrought orientalist account of experiences that deserve much more thorough analysis and exposition than Michael was able to supply.' He also suggests that the shortcomings of the book result from the fact that Ondaatje 'is not Sri Lankan, and has not been Sri Lankan for years'.

'Analysis and exposition' are generally absent from the novel. Ondaatje does not elaborate on the conflict itself, except in a brief editorial note, in which he writes:

> From the mid-1980s to the early 1990s, Sri Lanka was in a crisis that involved three essential groups: the government, the antigovernment insurgents in the south and the separatist guerrillas in the north. Both the insurgents and the separatists had declared war on the government. Eventually, in response, legal and illegal government squads were known to have been sent out to hunt down the separatists and the insurgents (Ondaatje 2011a: x).

References to 'insurgents' and 'separatists' occur throughout the novel, but there is little explanation of the militant Marxism and Tamil nationalism underlying each group's declarations of war. Rather than passing judgement on the sectarian resentments fuelling the violence, the novel frames the conflict in the broadest and most apolitical of terms, affirming that 'the reason for war was war' (Ondaatje 2011a: 39).

Anil's emotional evolution is similarly devoid of political detail. She may assert her Sri Lankan-ness, but her journey towards identifying as such is powered by a diversity of influences and blind spots, all of which are highly personal. The citizenship Anil assembles for herself lies outside the social strictures of ethnicity and religion that have been magnified into violent nationalisms by the Tamil/Sinhala conflict. Anil never invokes a Sinhalese identity, except as a reference to the 'lost language' (Ondaatje 2011a: 18) of her childhood. Instead, her version of citizenship is an eccentric pastiche of the things that have awakened kinship in her during her return: her relationship with her colleagues ('she was with Sarath and Ananda, citizened by their friendship' [196]), an affinity for nature and her induction into the 'national disease' of fear (49).

Anil's status as a returnee affects and complicates her role as a detective figure and informs her approach to the investigation. Ondaatje undermines the generic motifs of forensic truth-seeking and objective investigation by portraying Anil's immersion in her surroundings, enacting her re-citizenship through tactile and spiritual engagement. However, the thriller aesthetic that accompanies Anil's journey towards engagement creates certain elisions and silences, paradoxically undermining the reader's ability to connect with the specifics of the conflict.

Empathy and tactility

Anil's reconstruction of her Sri Lankan citizenship is a complex process, which should not be too sweepingly defined as a return to roots, or as a unilateral repudiation of 'Westernness'. In her article, 'Investigating Truth, History and Human Rights in Michael Ondaatje's *Anil's Ghost*', Emily S. Davis writes:

> Early in the novel, Sarath warns Anil that, as an outsider, she cannot understand the complex truths of the Sri Lankan civil war. His challenge to Anil as a Western detective is not just postmodern but postcolonial as well, because he questions the idea that a Western detective using Western methods can reveal the truth about Sailor (2009: 22).

However, it is too simplistic to describe Anil (as Davis does throughout her article) as a representative of 'Western detection', or even a Western character per se. Davis invokes crime literature tropes by describing Anil as the 'stereotypical hard-boiled loner' (2009: 18), but does not take note of the fact that Anil's solitude also speaks to her background as an emigrant and her failure to assimilate in either the West or Sri Lanka.

As Sandeep Sanghera notes, the young Anil's rejection of Sri Lanka is a calculated move that allows her profession to supersede nationality as her primary mode of identification: 'Citizenship is consciously let go. Anil then turns "fully to the place she [finds] herself in" [145]. And that place is the field, the classroom, and the lab where bodies are exhumed . . . and examined. She settles into her studies, drawing her books close to her' (2004: 3).

Anil self-identifies first and foremost as a scientist, but to interpret this nationalistically is to accept an orientalist framing of Western rationality versus Eastern intuition that is not upheld by the narrative. Speaking of ancient Sri Lanka, Sarath's brother Gamini, a local surgeon, says:

> This was a civilized country. We had 'halls for the sick' four centuries before Christ . . . The names of doctors appear on some rock inscriptions. There were villages for the blind. There are recorded details of brain operations in the ancient texts. Ayurvedic hospitals were set up that still exist . . . We were always good with illness and death. We could howl with the best. Now we carry the wounded with no anaesthetic up the stairs because the elevators don't work (Ondaatje 2011a: 188).

Science and medicine are not portrayed as imported disciplines in the Sri Lanka of the novel. In fact, the difficulty Anil must grapple with is not so much the fallibility of her 'Western methods', but the ethical implications of investigating her own country. Anil's arc as a character can therefore be more profitably read as a constant negotiation between involvement and distance (Farrier 2005: 84), rather than as a hard lesson about 'the inadequacy of Western detection' (Davis 2009: 23).

Initially, determined to maintain her status as a rootless loner, Anil uses scientific objectivity as a justification for maintaining her emotional reserve. On an abstract level, Anil's detachment from sectarian allegiances often makes her appear more moral than many of her local counterparts. She is at first the only character prepared to pursue the truth about Sailor's murder, upholding Theodor Adorno's assertion that 'the highest form of morality is not to feel at home in one's own home' (2005: 112). In other words, she holds a universalist view of morality, which she will not allow the particularities of the Sri Lankan conflict to touch. Upon arriving in the country, Anil has no qualms about implicating the government in her investigation and she plans to do so through impartial scientific evidence, 'same for Colombo as for Troy' (Ondaatje 2011a: 60). However, Sarath argues that her disregard for consequences betrays a lack of moral investment. He says: 'You can't just slip in, make a discovery, and leave' (40). Sarath fears what the truth can do in the hands of a protected observer with an escape route. In the context of the Sri Lankan war, as Wendy Knepper argues, 'the need to assert truth can be a violent impulse and have criminal consequences' (2006: 54).

Anil's move from untethered universalism (we are told that 'she had now lived abroad long enough to interpret Sri Lanka with a long-distance gaze' [Ondaatje 2011a: 7]) to involved citizenship entails immersing herself in the particular dangers of the conflict. This is in line with Edward Said's formulation of contrapuntal thinking, which differs from Adorno's concept of ethical rootlessness in that 'both the new and the old environments are vivid, actual, occurring together' and thus contrapuntal thinking represents a kind of independence that is achieved by '*working through* attachments, not by rejecting them' (Said 2013). It is therefore far more subjective and equivocal than Adorno's uncompromising insistence on moral objectivity.

In an early passage describing a colleague from Guatemala, Anil says:

> And Manuel. He is part of that community, so he has less protection than the others like us. He told me once, *When I've been digging and I'm tired and don't want to do any more, I think how it could be me in the grave I'm working on. I wouldn't want someone to stop digging for me* (Ondaatje 2011a: 30).

Anil begins to identify with Sailor in precisely the way Manuel describes. Here, 'it could be me in the grave' is not simply an expression of humanism, but carries a more literal meaning. Anil has been away from Sri Lanka for years, but had she stayed, she may well have been a casualty of war. Just as Manuel is differentiated from 'the others like us' (pathologists) when he is in Guatemala, so Anil finds that professional distance is harder to maintain when she could have been/could be the next casualty. In *Frames of War: When Is Life Grievable?* Judith Butler writes that 'in its surface and its depth, the body is a social phenomenon: it is exposed to others, vulnerable by definition. Its very persistence depends upon social conditions and institutions, which means that in order to "be," in the sense of "persist," it must rely on what is outside itself' (Butler 2010: 33). Anil's move to a Sri Lankan 'us' is powered by physical vulnerability: she can no longer hold herself apart from the context she is investigating because in this case the country's 'social conditions and institutions' are enacting the same threats upon her body as they do upon the rest of the country's citizens. Her reclaimed identity is therefore situational (predicated on her return) rather than essential.

As David Farrier states: 'To be in some way attached means to be vulnerable, because it implies a greater degree of intimacy . . . No longer the revered and sheltered forensic scientist, Anil must move from the cocooned "us" of Guatemala to a more intimate, and dangerous, *us*, altogether' (2005: 90). In Guatemala, Anil's group of pathologists had international protection and visible outsider status to prevent them from being subsumed in the civil war. However, Anil's ties to Sri Lanka put her at far greater risk. This dangerous solidarity is reflected in an early dream sequence, in which Anil finds she is not dissecting Sailor, but lying alongside him:

> *He was using the felt marker to trace her shape. You will have to put your arms down for a moment. She could feel the pen move around her hands and alongside her waist, then down her legs, both sides, so he linked the blue lines at the base of her heels. She rose out of the outline, turned back and saw he had drawn outlines of the four skeletons as well* (Ondaatje 2011a: 58).

When the examiner in the dream (presumably Sarath?) orders Anil to put her arms down, it is implied that Anil's affinity with Sailor renders her 'disarmed' or emotionally prone. Anil's dream of being a specimen is both reflective of a literal fear of death and part of a greater anxiety about being seen and categorised from without (indeed, the newspapers spread around her in the dream are aptly taken from the *Sunday Observer*). On her arrival in Sri Lanka she is jarred and irritated by the number of people who remember her childhood fame as a swimmer. She brushes off their recognition with flippant remarks ('a lot of blood under the bridge since then' [Ondaatje 2011a: 12]), but her defensiveness suggests a fear of being observed and recognised, even for such a benign achievement. Such recognition precludes the potential for 'privacy', which Anil cites as a treasured part of her life abroad (68).

However, by the end of the novel, Anil freely identifies herself as 'the swimmer' (Ondaatje 2011a: 267) during a phone call to Colombo, aligning herself with a communal 'us' by accepting the moniker the community has ascribed to her. Sanghera writes: 'That early (watery) celebrity citizens Anil to Sri Lanka. Although she has long been gone, her name lives on and that – her name remembered – matters poignantly for it is remembered in a place where names routinely, tragically go missing' (2004: 4). The incorporation of this past incarnation (or 'name remembered') into her present identity signifies the type of intimacy and vulnerability that Farrier describes. Anil is no longer simply compiling a report on the war: she is herself part of the narrative, a position that makes both objectivity and security impossible. Indeed, it is that same phone call to Colombo that brings the wrath of the government down upon her. Anil abandons detachment and caution and gambles on emotion, appealing to an old friend of her family's for help. She says: 'You knew my father. You worked with him. I need someone I can trust' (Ondaatje 2011a: 267).

Anil is not the only character in the novel who struggles to reconcile self-preservation with ethical involvement. Gamini, the trauma surgeon, has sacrificed much of his personal life. He lives in the hospital, snatching sleep in empty patient beds when he can. His marriage has ended ('She didn't love the smell of scrub lotion on my arms' [Ondaatje 2011a: 189]) and he fuels his days with amphetamines. The first time Anil encounters him he has 'blood on his clothes' (34). Like Anil, Gamini is a practitioner of science, but his black jacket (the opposite of the imposing, authoritative white coat) and his dishevelled state make her mistake him for the victim of an attempted murder. Later, watching him work, Anil again notes the similarities and lack of boundaries between Gamini and his patients: 'She noticed he wasn't wearing gloves, not even a lab coat. It looked as if he had just come from an interrupted card game' (126).

Vivian Nun Halloran argues that 'Gamini performs his solidarity with the victims instead of interacting through a dynamic of subject-Other such as the one affected by Western(ized) physicians with international affiliations, like Dr. Anil Tissera' (2007: 110). However, it is important to note that the 'subject-Other' dynamic is broken down over the course of the novel, at least for Anil. Her personal journey entails an emotional 'un-gloving', a willingness to be touched by the conflict and to be an actor, rather than an observer of it. As Milena Marinkova argues:

> Anil's insistence on preserving her position as an impartial external witness ascertaining the truth of Sri Lanka is untenable; nor can her brand of justice offer a solution to the situation. In contrast, Gamini . . . will not only denounce any humanist givens . . . but also immerse himself in the comfort of the smell of soap and the tender touch of a hand (2011: 82).

Anil moves closer to Gamini's mode of engagement as she begins to embrace tactility, rather than sterile distance.

In a flashback to Anil's early career, Ondaatje refers to the 'principle of necessary levity' common among forensic pathologists. We are given a snapshot of Anil's former laboratory mates in Oklahoma, whose work is accompanied by mordant humour and deafening rock and roll. They are insulated from the grieving relatives by their 'airtight' room, in which they freely refer to the bodies by irreverent, ghoulish monikers such as 'the Lady in the Lake' (2011a: 143). We are given to understand that this is a form of self-protective bravado, rather than genuine insensitivity:

> They snuffed out death with music and craziness. The warnings of *carpe diem* were on gurneys in the hall. They heard the rhetoric of death over the intercom; 'vaporization' or 'microfragmentation' meant the customer in question had been blown to bits. They couldn't miss death, it was in every texture and cell around them. No one changed the radio dial in a morgue without a glove on (Ondaatje 2011a: 143).

At the beginning of the novel Anil retains this sardonic approach to her work: we learn that she habitually greets the bodies in her lab with an ironic: 'Honey, I'm home!' (Ondaatje 2011a: 15). Although this is sometimes said in a 'tender' tone, the facetiousness of the greeting enforces distance between herself and the objects of her investigation. However, when Anil works with Sailor, she finds herself sincerely moved to cradle the skeleton in her arms:

> There had been hours when, locked in her investigations and too focused by hours of intricacy, she too would need to reach forward and lift Sailor into her arms, to remind herself that he was like her. Not just evidence, but someone with charms and

flaws, part of a family, a member of a village who in the sudden lightning of politics raised his hands at the last minute, so they were broken (Ondaatje 2011a: 166).

By holding the skeleton aloft from the exam table, she implicitly draws a comparison between Sailor's body and her own, measuring his frame against hers in order to 'remind herself' of their essential similarity. This is precisely the type of connection she eschewed in Oklahoma, where she was able to 'snuff out death' by refusing to see her own humanity reflected in her specimens. Her conception of Sailor as someone who once lived entails a frightening recognition of her own mortality. Her connection with the skeleton also creates a rapport between herself and the third member of the investigative team, the artificer Ananda. They do not share a language and Anil initially dismisses him as 'a drunk' (Ondaatje 2011a: 157). However, when she sees him carrying Sailor around the courtyard, she realises they share a way of communing with the dead. At this moment, she 'wished she could trade information with him, but she had long forgotten the subtleties of the language they once shared. She would have told him what Sailor's bone measurements meant in terms of posture and size. And he – God knows what insights he had' (166).

Eventually, Anil is able to gain the insights she craves. By touching Ananda's calves, she is able to identify the strictures she has found in Sailor's bones. This leads to the revelation that Sailor, like Ananda, must once have worked in a mine. However, the touch conveys more than forensic information: their initial dislike for each other is overcome as Ananda utters 'a dry laugh' (Ondaatje 2011a: 175). Later, when Anil dissolves into tears, Ananda comforts her without using speech: 'Now Ananda had touched her in a way she could recollect no one ever having touched her, except, perhaps, Lalitha. Or perhaps her mother, somewhere further back in her lost childhood' (183–4). Sanghera refers to this moment, saying: 'It is not just a touch that takes Anil into the past, it also [simultaneously roots] her in the present. It citizens Anil clearly to the Sri Lanka she stands in now' (2004: 7).

Throughout the text, physical contact is granted more weight and meaning than verbal speech: Sarath and Anil have long, philosophical conversations while working in the field, but she observes his guardedness by the fact that he 'had hardly touched her' (Ondaatje 2011a: 183). By contrast, Gamini, made unwary by drugs and exhaustion, falls asleep with his head in her lap the first time they are introduced, which makes Anil trust him at once. Similarly, when Anil goes to visit her old Tamil ayah, Lalitha, their embraces prove more eloquent than anything their translator can offer. Ondaatje's insistence on the superior power of tactility means that Anil can be 're-citizened' without having to recall her 'lost language' (18). Again, there is a certain democracy in the claiming of kinship: whereas Anil's use of English only enables her to communicate with middle-class Sri Lankans like Sarath and his brother, her physical proximity to Ananda enables him to 'citizen' her through touch. Farrier argues that 'touch and perception are important in the novel as facilities that allow a connection with the local' (2005: 89). However, it is important to note that, even as she establishes human connections, Anil's bodily approach enables her to avoid many of the barriers that would normally characterise 'local' life in Sri Lanka. The universality of tactility is used to transcend barriers of class and culture – the very barriers that fuel the leftist insurgency and the Tamil/Sinhala conflict, respectively. Tactile communication also elides the elements that mark Anil out as noticeably foreign, such as her halting Sinhala and 'Western' dress (Ondaatje 2011a: 22).

Through the use of tactility, Anil's journey from detachment to moral proximity is enacted upon the reader as well. Anil, cosmopolitan and broadly relatable, is used to lead international readers to Sarath and Gamini, part of a local family torn apart by war. Anil imagines herself 'in some way like a sister between them, keeping them from mauling each other's worlds' (Ondaatje 2011a: 282). In the same way, Anil performs as a multicultural mediator within the text, beginning with a forensic ('long-distance' [7]) gaze, but gradually establishing contact with the human element of the conflict.

The irony is that Anil must reincorporate Sri Lanka into her self-perception in order to re-establish her citizenship, but in order to bring international readers with her she must also remain as universal as possible, avoiding any 'ideological grid' or 'historical discourse' (Siddiqi 2008: 70). Her citizenship is not informed by the cultural specifics that underpin nationalism, but by shared geography and a common experience of mortality and physicality with which readers can identify. Indeed, one of the lines of poetry Ondaatje embeds in the novel is: 'I wanted to find one law to cover all of living. I found fear' (Ondaatje 2011a: 133).

Marinkova asserts that Ondaatje's 'haptic' prose (prose that is reliant on 'the bodily, the sensual, the material') is able to forge 'an intimately embodied and ethically responsible relationship among audience, author and text, as it renounces the Cartesian split between mind and body, the dialectical subsumption of the object into the subject, and the dehistoricization of a phenomenological subject' (2011: 4). However, Marinkova's argument (that Ondaatje replaces the dialectical subject/object gaze with the universal language of affective empathy) is rather sweeping and does not take into account Ondaatje's use of genre. Anil's connection to Sri Lanka through physicality and tactility is enacted upon the reader and lends an immediacy to the historical conflict. However, the 'haptic aesthetic' is unevenly applied.

In portraying the death of Sarath, Ondaatje comes closest to fulfilling the haptic ideal Marinkova describes. Sarath's murder effectively depicts the aftermath of the 'successful' investigation into Sailor's death, as he suffers the consequences of Anil's indiscretion. Like Sailor, Sarath is outlived by his own story. Sailor's story, however, is comparatively sparse: we learn that in life he was Ruwan Kumara. Kumara was a toddy tapper turned graphite miner who was 'disappeared' from his village, accused of being a rebel sympathiser. This, however, is as much as we ever know about him. Instead, it is 'the ghost of Sarath Diyasena' (Ondaatje 2011a: 305) that is left to haunt the reader. Of the forensic crime novel, Lee Horsley and Katharine Horsley suggest that 'by providing readers with not only a body of experts but an expert on the body the novelist allows them to listen to the voices of the dead' (2006: 9). In *Anil's Ghost*, however, the voice of Sailor remains elusive and summoning it remains beyond Anil's skill.

Through Sarath's death, Ondaatje illustrates the line Sarath took in life: he tells Anil that he wants her to understand 'the archaeological surround of a fact' (Ondaatje 2011a: 40). In the end Sailor's body is a fact (Ruwan Kumara: graphite miner) and Sarath's is a narrative. Instead of humanising the conflict by resurrecting Kumara, Ondaatje presents us with the dead body of a character we already know well. This intimacy is heightened by the fact that the scene takes place through the eyes of Gamini, his brother, who sees in the body the history of their relationship. Sarath's injuries (burns, broken bones) are common to many of the torture victims portrayed in the text, but our acquaintance with him lends them a horrible specificity. As Marinkova points out, this portrayal 'renounces the Cartesian split between mind and body' (2011: 4) by refracting the image of Sarath's body both through our experience of his character and through his brother's grief: Sarath's chest is described as 'gentle' and 'generous' (Ondaatje 2011a: 285) and he thus retains the humanity that Anil's forensic reconstruction has been unable to restore to Sailor/Kumara.

The images of Sarath's body are the most personal images of violence that appear in the text. In part, this underlines the difference between the 'unhistorical dead' (Ondaatje 2011a: 52) and the dead with whom one shares a past. Gamini is first made aware of his brother's death through a mortuary photograph. Sarath's face is concealed, granting him Sailor-like impersonality to anyone who did not know him in life. The image is brought in by a civil rights organisation that keeps track of torture victims (another set of investigators). Even without seeing his face, Gamini recognises his brother and finds him in the hospital morgue:

> Gamini didn't know how long he stood there. There were seven bodies in the room. There were things he could do. He didn't know. There were things he could do perhaps. He could see the acid burns, the twisted leg. He unlocked the cupboard that held bandages, splints, disinfectant. He began washing the body's dark-brown markings with scrub lotion. He could heal his brother, set the left leg, deal with every wound as if he were alive, as if treating the hundred small traumas would eventually bring him back into his life (Ondaatje 2011a: 284).

Ondaatje makes the reader a witness to the 'pietà' (Ondaatje 2011a: 285) between Gamini and his brother's body, changing the way that tragedy is framed: instead of an autopsy, this is an interactive lamentation, one which is the more affecting because in life we have previously seen 'no touching between [them], not a handshake' (125). When Gamini speaks in the mortuary, he abandons clinical language and his inventory of Sarath's injuries takes the form of a eulogy to their history together:

> The gash of scar on the side of your elbow you got crashing a bike on the Kandy Hill. This scar I gave you hitting you with a cricket stump. As brothers we ended up never turning our backs on each other. You were always too much of an older brother, Sarath (Ondaatje 2011a: 284-5).

Yumna Siddiqi contends that

> Anil repudiates an instrumental view of bodies that have been subjected to violence and asserts instead their affective moment. When Gamini cradles Sarath's battered body, he too reads the body in the language of shared memory and affect... By privileging these moments, the novel describes the bodily victims of political violence not in relation to an ideological grid or historical discourse, but rather in terms of the power they have to move (Siddiqi 2008: 70).

However, the novel's use of affect is selective, deliberately so, in a way that insists on the collaborative nature of truth. Ondaatje supplies an underdeveloped, fairly affectless sketch of Sailor's life to show the limitations of scientific truth. The second kind of testimony – 'intimate testimony' (Farrier 2005: 85), such as Gamini's – can only happen when the bereaved are left alone with their dead. Thus, we are given to understand that the intimate facts of Sailor's life can only be divulged once Anil and Sarath have carried the news to his village. The mystery of his death has been 'solved', but the story of his life becomes a ghost text: it does not appear in the main narrative, but is implicitly being memorialised somewhere just out of earshot.

Of the forensic thriller and its typical focus on the empirical, Linda Mizejewski writes, 'in these novels, medical forensics guarantee the authority of the main character... Readers are offered meticulous accounts of autopsies, descriptions of police procedures with homicide victims, and the process of profiling criminals through physical evidence' (2004: 55). In portraying this second, highly emotive reconstruction of the dead, Ondaatje reverses the conventions of the genre by undermining Anil's authority, showing the limitations of 'physical evidence'. In doing so, he argues for an approach to truth that addresses the effects of emotional and social trauma and 'the presence of truth beyond the evidential' (Farrier 2005: 89). In Sri Lanka, the text suggests, tragedy is not only diffuse, but also fathomless and it is the death of Sarath that ultimately reveals the comparative shallowness of dispassionate scientific truth.

Genre and suspense

In *Anil's Ghost*, Ondaatje subverts generic expectation by allowing the mystery of Sailor to recede and by undermining Anil's fixation on forensic truth. In other ways, though, the novel closely follows the techniques of the thriller. Marinkova states that *Anil's Ghost* makes use of 'the bodily, the sensual, the material' (2011: 4) to connect with its audience; however, in many cases the reader is kept at one remove by the fact that the 'body' in question is already dead. In many of these cases, the imagery fits seamlessly within the thriller aesthetic and thus serves quite a different function to the one Marinkova describes. Fear, the 'one law to cover all of living' (Ondaatje 2011a: 133) can be used to evoke suspense as well as compassion and in *Anil's Ghost* the persistent fear of bodily harm is used to hold the reader's attention as the narrative progresses.

In the course of the novel, multiple victims only appear during or after their deaths. In some cases they are reduced to their parts: 'Heads on stakes. Skeletons dug out of a pit in Matale' (Ondaatje 2011a: 7). Others feature in short inserts in which we witness only their murders or their dead bodies. Most of these characters remain anonymous and the narrative does not resurrect them. On one level, the profusion of anonymous bodies in the novel represents a comment on the nature of war. Near the beginning of the novel, we view the assassination of a government official through the eyes of his killer. The man is garroted and thrown from a moving train: '*He jerked the official off the ground and pushed him through the opening. The buffet of wind outside flung the head and shoulders backwards. He pushed him farther and then let go and the man disappeared into the noise of the tunnel*' (27). The reader is led to assume that this incident is related to the central mystery, until more vignettes of carnage follow. Their very ubiquity points to the impossibility of 'solving' the situation in Sri Lanka and the ease with which a life can disappear 'into the noise of the tunnel'.

In the sense that they depict violence as a way of life, rather than a solvable anomaly, the use of vignettes represents a subversion of genre. However, the fleeting presence of these victims has strong implications for the reading experience. As Judith Butler says: 'Specific lives cannot be apprehended as injured or lost if they are not first apprehended as living' (2010: 5). Because we return to the investigative team again and again, the snapshots of other lost lives risk being read as examples of foreshadowing, rather than fully 'apprehended' tragedies.

In his discussion of the thriller genre, David Glover writes:

> The world that the thriller attempts to realise is one that is radically uncertain in at least two major senses. On the one hand, the scale of the threat may appear to be vast, its ramifications immeasurable and boundless. Thus, the thriller trades in international conspiracies, invasions, wholesale corruption, serial killers who threaten entire cities or even nations . . . On the other, the thriller unsettles the reader less by the magnitude of the terrors it imagines than by the intensity of the experience it delivers: assaults upon the fictional body, a constant awareness of the physicality of danger, sado-masochistic scenarios of torture or persecution, a descent into pathological extremes of consciousness, the inner world of the psychopath or monster (2003: 130-1).

The many scenes of violence in the novel provide 'a constant awareness of the physicality of danger', evoking atmosphere, rather than distinct and fully 'grievable' characters, and in that sense they fit seamlessly within the thriller aesthetic. For the greater part of the novel, the danger the investigators face is 'implicit' (Nun Halloran 2007: 101), signified mainly by the dead and suffering bodies that surround them. The team conducts most of its research in out-of-the-way locations and while sympathetic characters like Gamini advise them to drop their interest in Sailor, nobody actively menaces them until just before the assembly scene. Instead, intermittent descriptions of carnage provide a grim and ominous surrounding to their stories.

Decontextualised scenes of violence from all over the country suggest 'immeasurable and boundless' danger, giving the impression that the war is closing in inexorably from every side while eliding the specifics of each perpetrator/victim relationship. At times they form a kind of litany: 'The disappearance of schoolboys, the death of lawyers by torture, the abduction of bodies from the Hokandara mass grave. Murders in the

Muthurajawela marsh' (Ondaatje 2011a: 154). Siddiqi writes: 'Ondaatje repeatedly makes equivalences between the carnage of the various groups. This has the rhetorical effect of flattening historical difference and essentializing violence' (2008: 201). By defying the government, Anil and Sarath are risking a very particular set of consequences. Their Sinhala identity also protects them from certain forms of ethnic violence, but the text does not distinguish between the fates that are likely to befall them and those that are more remote, making it appear that the investigators are opposed by the war in all its brutality, rather than by a particular side.

Even when a concrete threat emerges towards the end of the book, the enemy is rendered seamlessly and in one dimension. While the government is firmly implicated in Sarath's death, we never see his killers or learn their names. As Margaret Scanlan writes, the antagonists in *Anil's Ghost* are 'shadowy, nameless figures, encountered briefly; no police, no secret agents, no journalist heroes emerge to lock wits with them, hunt them down, or play the part of secret sharer' (2004: 302). The 'amorphous' portrayal of the 'omniscient' (Siddiqi 2008: 209) state both steers the novel away from 'historical discourse' (70) and produces suspense. At the climactic assembly, none of the officials (many of whom Sarath must have known quite well) is singled out by name or appearance. Instead, they are a hostile singularity. Glover refers to the thriller genre as relying upon 'the single-minded drive to deliver a starkly intense literary effect' (2003: 135). At the assembly, Anil and Sarath are the only characters who speak, while the hostile crowd listens in silence and the result is compelling, 'starkly intense':

> But now they were in danger. He sensed the hostility in the room. Only he was not against her. Now he had to somehow protect himself. Between Anil and the skeleton, discreetly out of sight, was her tape recorder, imprinting every word and opinion and question from officials, which she, till now, responded to courteously and unforgivingly. But he could see what Anil couldn't – the half-glances around the hot room (they must have turned off the air-conditioning thirty minutes into the evidence, an old device to distract thought); there were conversations beginning around him. He shrugged himself off the wall and moved forward (Ondaatje 2011a: 269).

Here, the government is shown as a faceless, hostile 'they', more terrible than the sum of those who work for it. Rather than depicting a more realistic vision of bureaucratic collusion in institutional violence (a more quietly terrifying phenomenon), Ondaatje suggests a seamless conspiracy, heightening the drama of the final chapters, which become a race against time as Sarath pretends to denounce Anil while actually ensuring her escape.

There is no indication of how or why individuals allow themselves to become part of a genocidal authority, or room given over to individuality. It is assumed, for example, that each petty officer Anil encounters while leaving the building will be aware of her transgression and punish her accordingly: 'Sarath knew they would halt her at each corridor level, check her papers again and again to irritate and humiliate her. He knew she would be searched, vials and slides removed from her briefcase or pockets, made to undress and dress again' (Ondaatje 2011a: 274). He is proved correct: Anil's belongings are confiscated and she implies that the guards have sexually assaulted her. There is no suggestion that any of the officials may have different motives or sympathies, or may simply be unaware of what has just occurred in the auditorium. The elision of agency among the perpetrators buries issues of complicity, collusion and the banality of evil.

Indeed, there is little banality of any kind depicted in the novel, as the mechanics of the conflict are smoothed into an anxious blur. What was the social contract like before the war? What drove citizens to turn on their neighbours? What elements of daily life were lost? The magnification of threat through the flattening of both victims and perpetrators means that these questions often go unanswered. As Siddiqi argues, this rendering tends to suggest the violence of the war as an ahistorical and innate feature of Sri Lanka. As a thriller device, it is effective even as it sacrifices realism. The undefined thriller-scape that results 'raises the stakes of the narrative' (Glover 2003: 138) by making us fear for the central characters who inhabit it, but at times the unknown dead portrayed in the novel risk being objectified, or reduced to ominous background noise.

Buddhism, genre and geography

Anil and Sarath spend much of the novel 'working in the field': they leave Colombo in order to get closer to the villages where Sailor might have lived and stay in a *walawwa*, or country estate. Here, the courtyard becomes Anil's makeshift laboratory. The isolation gives them some protection from government interference, but also prevents interaction between Anil and other citizens of Sri Lanka. Most of the time, she has contact only with Sarath, Ananda and Sailor.

This isolation impacts on Anil's evolution in two ways: first, it intensifies the intimacy between Anil and her colleagues. Ondaatje has used this technique before: the chief drama in *The English Patient* comes from the claustrophobic setting of the villa in which the characters take refuge after the Second World War. Deprived of other company, they sink deeper and deeper into mutual revelation. The other dimension is a spiritual one. Anil and Sarath find sanctuary in the prehistoric, 'humanless' (Ondaatje 2011a: 186) world outside the cities. As an archaeologist, Sarath specialises in ancient Buddhist iconography and these images have a strong presence in the text.

Discussing the role of religion in the Sri Lankan Civil War, Neil de Votta writes: 'With no meaningful checks to muzzle the influential *sangha* [Buddhist clergy] and Sinhalese nationalists, Buddhism was provided a special status and state patronage in the 1972 constitution. With Buddhism and Sinhala both afforded superior status, Sri Lanka was now nearer to being an ethnocracy than a full-fledged secular democracy' (2000: 61). In a violent protest against this perceived marginalisation, the Liberation Tigers of Tamil Eelam (LTTE) would drive a tank full of explosives through the iconic Temple of the Tooth in Kandy in 1998 (55). *Anil's Ghost* is set only a handful of years before this attack and yet its portrayal of Buddhism gives little hint of the faith's role in the conflict: instead, Ondaatje uses Buddhist iconography to symbolise nature, prehistory and a respite from violence. This toothless rendering of Buddhism provides another of the catalysts in Anil's transformation.

Buddhism is introduced to the narrative when Sarath takes Anil to the Grove of Ascetics to meet his mentor, Palipana. Palipana is a former archaeologist, now blind, who lives in seclusion among the ruins of an ancient temple. In the Grove, the narrative undergoes a dramatic slowing of pace:

> It felt to Anil as if her pulse had fallen asleep, that she was moving like the slowest animal in the world through grass. She was picking up intricacies of what was around them. Palipana's mind was

probably crowded with such things, in his potent sightlessness. I will not want to leave this place, she thought, remembering that Sarath had said the same thing to her (Ondaatje 2011a: 92-3).

The reference to 'potent sightlessness' is significant. Previously, Anil has been a strong advocate of rational inquiry, but here she subtly acknowledges that there are important ways of witnessing that do not depend on the empirical. During their stay in the Grove, she also (albeit uncertainly) agrees to Palipana's recommendation that they allow Ananda the artificer to attempt the reconstruction of Sailor's head. Palipana takes on a parental role for Anil, as he does for Sarath (Sarath says, 'We need parents when we're old too' [Ondaatje 2011a: 42]), imparting stories and wisdom that have little to do with science. In this way, he is of more help than the doctors she has consulted at the hospital in Colombo. He occupies the position of a sage: his advice goes unchallenged by Sarath and Anil, both of whom are usually assertive and vocal about their respective points of view. The atmosphere in the Grove is described as 'the spell of the old man and his forest site' (105) and the narrative itself falls under the same enchantment. This becomes problematic when one considers the version of Buddhism that Palipana puts forward.

In 'Representations of Buddhism in Ondaatje's *Anil's Ghost*', Marlene Goldman discusses the lessons Palipana imparts:

In Ondaatje's novel, Palipana warns Sarath and his co-investigator, Anil, that monks in Sri Lanka have never been able to transcend politics. Citing a story from the ancient Pali chronicles, Palipana relates how a group of monks fled the court to escape the wrath of the ruler, but the king 'followed them and cut their heads off' (87). At bottom, this story and the novel as a whole emphasize what a number of contemporary critics have observed, namely, that 'Buddhism has never stood outside the dynamics of power' in Sri Lankan society (Kapferer [1988]: 108). In keeping with this realization, rather than offer a sanitized, apolitical and ahistorical account that ignores Buddhism's enmeshment in nationalist politics, Ondaatje addresses in his novel the complex relationship between religion, politics, and violence in Sri Lanka (2004).

Goldman does not distinguish between political 'enmeshment' and culpability in this analysis. In Palipana's story, after all, it is the king who 'violate[s] a sanctuary' with a violent and vengeful act (Ondaatje 2011a: 83), rather than the monks themselves. Palipana cautions against the belief that a total retreat from society is possible, but he does not allude to the sangha as an active force in the social conflict. He says:

> 'Even if you are a monk, like my brother, passion or slaughter will meet you someday. For you cannot survive as a monk if society does not exist. You renounce society, but to do so you must first be a part of it, learn your decision from it. This is the paradox of retreat' (99).

Contrary to Goldman's interpretation, this does not directly address the issue of Buddhist militancy: there is, after all, implicit passivity in the idea of being 'met' by 'passion or slaughter', rather than instigating it. Palipana's use of the story as a parable therefore erases the agency of the monks involved in the modern conflict.

The narrative upholds Palipana's sanitised view of Buddhism: at the end of the novel, Ananda is working on the reconstruction of a smashed Buddhist statue. The area has become known as a site where the bodies of the disappeared are brought to be disposed of and we are told that 'these were fields where Buddhism and its values met the harsh political events of the twentieth century' (Ondaatje 2011a: 296). This not only positions Buddhism's 'values' in opposition to 'harsh political events', but locates it as standing outside of politics altogether. The existence of Buddhist artifacts and wartime casualties in the fields is depicted as a bitterly ironic coincidence, intended to be jarring, rather than representative.

The manner in which Buddhism is spoken of in the novel enacts a second form of erasure: when characters such as Palipana refer to 'monks' and 'temples', they most often use the words to invoke Buddhism without identifying it explicitly. It therefore appears as the default religion within the novel. Even though Ondaatje is careful not to explicitly address the rights and wrongs of the ethnic conflict, his easy conflation of Buddhism with Sri Lankan prehistory becomes indistinguishable from the Sinhalese origin story.

In 'In Defense of *Anil's Ghost*', Chelva Kanaganayakam summarises Qadri Ismael's eviscerating critique of the novel's portrayal of Buddhist artefacts as follows:

Ondaatje's bias in the novel, according to Ismail, is clearly in favour of a monolithic Sri Lanka in which the minority groups are irrelevant: 'Sri Lankan history, to this text, is Sinhala and Buddhist history. A more humane history than we are used to hearing, yes; but not a multi-ethnic history, either. We now know whose side this novel is on' (2006: 13).

It is facile, of course, to argue that Ondaatje's portrayal of Buddhism makes the novel a piece of pro-Sinhalese propaganda. While the depiction of Sri Lankan pre-history at times sails perilously close to Sinhalese nationalist rhetoric, Ondaatje (as Kanaganayakam notes) also portrays the atrocious violence of the pro-Sinhalese government. Rather than indicating that Ondaatje has chosen a 'side' in the conflict, the portrayal of Buddhism can be read as an appeal to an international readership with limited local knowledge.

In *The Foreign in International Crime Fiction: Transcultural Representations*, Jean Anderson, Carolina Miranda and Barbara Pezzotti claim that one way that 'postcolonial authors attract global audiences of cultural outsiders is by constructing "glocal" settings that play on the contrast between the particularly exotic and the universal, and the related continuum between strangeness and familiarity' (2012: 13). Anderson, Miranda and Pezzotti go on to refer to Graham Huggan's argument that the inclusion of exotic elements favours 'a particular mode of aesthetic perception – one which renders people, objects and places strange even as it domesticates them, and which effectively manufactures otherness even as it claims to surrender to its immanent mystery'. Ondaatje 'foreignises' Sri Lanka by taking us away from Colombo and into the Grove of Ascetics. However, the message the investigators take away is very much a 'domesticated' or universal one.

Anil does not 'become a Buddhist' (or revert to Buddhism) in any doctrinal or culturally specific sense. Rather, she associates the broadest and best-known principles of the philosophy – in particular, denial of the self – with her journey of return. Any references that are not explicitly signposted (for example, Palipana's explanation of the Nētra Mangala ceremony, in which an artificer must blindly paint eyes on a statue of the Buddha) are easily understood using only the pop-cultural common knowledge colloquially known as 'Dharma-lite' (Willis 2009: 10).

Ondaatje's universalisation of Buddhism is problematic in that it reinforces the shorthand definition of Buddhism as a philosophy of peace, despite the violent Sri Lankan context. Stanley Jeyaraja Tambiah refers to 'a certain standard perception of Buddhism as a philosophy and "religion" dedicated to nonviolence and liberation from suffering' (1992: 3) and Ondaatje's depiction does nothing to correct or complicate this belief. However, it is less a propagandist tactic than another attempt to make Anil's transformation as broadly understandable as possible. When Palipana refers to the paradox of retreat, for example, his words elide the complexity of the national situation, but can be comfortably understood as a life lesson for rootless, professionally obsessed Anil. His parable can therefore be interpreted as a general plea for social engagement over individualistic detachment.

Mark Siderits writes:

> Buddhism teaches that there is no self, and that the person is not ultimately real. Buddhists also hold that the highest good for humans, nirvana, is a state that is attained through abandoning belief in a self. And it is claimed as well that those who enter this state will naturally devote themselves to helping others overcome suffering (2007: 283).

Ondaatje does not explore the metaphysical implications of this belief, but provides a practical illustration of self-renunciation in the figure of Gamini. Gamini's way of life exemplifies the paradox of retreat. He has renounced his marriage, his class status and even his house in order to help those wounded in the war. He describes the self-effacing delirium of working in the emergency ward as a 'state of grace' (Ondaatje 2011a: 219) and pauses to touch a small statue of the Buddha as he makes his way through the hospital. He refuses to pass political judgements on the conflict, but immerses himself in alleviating the suffering it causes, reflecting: 'You were without self in those times, lost among the screaming' (115).

Anil, by contrast, is initially intent upon observing society rather than participating in it. Her first attempts to understand Sri Lankan society are futile because she still refuses to acknowledge that she is part of it. The job of the conventional literary detective is to exert power over her surroundings and restore them to order, but *Anil's Ghost* insists that its protagonist must become one with those surroundings before she can claim any kind of authority. In part, the text's advancement of a 'Buddhist' philosophy of engaged selflessness suggests the egoism implicit in established forms of international intervention. As Teresa Derrickson states, in *Anil's Ghost*, international human rights investigations are portrayed as 'broadcast[ing] an arrogance that is culturally belittling . . . they provide us, according to Ondaatje's novel, with ample reason to rethink methods of adjudicating human rights violations' (2004: 132). Ondaatje's invocation of Buddhism can therefore be interpreted as a call for humility and cultural receptivity, rather than the superimposition of narratives and solutions from above. It is implied that Anil must renounce her 'arrogance' and entitlement before she can 'learn [her] decision' from Sri Lanka (Ondaatje 2011a: 303).

While Gamini finds a spiritual aspect among the wounded in the hospital, Anil's own move towards selflessness is largely enacted through environmental rather than social immersion. Her interest in Buddhism is inseparable from her appreciation for nature: often, her relationship with her natural surroundings is described in religious terms and she enacts the principle of self-transcendence by merging with her environment. For Anil, grace is a geospiritual experience, a spiritual affinity for nature that can be claimed through the body and does not require language or other social calling cards.

Initially, her feeling of belonging in Sri Lanka is brought about by sense memories from her early years. Her first awareness that she is glad to have returned is brought on by the sound of rain and the 'duck-like horns' hooting in the traffic: 'Suddenly Anil was glad to be back, the buried senses from childhood alive in her' (Ondaatje 2011a: 11). Upon her arrival in the Grove of Ascetics, she bathes at the well and we are told: 'She understood how wells could become sacred. They combined sparse necessity and luxury. She would give away every earring she owned for an hour by a well. She repeated the mantra of gestures again and again' (86). Anil's actions are not part of any established ritual, but Ondaatje uses religious terminology ('mantra') to describe them. Mantras are traditionally comprised of repeated words, but Anil replaces language with gestures, composing her own rite, which bypasses the need for language. Later in the novel, Ondaatje elevates Anil's appreciation of the natural landscape into a form of trance. One morning outside the *walawwa*, she enacts her own form of ritual to music:

> It is wondrous music to dance alongside – she has danced to it with others on occasions of joy and gregariousness, carousing

through a party with, it seemed, all her energy on her skin, but this now is not a dance, does not contain even a remnant of the courtesy or sharing that is part of a dance. She is waking every muscle in herself, blindfolding every rule she lives by, giving every mental skill she has to the movement of her body. Only this will lift her backward into the air and pivot her hip to send her feet over her.

A scarf tied tight around her head holds the earphones to her. She needs music to push her into extremities and grace. She wants grace, and it happens here only on these mornings or after a late-afternoon downpour – when the air is light and cool, when there is also the danger of skidding on the wet leaves. It feels as if she could eject herself out of her body like an arrow.

Sarath sees her from the dining room window. He watches a person he has never seen. A girl insane, a druid in moonlight, a thief in oil. This is not the Anil he knows (Ondaatje 2011a: 177-8).

Although she is listening to a pop song on a Walkman, Anil is described here as a devotee in the throes of religious bliss. Appropriately, the song is 'Coming in from the Cold' and she uses the familiar song as an initiation into the landscape, melding the local and the cosmopolitan. Of the dance sequence, Sanghera writes: 'Anil, for the first time, echoes the place that she is in' (2004: 7). Nature is depicted as an active participant in Anil's ritual: 'She stops when she is exhausted and can hardly move. She will crouch and lean there, lie on the stone. A leaf will come down. Its click of applause' (Ondaatje 2011a: 178). The scene represents an effacement of the rationality that usually constrains her ('blindfolding every rule she lives by'), but it is a hybrid, self-created rite, requiring no specialist knowledge on the part of the reader. Within the story, the scene is used to demonstrate a different side of Anil to Sarath, who is accustomed to her scientific precision and uneasy social demeanour.

Anil's rhythmic initiation into the landscape stands in contrast to her earliest reaction to return. When she first travels with Sarath, she lapses into a tropical fever, finding herself 'delirious, nearly in tears' (Ondaatje 2011a: 56), unable to tolerate the heat. In the course of her journey, she is able to move from fragmented delirium to the fluid grace of the dance sequence. Her return is partly enacted through a literal process of acclimatisation as she moves from physical resistance of her surroundings towards an equally physical celebration of her environment.

In *The Poetics of Prose*, Tzvetan Todorov notes 'the thriller's tendency toward the marvelous and exotic, which brings it closer on the one hand to the travel narrative, and on the other to contemporary science fiction' (1977: 48). *Anil's Ghost* is such a narrative and the tropical, unpredictable patterns of the island are firmly entwined with Ondaatje's depiction of the civil war and Anil's journey towards re-citizenship. Discussing the anarchic quality she perceives in herself and other Sri Lankans, Anil describes it in terms of weather, asking: 'What is that quality in us? Do you think? That makes us cause our own rain or smoke?' (Ondaatje 2011a: 303). Ondaatje focuses on extremities of climate as much as he does extremes of morality, and the two types of excess echo and address each other.

The conventions of the genre, in which 'prospection takes the place of retrospection' (Todorov 1977: 47) mean that the reader experiences a swift and full immersion into the 'marvelous and exotic' setting (48), but the immediacy of the narrative also means that there is no countering ('retrospective') image of what the country might have looked like in peacetime. Anil's childhood is so lightly sketched that the reader does not see her everyday relationship with the milieu, but only her return, which is enacted through murders and marvels, rather than everyday routine. This means that the extremity and violence Anil encounters can seem to be innate, written into the landscape itself.

Anil adjusts to her surroundings without ever establishing a sense of normalcy. Instead, she alters her tempo to imitate her environment, pushing herself into 'extremities and grace' (Ondaatje 2011a: 178), herself becoming strange by 'blindfolding every rule she lives by' (74). The landscape resonates with her, but it is always a resonance that suggests a numinous connection, rather than an everyday one. Her dance in the courtyard is wild and risky: there is 'the danger of skidding on the wet leaves' (177), she cuts her foot and begins to weep as she dances. By emphasising Anil's sense of wonder, Ondaatje suggests a primal melding, rather than a considered assimilation. In doing so, he portrays an atmosphere of extremes, alive with both violent and spiritual possibilities. Thus, while Ondaatje departs from the crime genre by chipping away at Anil's authority, he nonetheless maintains the kind of exotic and evocative backdrop commonly used to build atmosphere in the thriller, eschewing worldly explanation in order to heighten scopic effect. It must be said that this combination of the atrocious and the exotic does little to unsettle orientalist stereotypes of postcolonial South Asia. The reliance on nature to provide a sense of belonging can also be interpreted as an evasion of sorts: one can argue that Ondaatje uses it as an alternative to giving Anil the difficult work of exploring and interpreting Sri Lanka's social structure, and finding her place within it.

Conclusion

At times, the novel's universalism means that a real conflict risks being reduced to a sensational backdrop, or to a learning experience in the protagonist's personal journey towards self-actualisation. Specificity falls by the wayside, allowing for a more general story of the value of belonging and engagement, a story that, ironically, struggles to apply these values to its sociopolitical setting. Anil's return is enacted through an embrace of the tactile and the numinous, but these features are seldom given the 'archaeological surround' (Ondaatje 2011a: 40) that Sarath insists must attend local knowledge. These elisions effectively produce swiftness and suspense, bolstering the novel's appeal as a thriller, but gloss over details that could perhaps benefit from further magnification and decoding.

3

Death of an Idea

Francisco Goldman's *The Long Night of White Chickens*

The Long Night of White Chickens by Francisco Goldman (first published in 1992) is set during the period of Guatemala's civil war and much of the novel is set contemporaneously with the action in *Anil's Ghost*. However, Goldman's novel takes the form of a family history and the non-linear narrative moves between the 1960s, 1970s and 1980s and between Guatemala and the United States.

The plot ostensibly revolves around the murder of Flor de Mayo Puac, the head of Los Quetzalitos orphanage in Guatemala City. Instead of conforming to the standard process of elimination in detective stories, however, the novel increases in scope as it progresses, accumulating possible motives and perpetrators, rather than ruling them out. The novel is lengthy and intimately detailed, but Flor's murderer is never conclusively revealed. The narrative sacrifices closure and solutions in order to emphasise certain elements of life in Guatemala during the civil war. Michael Holquist refers to the metaphysical detective story as 'drama[tising] the void' through its lack of closure (1971: 155). In *The Long Night of White Chickens*, the 'void' is both existential and political.

Goldman's decision to withhold the identity of the perpetrator impacts on the novel in three different ways. Firstly, it allows Flor's life and death to be read as a national allegory – her unresolved murder represents a comment on the collaborative nature of Guatemala's civil war. Flor, a Guatemalan orphan, grew up as an indentured domestic worker in an American household, an ambiguous position that had a lasting impact on her life. While sifting through the complexities of her history, the detective figures begin to see her death as the outcome of personal, transnational and familial complicity, rather than as the consequence of a single criminal act. Attempts at uncovering a 'true' version of the living Flor prove equally difficult. Her elusive and unstable characterisation emphasises the difficulty of understanding a small country caught in the violent cross-currents of global politics and neocolonialism.

Secondly, the lack of narrative closure provides a commentary on the nature of return. Roger's attempts to solve the case are part of a sustained attempt to locate himself in relation to Guatemala. Like Goldman himself, Roger is the son of an upper-class Guatemalan woman and a working-class Jewish man from Boston. His return to Guatemala, in the immediate aftermath of Flor's death, throws his identity issues into sharp relief. Roger's attempts to solve Flor's (increasingly baffling) murder therefore mirror his attempts to grapple with the riddle of his own identity.

Thirdly, Goldman reneges on generic expectations in order to show the complexity of accusation and exoneration in the context of civil conflict. Goldman's eschewal of a linear narrative highlights the destabilising impact of civil war on ideas of identity, plausibility and culpability. This is best exemplified through the portrayal of the text's second detective figure. Luis Moya Martinez ('Moya') is a young dissident journalist from Guatemala City and a former lover of Flor's. Unlike Roger, whose American upbringing has armed him with an expectation of justice, Moya embarks on the investigation knowing it may well be futile, but also that the chronicle's very incompleteness will provide an important illustration of life under totalitarianism.

Who killed Flor de Mayo?

Laura Marcus writes that detective fiction typically contains a 'complex double narrative in which an absent story, that of a crime, is gradually reconstructed in the second story (the investigation)' (Marcus 2003: 238). In *The Long Night of White Chickens*, there is some dispute as to what this crime actually is: the events of Flor's death are so inextricably bound up with her own troubled history, and that of Guatemala, that it becomes impossible to discern the moment at which things fall apart.

Flor operates as a fairly obvious allegory within the text. Her relationship with Roger mirrors the relationship between Guatemala and the United States and the allusions to her many lovers (all possible suspects in her killing) can be read as a metaphor for the international collaboration that brought about Guatemala's civil war. The fact that the murder is never solved conforms to the novel's peculiar logic: just as it is impossible to say who 'killed' Guatemala, so guilt (and, correspondingly, innocence) cannot be established in the matter of Flor's murder.

The weightiness of Flor's characterisation (the nation as murder victim) sometimes threatens to overwhelm the narrative: the novel initially seems to promise a solution, but the more metaphorical value Flor accrues, the more the events of her actual death are allowed to recede. Of the novel, Jonathan Coe writes:

> If it just fails, in the end, to pack the emotional punch which it constantly seems to be promising, this is because Flor - although ostensibly the main focus of attention - is never allowed to become more than the sum of the questions which her (male) investigators ask of her. It looks as though there is going to be a strong female presence at the centre of the novel, but what we actually get is a knot of enigmas, contradictions and unsolved riddles: in this respect the task Goldman wants her to perform - functioning largely as a metaphor for Guatemala itself, maddening but at the same time irresistible - seems finally too reductive, too objectifying (1993).

Coe's assertion that Flor 'is never allowed to become more than the sum of the questions which her (male) investigators ask of her' is largely accurate. Although Flor's voice comes alive in places (notably, in the letters she writes), we seldom see her without the mediation of the male gaze. Her two-dimensionality is compounded by the lover's-eye view of the narrative: the investigation is conducted by two men, both of whom view Flor through a lens of sexual longing and loss. Much of the prose has the quality of a love poem and the novel opens with a poetic lament by Rubén Darío ('*and beneath the window of my Sleeping Beauty, / the continuous sobbing of the running fountain / and the neck of the great white swan that questions me*' [Goldman 2007: 17]).

The reader is introduced to Flor after her death, as Roger and his father are called to identify her body at the morgue in Guatemala City. Despite the grimness of the scene, Flor's physicality is evoked in tender and even erotic terms, which sets the tone for the way she will be described throughout the book. This has generic implications. As Mary Evans notes, the body of a young and beautiful woman is a recurring motif in the crime genre. In *The Imagination of Evil: Detective Fiction and the Modern World*, Evans writes:

> The gender distribution of the dead in crime fiction has not yet been quantified but what is noticeable is that young and attractive women (across cultures and throughout the twentieth century) are often the victims of murderers. In this context, crime fiction identifies one of the schisms of western culture: its veneration for female beauty but the ancient fear of its disruptive possibilities (2009: 72).

Evans argues that the presence of a beautiful female victim evokes anxieties about transgression (for example, the possibility of sexual predation), while also justifying the investigation through an aesthetic appeal to both the reader and the investigator. Beauty, she argues, can 'inspire men to exceptional actions' (2009: 72). Here, Evans codes the investigator (or even, potentially, the murderer) as a male self whose agency is 'inspired' by a female other. This dynamic is very evident throughout *The Long Night of White Chickens*. In the morgue scene, we are introduced to Flor as the catalyst of the investigation – and, in fact, of the narrative itself. However, the pathos of the scene is evoked through scopic appeal as opposed to haptic identification with her pain.

The sparseness of Flor's injuries (there is a single, neat slash to her throat) stands out in a text marked by far more lurid violence. In the same room, Roger encounters the brutalised bodies of two unnamed torture victims. Goldman describes the two men's injuries in merciless detail, which is noticeably absent from his description of Flor:

> Stretched out on slabs, skinny but pigeon chested, their open eyes, like Flor's, full of the empty, astounded, fed up stare of the dead or maybe that stare only belongs to the just murdered dead. Both of them had horribly battered faces but one hadn't been washed off yet, his face was a mask of not yet completely congealed blood, he was still bleeding a little I think – and his lower lip looked just torn off. And the other had a cleaned-out gunshot wound in his temple and a clean-looking slice where his penis had been. Both of them were speckled with what I now realize must have been cigarette burns. I'd barely glanced,

but even in my dizziness, spaciness, the nausea of the heaviest rage . . . I took it in. That carnage was in contrast to the clean, nearly pristine, unbearable visage of Flor's nakedness, the slash in her throat clean and nearly stitched - so cleanly, precisely, delicately stitched that it smacked of her own fastidiousness, as if she'd sewn up her own mortal wound in defiance of the many forced indecencies of death (I mean here we were, looking at her) (Goldman 2007: 71).

The description of the men's bodies forces the reader to imagine the 'tearing', 'slicing' and 'battering' that has taken place. It humanises the victims by appealing to the universality of bodily pain, but also depersonalises them by removing or 'mask[ing]' their identifying characteristics through battering and castration. By contrast, Flor might be the 'Sleeping Beauty' of the Darío poem. The image of the dead Flor is consistent with the one we will be given of her in life: she retains her markers of individuality (her 'sweetness of expression' [Goldman 2007: 73]) and her femininity ('plush lips no lipstick long lashes traces of eye makeup wide-open eyes'). We are not encouraged to identify with her bodily suffering, but with Roger, who gazes down at her from above and says: 'I looked and looked and looked.' Even in death, she remains an icon of male desire: naked, beautiful and forever out of reach.

The contrast between Flor's body and those of her male counterparts is significant. In *Over Her Dead Body: Death, Femininity and the Aesthetic*, Elisabeth Bronfen writes:

> To represent *over her dead body* signals that the represented feminine body also stands in for concepts other than death, femininity and body - most notably the masculine artist and the community of the survivors. These find an allegorical articulation even though they are not the literal meaning of the image. In other words, what is plainly visible - the beautiful feminine corpse - also stands in for something else. In so doing it fades from our sight and what we see, whenever an aesthetic representation asks us to read tropically, is what is in fact not visibly there. As we focus on the hidden, the figurative meaning, what is plainly seen may not be seen at all (1993: xi).

Indeed, the image of Flor as an almost perfectly preserved beauty moves the reader away from speculation about her last moments and towards a reading of her as a lost love object freighted with symbolic meaning. Looking at her hands, Roger notes:

> Her tawny palms, which always astonished palm readers, professionals as well as amateurs, because one palm was nearly smooth and the other so filled with crisscrossed wrinkles as to be indecipherable, as if clutching there as loosely as a handful of fine sand the layered, lacy palimpsests of all her lived lives: one palm told no story at all and the other held the record of three lives for every century going back to the beginning of time and who could find the future in that muddle? (Goldman 2007: 74)

In her very doubleness (on the one hand, she is young; on the other, ancient), Flor invites two contradictory forms of mourning: for the brevity of her literal life and for 'centuries' of Guatemalan suffering.[1] However, as Bronfen writes, one form inevitably eclipses the other and what is 'plainly seen' (a woman who has been slashed to death during the civil war) risks being eclipsed by the image's allegorical implications.

From a historical point of view, Flor's death is consistent with a chilling trend of violence against women in Guatemala. In 'Guatemala as a National Crime Scene: Femicide and Impunity in Contemporary U.S. Detective Novels', Susana S. Martínez makes this very clear:

> Regrettably, the fate of the disappeared and murdered women in [these novels] reflects the shocking trend of contemporary cases of femicide in Guatemala. There are several disturbing aspects that unite these works of fiction to actual cases of gendered violence and femicide in Guatemala, namely: the cases are not investigated in a timely manner by local authorities; the sexual lives of the victims are openly questioned – with victims often being blamed for their deaths; and the crimes remain unpunished (2008: 14-15).

---

1. One of the books Roger reads about Guatemala is *Guatemala, las líneas de su mano* by Luis Cardoza y Aragón, first published in 1955. In English, 'Guatemala, the lines of her hand'.

Goldman's depiction of Flor touches upon the issue of femicide in Guatemala, but then frames it as a metaphor for the country's own death, divesting it of its immediacy and specificity.

In postcolonial literature, the language of national loss, through invasion or colonialism, has often been couched in terms of violence against women: the country is said to have been 'prostituted' or 'raped'. Ania Loomba writes: 'From the beginning of the colonial period till its end (and beyond), female bodies symbolise the conquered land' (2015: 154). In 'The Mother Africa Trope', a chapter in *Contemporary African Literature and the Politics of Gender*, Florence Stratton discusses the tendency towards gendered national allegories in African literature. She identifies two ways in which women are commonly used as national allegories: the 'pot of culture strand', in which the woman character is used to symbolise a pre-colonial or pastoral utopia, and the 'sweep of history strand', in which she functions as an 'index' of the ever-changing fortunes of the nation (2002: 41). Often, in the latter strand, colonialism is depicted through the female character's victimisation through rape or prostitution. Stratton writes: 'The national subject is designated as male. A feminized Africa thus becomes the object of the male gaze ... He is the active subjectcitizen, She is the passive object-nation. She symbolizes his honour and glory or his degradation as a citizen' (51). Flor's characterisation contains elements of both the strands that Stratton describes, although there are variations, reflecting the different geopolitical contexts.

When Roger identifies Flor at the morgue, he remembers a 'famous nineteenth-century explorer's description of a young and beautiful Indian girl's funeral' (Goldman 2007: 72). In the same passage, he refers to Flor's 'haughty Maya Princess' features and 'brown skin'. It is significant that Guatemala during the civil war is pictured not only as a beautiful woman, but as a slain 'Maya princess'. During this period, the government massacred entire indigenous villages and the American coup was largely enacted to prevent land being returned to these communities as a form of reparation for years of feudal labour practices dating back to 1871. The text repeatedly invokes the indigenous elements of Flor's background, thereby stressing 'Indian blood' as the historical foundation of Guatemalan identity and foregrounding indigenous Guatemalans as victims of political murder. At times, these two emphases are at odds. In keeping with the 'sweep of history' strand, Flor undergoes an evolution that mirrors Guatemalan history. However, the fact that she is *mestiza* (mixed-race) and moves away from her childhood home in the desert to become an urban, American-educated woman tends to relegate indigenous women to the nostalgic past tense.

The pre-conquest ideal is suggested by Flor's first 'incarnation' (Goldman 2007: 246). Her early life was spent with her (probably Mayan) father in rural Chiquimula. He raised her alone and she never knew who her mother was. When Flor returns to visit the region, she finds that the villagers have believed her to be dead for years. Her father, who was murdered in a dispute over well water, is said to walk the night and his ghost is known as 'El Sed' or 'The Thirst' (253). After his death, the ghost of the child Flor was also said to cry at night, 'from several places in the desert all at once' – evidence, the villagers believed, that she had been hacked to death and scattered in different places. Flor's violent exile from the pueblo (symbolising colonisation and urbanisation) is implied as a figurative death, or another kind of scattering. Describing her return to Chiquimula, she writes: 'Idea for a short story: the possibility that all my life I have been a ghost' (244).

The novel is similarly haunted by the image of the child Flor. The narrative shifts between Roger's first-person point of view, Flor's letters and a third-person narrative that shadows Moya, but all three strands are preoccupied with this image. Moya glimpses 'a little Indian girl in a snowsuit, one of the orphans, he *swears* from Flor's orphanage, playing with some other children in a snowy yard' (Goldman 2007: 172). In his mind, the girl becomes a stand-in for Flor herself: 'Soon, wherever Moya went in Boston, he felt as if his actual shadow was snagging on Flor's shadow . . . the actual and innocent shadow of her past.' Indigineity and the 'innocent' past are thus presented as being interlinked.

The idea that Flor has lived her life in successive incarnations (or has different 'layers of skin' [Goldman 2007: 246]) tends to dehistoricise indigenous identity and, at times, to sexualise it as well. Indigeneity is depicted as something atavistic and essential. Even though Flor has left the pueblo far behind, it manifests itself, primally, through her sexuality. Roger states,

> But there was desert anarchy and near paganism in Flor's early unreligious upbringing. And I think that wild empty space, that small desert world inside of her, was merely surrounded by her

seven years in the convent orphanage; it was an outer layer of sorts but one she felt compelled to live in too, her second incarnation. Later love plunged her back into the small wild place: Flor gave herself to Tony – in the Namoset woods, just once in her basement room when no one else was at home, she'd finally tell me in later years – like a young desert girl who has never learned anything about making love except that everyone around her seemed to consider it a great and necessary joy (Goldman 2007: 265).

Roger goes on to recount his memories of the teenaged Flor changing out of her school uniform, stating: 'For those few seconds when she was almost naked, I always thought Flor looked just like Pocahontas' (Goldman 2007: 266). The description suggests Flor's schoolgirl persona as a recent and impermanent acquisition. It is only when she shrugs off the uniform of her new life that Flor reveals herself in her original incarnation – that is, as 'Pocahontas'. The image carries a duel burden of naivety and sexuality: in 'The Pocahontas Perplex', Rayna Green discusses 'the exotic and sexual, yet maternal and contradictorily virginal image of the Indian Princess' (1975: 709-10) as a gendered personification of the 'earthly, frightening, and beautiful paradise' (701) encountered by explorers of the New World. Flor is depicted as being most 'Indian' in the years of her early childhood, in her natural state of nakedness and when she is laid out after her murder. All this tends to depict Mayan women as nostalgic and exotic icons of loss.

Flor's death can be read as a lament about colonialism and ethnic genocide, but as an urban *mestiza* woman she is not a victim of that genocide. She is used to represent something that is not her experience, while her literal experiences (with the exception of her letters) are ventriloquised and allegorised by narrators who do not have access to her thoughts. Her lack of interiority makes the national allegory less stable and more self-reflexive: the narrators do not claim to understand Flor and the project of defining the nation is subject to their confessed unreliability. However, although speculative rather than definitive, this refracted rendering of Flor reinforces the gender stereotypes that commonly underlie nationalism by denying her a private voice and identity. Discussing gender and nationalism, Anne McClintock notes:

The temporal anomaly within nationalism – veering between nostalgia for the past, and the impatient, progressive sloughing off of the past – is typically resolved by figuring the contradiction as a 'natural' division of *gender*. Women are represented as the atavistic and authentic 'body' of national tradition (inert, backward-looking and natural), embodying nationalism's conservative principle of continuity. Men, by contrast, represent the progressive agent of national modernity (forward-thrusting, potent and historic), embodying nationalism's progressive, or revolutionary principle of discontinuity. Nationalism's anomalous relation to *time* is thus managed as a natural relation to *gender* (1993: 66).

Like McClintock's formulation of nationalism, the crime fiction format has an 'anomalous relationship to time'. The 'complex double narrative' (Marcus 2003: 245) means that the story of the inquiry can only progress through a process of retrospection. The detectives are the 'agents' of this progress, while the murder victim is inevitably consigned to history. Flor represents an ideal of Guatemala, but she is largely without agency, even though she is the ostensible driving force of the narrative. In death, she forges a bond between Roger and Moya (the 'community of the survivors' [Bronfen 1993: xi]), but she is excluded from being part of the group herself: she is not one of the 'active subjectcitizen[s]' (Stratton 2002: 51), but only the common ground that makes them compatriots.

As Coe suggests, the novel loses some 'emotional punch' (1993) by rendering Flor so unknowable: she effectively suggests the 'riddle' of Guatemala, but the pathos of her own demise is somewhat lost in its suggestive import. However, the use of allegory is more successful in another part of the world-making project the novel undertakes – in conveying the clash between the intimacy implicit in neocolonialism and civil war, and the idea of 'crime' itself. Goldman uses the motif of familial abuse, love and betrayal to highlight the difficulty of extracting a culprit from these tangled bonds and to represent the nebulous boundaries between humanitarianism and exploitation.

In the world of the novel, help and harm are often indistinguishable from each other. The Graetzes have 'helped' Flor, just as Flor has 'saved' numerous orphans, but none of them emerges from the narrative in a heroic light. Roger becomes consumed with the idea that he and his family are somehow responsible for Flor's death. Regretting his support of her decision to return to Guatemala, he finds himself reacting 'like it was my fault' (Goldman 2007: 346). Flor herself occupies an ambiguous space between victim and perpetrator: after her death, she becomes the centre of a media storm. Reporters allege that she has been running a 'fattening house', where orphans are cared for until they are presentable enough to sell in illegal adoptions. At times, therefore, the detectives' work seems to be motivated by the hope of exonerating Flor, rather than finding out who killed her.

One of the suspects in Flor's death is a displaced child named Lucas Caycam Quix. Flor is said to have had Lucas's sister adopted, despite the fact that this meant the children would be separated. Lucas is therefore both a suspect in the murder inquiry and a potential witness and victim of Flor's involvement in child trafficking. When Roger imagines confronting him, he places more emphasis on what Lucas will be able to tell him about Flor's possible crimes than on extracting a confession. He says:

> I wanted to tell him that we had *both* been cruelly wronged, and wanted to at least try to make amends with fate. I wanted to hear what he had to say for himself and look into his eyes and decide then what to feel about him once and for all (Goldman 2007: 664).

Roger's desire to 'hear what he had to say for himself' (Lucas's possible motive for killing Flor) is actually an attempt to 'decide what to feel' about Flor, whom he hopes to absolve of the rumours that have surrounded her in death. As he combs his memories of her for clues, he becomes increasingly focused on proving that she was, after all, the person he had known and loved all his life. The text therefore includes a far wider scope of recollections and emotions than those relating to the murder itself, expanding into a family history. The novel's existential inquiry, which questions what it means to be Guatemalan in the time of neocolonialism, is largely mediated through the lens of this family drama.

In *The Last Colonial Massacre: Latin America in the Cold War*, Greg Grandin refers to the 'intimacy' of Guatemalan politics, noting that 'the plantation culture that arose within the close quarters of its borders was forged from familiar, often bodily attachments . . . Plantation life rested as much on rape and sex as it did on forced labour' (2011: 32). Grandin continues:

> Given the closeness of this society, it is not surprising that local explanations of national events are often expressed in terms of physical intimacy and sexual power. Behind every official history lies another not so hidden story – *secretos a voces* – of faithlessness, of furtive passions, of filial grudges. Arbenz's 1953 Agrarian Reform, the most serious challenge to this system of political intimacy, elicits from Guatemalans a creative kind of historical hearsay, one that translates social histories of migration, gender, class and race into family fables, sordidly accessible histories from below (2011: 33).

The Long Night of White Chickens follows this tradition of transmuting politics into 'family fables'. In one of her letters, Flor writes: 'In a way, I have come to realize, you don't live *in* a small country so much as *with it*, in a way comparable to how you might find yourself sharing your life with a not necessarily complex but completely involving and painfully demanding person' (Goldman 2007: 270). In the context of the novel, Flor is this person: she functions as a national allegory and her death symbolises the tragedy of the country itself. The intimacy and ambivalence of Flor and Roger's relationship can be read as an extension of this metaphor. Roger and Flor have grown up together, but the dynamic between them is nebulous and difficult to define: it is at once a bond of feudal obligation (in that she has spent years working for his family), a sibling-like connection and a quasi-incestuous, unspoken love affair. This dynamic echoes the historical relationship between the United States and Guatemala.

In 1954, the Central Intelligence Agency (CIA) of the United States engineered a coup to unseat the democratically elected president of Guatemala, Jacobo Árbenz, precipitating the civil war. As Eduardo Galeano writes: 'Árbenz's fall started a conflagration in Guatemala which has never been extinguished' (1997). Árbenz had begun instituting agrarian reform in the country, a project that threatened the interests of the United Fruit Company, an American enterprise that was deeply entrenched there. In *The Blood of Guatemala: A History of Race and*

Nation, Grandin asserts: 'There is debate today as to whether it was anticommunism or the economic interests of the United Fruit Company that compelled the Eisenhower administration to act against Arbenz. The question is moot: the culture of anticommunism cannot be separated from the political economy of the Cold War' (2000: 202).

Formally speaking, the United States had no 'active role' in the coup: it trained a force of Guatemalans, led by Castillo Armas, to undertake the overthrow of the Guatemalan president. Roger, the last of an upper-class Guatemalan family, refers to his grandmother 'lighting a charcoal in a pit in her patio' (Goldman 2007: 310) to guide the air force towards the National Palace that night. It is this atmosphere of collaboration that informs the novel as a whole. Roger characterises the hole left in Abuelita's patio as the portal through which civil war entered Guatemala, but he frames this as an act of collaboration, rather than a straightforward invasion. He says: 'Hardly anyone entered Guatemala through the hole in Abuelita's patio. Tools were passed through it, that's true, such as killing tools for vile apes, all the tools they needed' (328).

Flor is Roger's sister/servant and would-be lover, but like the United States/Guatemala connection, there is no official term to describe their complex relationship. After her death, Roger says: 'I didn't know what I was trying to heal. Had I lost a relative, a sister as it were? A best friend? A myth? A metaphysical lover? A lie? My own history?' (Goldman 2007: 347). His confusion is compounded by the tacit conflicts within his family: his American father Ira treated Flor like a daughter, but never officially adopted her. Roger's mother Mirabel viewed Flor's 'allowance' as her pay packet and resented the role she came to occupy in the household. Flor, for her part, never stopped addressing Mirabel as the more formal '*usted*' (you), rather than switching to the familiar '*tu*' or the more intimate '*vos*'. These two different parental attitudes suggest that even supposedly benevolent paternalism inevitably has a darker obverse side and that the language of rescue can be used to mask exploitation and abuse.

In 1978, the Congress of the United States cut off funds to Guatemala because of its growing reputation for appalling human rights abuses, a change of policy Susanne Jonas describes as a symptom of 'Vietnam syndrome' (1996: 148). The United States, Jonas argues, turned the Guatemalan army into a 'killing machine' (147) and then turned its back in order to preserve its own image. Both actions were framed as attempts to 'save' Guatemala, first from the spectre of 'Communism' and then from a civil war. In *Human Rights, Inc: The World Novel, Narrative Form, and International Law*, Joseph Slaughter writes:

> The banalization of human rights means that violations are often committed in the Orwellian name of human rights themselves, cloaked in the palliative rhetoric of humanitarian intervention, the chivalric defense of women and children, the liberalization of free markets, the capitalist promise of equal consumerist opportunity, the emancipatory causes of freedom and democracy, etc. (2007: 2).

Roger becomes obsessed with the idea that his family may have similarly condemned Flor with their patronage, exploiting her even as they were 'saving her from a suburban maid's life and God knows what after' (Goldman 2007: 86). Even 'innocent' memories retrospectively take on a sinister cast. Roger describes games played during his childhood, in which he would design mock-murderous contraptions while Flor looked after him during the day. He recalls: 'They were all theoretically designed to execute Flor, and she was my willing accomplice, holding the stepladder for me if I needed to climb up to some hard-to-reach place and so on' (267). The childhood story provides a powerful reflection of the collaborative mechanics of the 1954 coup and much of the violence that followed.

In the novel, neocolonialism is intimate and indivisible, and resists crime fiction categories that separate victims and perpetrators. In 'The Novel of Human Rights', James Dawes argues that in *The Long Night of White Chickens* the 'desire to "find out" is finally characterized as morally suspect' (2016: 144). Dawes contends that this immorality comes from the drive to 'individual[ise] narrative answers to complex social problems'. As discussed later in this chapter, Dawes's formulation delineates the private and public spheres in a way that the novel does not uphold: Goldman's text is concerned with the confluence of the public and the private in the context of civil war, rather than with privileging one over the other. Dawes is correct in stating that Roger's mission becomes 'morally suspect', but this is because Roger is attempting to pass judgement on a situation in which he has played a critical and possibly destructive role. Flor, the person he loves most, arrived in his life thanks to the one-way child traffic between Guatemala and the United States and he has been a direct beneficiary of that traffic.

Looking at a photo of Flor and the orphans at Guatemala City Zoo, Roger notices that 'a giant Marlboro Man stands up against the sky' (Goldman 2007: 122). Just as the United States is still economically entrenched in Guatemala, so the shadow of his own family looms large over Flor's story, making objectivity impossible. As the narrative progresses, he realises that he cannot separate his family's 'crimes' against Flor from everything that has followed, even if they were committed far away in the apparent safety of the family home. As with foreign policy, actions undertaken lightly in closed rooms in the United States have caused violent and terrible reverberations abroad.

Motive and the detectives

Throughout *The Long Night of White Chickens*, Goldman associates Flor's unsolved murder case with two further forms of irresolution, each one tied to the detective figures' respective positions in Guatemala. As Moya says: 'We may be in separate labyrinths, Rogerio, but we are hunting the same minotaur' (Goldman 2007: 187). The image of the labyrinth is a recurring one and is reproduced in the structure of the narrative, which is circuitous and punctuated by dead ends.

Even though much of his family hails from Guatemala, Roger openly identifies Flor as his strongest tie to the country. When she returns there to run the orphanage, he begins collecting books about Guatemala, even though he is living in Brooklyn, claiming that 'a separate part of me went on living in Guatemala with Flor and the ghosts of centuries' (Goldman 2007: 288). After she dies, he gives up his reading ('all those Guatemala books turned instantly to hateful junk'), as though her absence has forever debarred him from understanding one part of his culture. The investigation gives him the opportunity to return to decoding the 'knot of enigmas' (Coe 1993) that is Guatemala, but both inquiries prove inconclusive.

At times, the text takes on the quality of a travelogue. Roger recounts his experiences as he journeys through the bars and brothels of Guatemala City, sets himself up in his family's ancestral home and takes a bus journey through the highlands. The novel ends just as he is temporarily leaving the country for Mexico. Despite the smallness of Guatemala, his travels through the country have yielded few true conclusions about who Flor really was, or precisely what it is he has lost.

Flor's death and the subsequent investigation mirror the imperfection and irresolution of the act of return: in *Rites of Return: Diaspora Poetics and the Politics of Memory*, Marianne Hirsch and Nancy K. Miller assert: 'To some extent, the desire for return always arises from a need to redress an injustice, one often inflicted upon an entire group of people caused by displacement or dispossession, the loss of home or of family autonomy, the conditions of expulsion, colonization and migration' (2011: 7). In *The Long Night of White Chickens*, the need for redress is writ large in the form of the unsolved murder case, but Roger's decision to delve through the 'layers' of Flor's life is also driven by a need for self-actualisation. As Dawes puts it: 'Roger's investigation into [Flor's] murder was always, at its heart, a form of self-investigation, a struggle to come to terms with the fractures of his own identity' (2016: 149).

Roger's 'fractured' identity is a result of his mixed heritage: his father, Ira, is a Jewish American with Eastern European ancestry. Ira has working-class Boston roots, while Roger's mother Mirabel is from an upper-class Guatemalan family. Roger says:

> Even during happy times, never mind the cataclysmic, origins such as mine – Catholic, Jewish, Guatemala, USA – can't always exist comfortably inside just one person . . . you've been born into a kind of labyrinth, you have to pick and choose your way through it and there's no getting back to the beginning because there isn't any one true point of origin (Goldman 2007: 285).

Roger attempts to navigate his way by becoming more acquainted with his Guatemalan side, but – as Flor's ever-changing 'layer[s] of skin' (Goldman 2007: 246) attest – even the word 'Guatemalan' can signpost a labyrinth. Moya asserts that the country's history of colonialism means that all Guatemalans are 'at least tricultural . . . or at least there is this opportunity. Spanish, Indian, the synthesis' (369). Roger's position in the United States is equally ambiguous. For much of his early childhood he lived in Guatemala because of the temporary break-up of his parents' marriage. His arrival in the 'strange new place' (82) that was the United States coincided with Flor's and she nursed him through his recovery from tuberculosis. Of this time, he says: 'It was an ideal and lyrical beginning – the other kind or kinds of love came later but were often hard to distinguish from the first. After all, our lives, mine and yours, needed a shape that we could express. A yearlong quarantine is an eternity at that age.' The quarantine period suggests Roger's ambiguous position in the United States: he is in the country, but not entirely of it. Of the months he spent confined to the house, he says: 'I hardly had any idea of where we lived ... So the world that I still live in begins for me then and there, with you stepping in from the breezeway so that we could be infiltrated into it together.' The adult Roger, too, turns to Flor in order to give his life 'a shape', struggling to keep her in place as his 'point of origin' (285). Flor's essential unknowability makes this more and more difficult. In this way, Roger's futile process of investigation becomes reflective of the drama of multicultural identity and transnational return, suggesting that, at best, it can end in an acceptance of contradictions, rather than settling upon a 'solution' to one's own ambiguity.

Roger's return to Guatemala is enacted over and over again, but he never locates the centre of Flor's story, or his own. In the final pages, he has left the country for a period of time in order to drop below the government's radar, but it is plain from the novel's irresolution that his performance of return could be repeated indefinitely without any prospect of cohesion or consolation. The novel opens with the title line from a Darío poem, '*yo persigo una forma*' (I pursue a form). In the course of the narrative it becomes increasingly clear that the 'form' that Roger pursues through Flor's history is not, after all, a shadowy killer, but an elusive image of self.

Roger's hopes of revelation wane with each new obstacle in his path, but Moya - despite being the instigator of the investigation - appears bitterly disillusioned from the start. As a political columnist, he lives under constant threat and has no faith in Guatemala's corrupt legal system. When Roger half-heartedly suggests they go public with some of the information they have found, Moya launches into a caustic tirade: 'What he was more or less saying was Oh yeah, great idea man, just great that they stomp on us, machine-gun us, break our faces, dump a thousand tons of shit on us, fuck us up the ass, *vos* [man], and I don't know what else, *vos!*' (Goldman 2007: 422). Roger's suggestion, which might be reasonable in another cultural context, is outlandishly ludicrous in Guatemala in the 1980s. If Moya strikes Roger as being jaded, Roger in turn comes across as suicidally naive. Here, the well-worn path towards revelation (the generic trajectory of crime fiction) does not lead towards justice, but only towards more violence and death.

As committed as Moya is to the investigation, it is plain that this commitment does not come with any expectation of any resolution, or of just punishment for the perpetrators. However, the very act of investigating, and of writing, proves to be an end in itself. The act of investigation is significant for Moya (but not necessarily for Roger) because Moya has become habituated to the oppressive silence necessitated by life under the Guatemalan regime. In Moya's life, 'secrecy is a church' (Goldman 2007: 367) and possibly his only chance for refuge and salvation. This is a fundamental aspect of his character: the sections detailing his thoughts and feelings appear intimate, but towards the end of the novel are revealed to be a glaringly incomplete version of his life. After hundreds of pages of denials, it emerges that persistent rumours about Moya's involvement with guerrilla organisations are true. This is something Moya has never once articulated in the many chapters that gloss his thoughts. That the information remains buried for so long demonstrates Moya's assertion that 'in Guatemala ... you can't even confide in your own shadow' (444).

In the light of this, Moya's commitment to a potentially unsolvable investigation becomes more understandable: in his world, merely posing a question can constitute an act of rebellion. Asking questions can shed a little light on the 'bottomless grief' (Goldman 2007: 273) in which his country is mired, even if there is little hope of the questions being conclusively answered. Of the investigation, he reflects: 'True, he had always known that it *might* not go anywhere, and that this alone would not mean that it was not worth chronicling' (436). At times, Roger interprets this 'chronicling' as a cynical attempt to prove a point: 'Come and investigate a murder in Guatemala. It won't go anywhere! See? See what it's like here America?' (421). To Roger this attitude seems exploitative ('Could Moya really use Flor like that?'), but in Moya's world even an unfinished chronicle can perform important work.

In many ways, Moya's project mirrors that of *The Long Night of White Chickens* itself. The novel's failure to fulfil the crime genre's generic expectation of solution dramatically demonstrates the inadequacy of traditional ideas of justice in the world it evokes. Marcus describes 'postmodern detective fiction' as representing a departure from the process of elimination and the epistemological quest for answers:

> Postmodernist literature, and postmodernist detective or 'anti-detective' fiction in particular, are ... placed on the side of a 'negative hermeneutics' (in which the quest for knowledge is doomed to failure) and/or the realms of 'ontology', in which the focus is not on the problematics of knowledge (as in the epistemological field) but on world-making (2003: 239).

Goldman's novel makes precisely this kind of departure, but the 'world-making' in question is weighted with a political gravitas best described using Edward Said's formulation of worldliness – 'a knowing, unafraid attitude to the world in which we live' (2013). The 'quest for knowledge is doomed to failure' here because of the inaccessibility of justice in the sociopolitical context, and the multiplication of possibilities illustrates a world too tangled and interdependent to be effectively rendered by a narrative that narrows towards a single truth.

The novel also conforms to Marcus's formulation in its focus on 'ontology', although once again this carries specific political significance. The novel repeatedly revisits the question of what it means to be Guatemalan. This is suggested through the very thwarting of the epistemological inquiry: to be Guatemalan during this period means to be without answers. As Coe suggests, the novel suggests an analogy 'between [the] convolution and apparent purposelessness of the narrative, and the endless frustration, gridlock and unreality of life in Guatemala itself' (1993). Both the novel and Moya's metatext are preoccupied with world-making and their very shapelessness represents a comment on life under dictatorship. This is best illustrated by comparing the form of *The Long Night of White Chickens* with that of Goldman's investigative journalism.

Goldman's investigative piece, *The Art of Political Murder: Who Killed Bishop Gerardi?* (2010) is a compelling, lucid account of a post-war extrajudicial killing in Guatemala. The book charts the progress of one of the first post-war trials to result in the conviction of army and government officials on human rights charges. There is a background atmosphere of terror throughout: witnesses go missing and prosecutors and judges are forced to flee for their lives. However, the trial continues and the (slow) progress of the justice system gives the volume its form. Goldman divides the book into sections titled: 'The Murder', 'The Trial: Witnesses', 'The Third Stage: Purgatory' and 'Deciphering the Truth: Victory and Death'. In its apparent formlessness, *The Long Night of White Chickens* seeks to project a society in which there is not, yet, any such judicial procedure. Roger says: 'Moya insists that any such phrase as *rule of law* is just not in play here and debate over whether or not that is "really as true as it seems" is off the table' (Goldman 2007: 423).

In the absence of rule of law, the mystery of Flor's death cannot be 'broken through', but can only be retraced and relived from many different perspectives. In their analysis of the metaphysical detective story, Patricia Merivale and Susan Elizabeth Sweeney assert that 'in metaphysical detective fiction . . . the mystery is a maze without an exit' (1999: 9). The formal subversion here is similar and Goldman repeatedly invokes the image of the labyrinth, but its political investment means that the novel requires a different kind of reading. In *The Long Night of White Chickens*, the circuitous narrative is not an example of 'playful self-reflexiveness' (Merivale and Sweeney 1999: 2), but suggests the experience of living under constant terror, without even the guiding form of judicial process. Moya says: 'Trials are much more than a symbol. They are our only hope for becoming civilized' (Goldman 2007: 417). In the same conversation, he refers to 'the cleansing and inaugural rite of justice', stating: 'If my side doesn't win this one . . . we may never win anything else, with or without elections. To me, this is the only so-called ideological battle that matters.' Without these trials, grappling with issues of human rights is depicted as a futile process of 'blasting away at that black-and-white, obsidian-and-diamond-hard riddle of social injustice, of just a handful of rich and everyone else poor, thus so much and so many kinds of murder' (395).

Since Moya's disillusionment precludes the hope of 'winning' justice, his task becomes one of representation. Throughout the novel, Moya's running catchphrase is '*Guatemala no existe*', which gestures towards the absurdity and unpredictability of life in the country, as well as its invisibility on the world stage. As Coe notes, Goldman's writing follows the tradition of Gabriel García Márquez in its 'profusion of horrors and miracles' (1993). In García Márquez's 1982 Nobel Prize acceptance speech, he referred to the difficulty of conveying the dramatically brutal reality of life in Cold War Latin America:

> I dare to think that it is this outsized reality, and not just its literary expression, that has deserved the attention of the Swedish Academy of Letters. A reality not of paper, but one that

lives within us and determines each instant of our countless daily deaths, and that nourishes a source of insatiable creativity, full of sorrow and beauty, of which this roving and nostalgic Colombian is but one cipher more, singled out by fortune. Poets and beggars, musicians and prophets, warriors and scoundrels, all creatures of that unbridled reality, we have had to ask but little of imagination, for our crucial problem has been a lack of conventional means to render our lives believable. This, my friends, is the crux of our solitude (1982).

Similarly, Moya's intention is not to tame the 'unbridled reality' of Guatemala by solving a murder mystery, but to 'render it believable' in all its complexity and horror. Goldman commits to a similar undertaking in the foreword to the novel, in which he writes:

The Guatemala that forms the backdrop of a portion of this novel is a fictionalized country – nonexistent – despite occasional references to actual events, institutions, and prominent personages. Its greatest unreality may lie in its omissions: impossible, through a mere story like this one, to fully convey – or to exaggerate – the actual country's unrelenting nightmare (Goldman 2007: 17).

Moya's (and Goldman's) favoured metaphor of non-existence carries García Márquez's idea of solitude to its melancholic conclusion: Guatemala is so lonely and isolated that it may as well have dropped off the face of the earth. In envisioning a chronicle that will be read elsewhere, Moya hopes to place Guatemala firmly in the global consciousness – to make it exist – even if Flor's murder remains unsolved and she herself goes unavenged. By producing a narrative that is in many ways the opposite of a procedural crime story, Moya hopes to highlight the desperation of a place where meaningful judicial procedure is absent.

The nature of truth

While the novel declines to provide a solution to the crime at its heart, it also avoids ruling out possibilities, so that no one solution emerges as more likely than any other. Within the text, 'fact' and 'hearsay' are seldom distinguished. Gill Plain writes: 'Crime fiction in general, and detective fiction in particular, is about confronting and taming the monstrous. It is a literature of containment, a narrative that "makes safe"' (2001: 3). The genre's capacity to 'contain' is subverted in this case by the text's refusal to eliminate or demarcate. Even in its textual make-up, *The Long Night of White Chickens* eschews the idea of containment, insisting that monstrosity, like criminality, is a fluid and elusive designation.

At the beginning of the novel, Flor's murder has already been 'solved' in a lurid trial-by-media. It is commonly accepted as fact that Flor's orphanage was a 'fattening house' in which local children were sold into adoption, or even dismembered for use in the organ trade. In the media's rendering, Flor is a *gringa* (American woman) who has been assisting the CIA with child abductions and her death (supposedly at the hands of a fellow trafficker) is popularly considered an example of justice, rather than a crime. When Roger and his father first arrive to view Flor's body, we are given a snapshot of the gulf between two cultures. Ira Graetz is informed of the baby-selling rumours surrounding Flor and protests her innocence in the face of all the evidence presented to him:

> 'Call it a gut hunch if you want,' said my father. 'But I did some police work myself once, long ago, back when I was in the service. And two of my brothers have been district attorneys in Boston, and one is now a judge. And I will tell you this, no one who knows about police work will disregard a hunch just like that, no matter what the evidence to the contrary looks like. In a courtroom you learn that the truth does ring true' (Goldman 2007: 106).

The rest of the novel works against this premise: we are given to understand that, in Guatemala, the truth very often rings false and vice versa. Ira's conception of truth is too narrow to allow for what García Márquez terms 'unbridled reality' (1982). The absurdities of life under a dictatorship (the government orders the traffic to run backwards one day, causing massive casualties) mean that even established 'facts' can no longer be relied upon.

Goldman's prose style, too, is inherently inconclusive: the text is awash with parentheses and run-on sentences, a technique that once again evokes García Márquez. In the space of a single pair of brackets, Goldman offers the following description of Ira and Roger's conversation with an American reporter shortly after they have identified Flor's body:

> *Well yes, you know it's like that in there almost every day and the press here, you know, they're not exactly antiestablishment and even if they are, there's all that fear* . . . And I said, *My old friend Moya was one of them*, and she said, *Luis Moya, you know him then?* And I said, *Yeah, he was there*, sort of too angrily and defiantly and she started to say something but just nodded, you could see her thoughts working, a kind of tiredness with the failure of her enterprise – particular or general, I don't know, but she was realizing we had nothing newsworthy to tell her about Flor and she was tired of bothering us, tired of our innocence too perhaps (Goldman 2007: 71).

Paradoxically, the lengthiness of the transcription prevents the true nature of the exchange from being pinned down. Peppered as it is with qualifiers such as 'perhaps', 'kind of' and 'I don't know', the sentence confesses its own fallibility at every turn. The ellipsis at the end suggests a derailed train of thought with the potential to rush in any direction. The novel's textual structure, which is often rambling and filled with syntactic self-doubt, means that competing truths can exist at the same time, as possible explanations are juggled without ever being conclusively set down.

Dawes discusses the progress of the narrative and the different theories that emerge regarding Flor's murder:

> Roger's final hypothesis about Flor's murder synopsizes the competing moral and narrative pressures of the individual/social binary. Flor was involved in a love affair with a political figure that went terribly wrong; in her distraction after the breakup, she arranged for a young girl to be sent to France for adoption. Years later, it becomes clear that the girl had a surviving older brother because Flor (purposefully and illegally? Negligently in her depression over the breakup?) conducted the adoption as if he didn't exist (2016: 144).

However, it is misleading to suggest any of Roger's hypotheses as being 'final', unless it is in a strictly temporal sense: the story ends because the two detective figures are forced to leave the country, rather than because their questions have been laid to rest. Dawes's reading suggests a confluence between termination and closure, which Goldman's novel does not uphold. In 'Closure and Detective Fiction', Eyal Segal distinguishes between 'closure' and 'ending' as follows:

> What do we mean by saying that a narrative (text) has 'ended'? It may be simply that the tale has reached its termination point, in which case we are referring to an inevitable (and hence 'obvious') phenomenon, since every narrative text has to end somewhere. On the other hand, we might be referring to the sense of an ending (Kermode 1967), that is, not to the textual termination point itself but rather to a certain effect, or perceptual quality, produced by the text (2010: 155).

The Long Night of White Chickens appears to conclude only because it 'has to end somewhere'. There is no 'sense of an ending' and thus it allows for the possibility of infinite new theories and guesses about Flor's death.

Dawes aligns two of Roger's competing theories with the private and the public sphere, respectively:

> Roger considers the possibility that Flor was murdered to clean up the politician's love affair, but then comes to believe that the orphaned brother came back to murder Flor in revenge. Here, the scope of social concern in the narrative is expanding at the same time that narrative focus is contracting. Flor's murder is the result of social breakdown so chaotic and severe that siblings can be orphaned and then separated as a matter of course ... to focus on the turbulent romance, by contrast, is to focus on the individual. The romance plot is effectively depoliticizing, turning our attention away from patterns of public life toward the satisfactions of peeping into the private (2016: 144-5).

While Dawes is correct in stating that the 'scope of social concern' expands throughout the novel, the narrative focus cannot really be said to 'contract'. Rather than conforming to a process of elimination, the text is concerned with the multiplication of ideas and possibilities. The individual and the political are so intertwined that it becomes impossible to separate the two and it is this blurring of spheres that makes the notion of 'guilt' appear so fluid.

Flor's orphanage is literally in the business of constructing families. Even if the orphan crisis is the result of 'social breakdown', we are invited to remember that it comprises thousands of individual tragedies. This is emphasised in the photo of Flor and the orphans on their outing to the zoo. Roger says:

> For a while Flor liked to put a single plaited braid into her hair along the side, though you can't see it in the picture. But if you look closely you can see that the girls – rounded Indian faces and Kewpie doll eyes, straight black hair – and even brunette Belinda have put braids into their hair in imitation of Flor (Goldman 2007: 123).

Something of Flor is replicated again and again in her young charges. The drama of her displaced childhood is simultaneously striking and banal – the children are both a 'pattern of public life' (Dawes 2016: 145) and a reflection of her own formative trauma.

In *The Art of Political Murder*, Goldman describes this confluence of the public and the private with a remark he attributes to Joseph Brodsky: 'Small countries have big politics' (2010: 98). In an interview with Daniel Peña, Goldman elaborates:

> 'There's a certain advantage to living in a small country like Guatemala, I think. You don't feel so distant from political reality there. When things happen, they almost seem to happen on a Shakespearean stage with the audience so close they can become actors too. This is partly what Joseph Brodsky meant when he wrote that small countries have big politics. Sometimes booming politics!' (Peña 2015).

In *The Long Night of White Chickens*, the dramatic convergence of the public and private spheres is perhaps best exemplified by Moya's farcical encounter with an American political analyst. The influential analyst, Sylvia McCourt, has power over Guatemalan life and death – Moya imagines her as a 'Delphic oracle, a potential unleasher of war, plague and famine' (Goldman 2007: 415). However, she suffers a 'crisis' when Moya cheerfully remarks that their hotel room is probably bugged and commands him to comfort her, in a bizarre reversal of power dynamics. They spend the night in each other's arms, discussing love and foreign policy while the state listens in. The novel as a whole maintains these absurd juxtapositions, rather than 'narrowing the focus' to privilege one or the other. Dawes argues that 'Goldman desires both that we study the deep histories of his primary characters as a way of understanding their individualized rights-narratives, and that we resist the insistent pull of the individual' (2016: 145). However, it is perhaps more accurate to say that the Guatemalan characters in the novel do not have the luxury of a private or 'individual' life at all: they are all 'actors' in the war, forced to inhabit a zone of moral ambiguity.

The narrative never fully implicates Lucas as the murderer but neither does it affirm or disprove the charges against Flor. Rather, it uses the rumours about her as a way of depicting the dangerous overlap between exploitation and humanitarianism. Flor's adoption business can be viewed as both an act of cultural confiscation (in which children are abruptly removed from their place of origin) and as an attempt to secure them a safer and better life.

Around the time of Flor's murder, the government is engaged in appalling atrocities, fuelling the influx of orphans into Los Quetzalitos. Because wealthy local families are turning a blind eye to the massacres, the orphans can only be resettled abroad. Flor says bitterly: 'So they'll adopt a baby parrot, a macaw, a monkey, a curlew, but an Indian orphan, *olvidate*, forget about it. Not one Guatemalan has ever tried to adopt a kid from my orphanage. Not one' (Goldman 2007: 233). Despite the lack of better options, Flor suffers anxieties about what she is doing. During her relationship with Moya, she expresses her ambivalence and self-accusation:

> There was a *mistica* [mysticism] to it. These were whole and often very complicatedly begun little lives she was signing over. It was important to have a sense of how the future would guide the past, you know what I mean? The power she had was incredibly intimidating; she said she needed nerves of steel sometimes, when faced with such a decision. It was just that she trusted herself to get it right more than whoever else might try to. No one knew, she told Moya, during those five brief and turbulent weeks when they were actually lovers, how often she had silently called herself a monster, how bitterly she'd derided her own conceits and prejudices (Goldman 2007: 462).

The anxiety and *mistica* accompanying the process are compounded by the fact that there are no clear legal lines governing transnational adoption. The ambassador who meets with Roger says: 'This so-called illegal adoption business, at least by Guatemalan legal standards, often turns out to be more a matter of ethically disturbing activities, say, than an actual violation of the laws here, because those laws just *aren't* very clear' (Goldman 2007: 99). Indeed, as recently as 2000, Guatemala was reported to have 'the weakest adoption laws in Central America', allowing for 'lucrative business deals' between private agencies and (predominately American) adoptive parents (Siegal 2011: 90). In Flor's case, the lack of legal definition means that judgement of her actions is left entirely to the ethical imagination: it cannot be called 'criminal', but the laws do not have sufficient moral content to mean that her adherence to them automatically exonerates her from wrongdoing.

While there is no evidence that she has been selling the orphans for parts, a different kind of 'transplant' is taking place. As David Samper writes in 'Cannibalizing Kids: Rumor and Resistance in Latin America', anxieties about 'outside adoption' have sparked recurrent legends about child-snatchers throughout Latin America. The whispers that swirl around Flor have their basis in this historical panic: there were several incidents in which American tourists and aid workers were brutally attacked because they were suspected of being kidnappers. Samper writes:

> What led to these violent and sometimes fatal attacks in Guatemala, and to many similar incidents throughout Central America? What could have motivated such violent fervor? It was a rumor. The people of San Cristobal Verapaz believed that their children were being kidnapped, killed, and their organs harvested for transplantation into wealthy North American children (2002: 2).

In Samper's rendering, the proliferation of this rumour communicates a particular truth, albeit a figurative one, about the conduct of the United States in Latin America during and after the Cold War. After installing its own preferred leader in Guatemala, the United States was free to entrench itself economically. Guatemala's natural reserves were 'gutted' for export by American corporations (for example, the United Fruit Company), hence the fear of foreigners feeding upon the country's most precious resources. Samper clarifies: 'Though untrue, the rumor is not a figment of the media's imagination or a political fabrication. Instead, it is rooted in the everyday lives of Latin American people, expressing real concerns and heightening real fears' (2002: 11). However, Samper qualifies this by acknowledging that the rumours have been used to further certain political agendas, including that of conservative anti-adoption campaigners.

The Long Night of White Chickens is less concerned with the idea of rumours as a form of grassroots resistance and more with the idea of such legends being harnessed in order to direct anger outwards. In *Speaking with Vampires: Rumor and History in Colonial Africa*, Luise White states that widespread rumours of vampiric Europeans in colonial Africa 'report[ed] the aggressive carelessness of colonial extractions and ascribe potent and intimate meanings to them' (2000: 3). In *The Long Night of White Chickens*, Goldman takes care to note that the rumours about Flor are deliberately focused on neocolonial 'extractions' in order to erase local complicity in various atrocities. It emerges that the family members of a prominent general have bribed journalists to report on Flor's supposed human rights abuses in order to divert attention from their own:

> So here was a chance to put an end to embarrassing rumours about the sister and sister-in-law of Lopez Nub and focus all hatred of baby sellers on Flor as well. Which excited the *faferos* [corrupt journalists], because here was their chance to make great patriotic rhetoric against baby sellers and make it sound like they were blaming the hypocritical *gringo* slanderers of Guatemala all in one murder, simply by accepting everything that the police said as true (Goldman 2007: 354-5).

When Flor is accused of 'vampirism' on the basis of her supposed 'Americanness', the claims are considered attempts to whitewash local complicity through scapegoating. The myth of the *patria* (homeland) can only be sustained if all blame is shifted towards an outside source (in this case, the United States). However, even knowing the source and the function of the rumour does not remove its content from the realm of possibility.

The Long Night of White Chickens subverts the idea that monstrosity can be defined in the Guatemalan context: like criminality, it proves to be a fluid designation. Roger wants to liberate Flor from being perceived as 'the moral monster of the Western World' (Goldman 2007: 70), but Flor is self-aware enough to see this monstrosity in herself as she is deciding the orphans' fates. Similarly, when Moya refers to Bram Stoker's *Dracula* as 'the best book about Guatemala ever written' (287), this initially seems to be a comment on government atrocities. As a student, he stars in a university production of *Dracula*, in which the terrorised Transylvanian villagers appear dressed in Guatemalan peasant *traje* (costume), as a reference to the government's campaign of genocide in the highlands. Years later, though, Roger accuses Moya himself of 'vampirism', or of using people for his own journalistic purposes. He says: 'So Moya's a little bit like Dracula after all' (421).

It is worth noting that Stoker's novel is not just about a single monster, but also about monstrosity as a form of contagion. A large part of the plot features the transformation of a virtuous young woman into a child-stealing vampire. The change is gradual. Lucy Westenra's health and soul gradually ebb away, until at last we read: 'She seemed like a nightmare of Lucy as she lay there, the pointed teeth, the blood stained, voluptuous mouth, which made one shudder to see, the whole carnal and unspirited appearance, seeming like a devilish mockery of Lucy's sweet purity' (Stoker 2011: 201). The characters in *The Long Night of White Chickens* are similarly faced with the possibility that the civil war will make monsters of them all:

> The last thirty years of violent repression – not to mention the centuries before – had perhaps bred a new kind of human being, as if in a poisoned petri dish. Resolutely silent, suspicious, dishonest, full of denial, quick to believe the worst of anyone, guilty when guiltless, guiltless when guilty. Noisy in the cantinas, but, even then, the desperate noise of the stifled. And such a capacity for delusion. Even the religious landscape had for many become one of confusion and delirium, because how to speak to the soul without addressing the terror so many felt there, and how to name the devil without increasing the terror? (Goldman 2007: 446)

In the world of the novel, rumours can be both true and untrue, and humanity and monstrosity can live side by side in the same people. Roger and Moya are both deeply implicated in Flor's murder, even if their 'crimes' seem trivial from an outside perspective: Moya makes an offhand comment about his affair with Flor and Roger gives her bad advice about where she should live. In the context of an extremely violent society, this is all it takes to become a killer. The intimacy of civil war means that everyone, including Flor, is 'guilty when guiltless, guiltless when guilty'.

Conclusion

The Long Night of White Chickens synthesises a number of literary forms and techniques into a single story. It is at once a crime novel, a family fable, a travelogue and a story of national breakdown and loss. The incompleteness of the synthesis reflects the difficulty and complexity of the subject matter: English and Spanish sit side by side, and real and imagined versions of events accumulate and remain indistinguishable, while lines of inquiry are abandoned for apparently irrelevant detours. This makes for a challenging read, but the challenge is not merely stylistic, operating as a type of politically charged defamiliarisation. Coe describes the novel's 'intent' as 'the hacking away of whole indecipherable jungles of irony in order to uncover the raw, disturbed heart at the centre (1993). He further comments that 'one awkward side-effect, certainly in the early stages of the book, is that Goldman has been so scrupulous at rendering this indecipherability that he is himself occasionally indecipherable'. However, it is perhaps more accurate to say that Goldman's rendering of the 'raw, disturbed heart' of the country *encompasses* absurdity, mystery and irony, rather than being obscured by them.

By using the form of the unsolved murder story, Goldman suggests Guatemalan identity as an unsolvable riddle, while simultaneously projecting an image of a society trapped in the violent 'gridlock' (Coe 1993) of dictatorship. At the same time, he suggests multicultural identities such as Roger's as irreducibly complex, defying solution at every turn. Sometimes readability and suspense are sacrificed, as the story unspools into repetition and futility, but the text's very difficulty highlights the intractability of its subject matter. While the murderer's trail is allowed to go cold, Goldman's chaotic projection of a world forces one to conclude that reports of Guatemala's non-existence are greatly exaggerated.

4

A Foreign Country
Gillian Slovo's *Red Dust*

Like *Anil's Ghost* and much of *The Long Night of White Chickens*, Gillian Slovo's *Red Dust* (first published in 2000) takes place during a period of political turmoil in the early 1990s. In this case, the setting is South Africa and the novel focuses on the Truth and Reconciliation Commission (TRC). The TRC was convened in 1996 and was one of the conditions agreed upon in the negotiations leading up to the dismantling of apartheid. The TRC differed from earlier examples of the truth commission model. Rather than offering 'blanket amnesty' to perpetrators, it assessed each case on its own merits. Chief among the qualifying criteria for a perpetrator to receive amnesty was proof of political motivation. In other words, perpetrators needed to demonstrate that their actions were part of systemic violence, rather than individual or rogue acts. Full disclosure was mandatory, but remorse was not a condition of amnesty. The hearings also differed from previous truth commissions (for example, those held in Chile in 1990-1) in that they were held publicly and broadcast on national television, in an effort to further the redress of the historical record through transparency (Bhargava 2002: 1307).

Sarah Barcant, the novel's protagonist, works as a prosecutor in New York. At the request of her mentor, a left-wing lawyer named Ben Hoffman, she travels back to her hometown of Smitsrivier, where she will represent Alex Mpondo at the amnesty hearing of Dirk Hendricks. Alex agrees to participate, not on his own account, but at the behest of the Sizela family. The Sizelas believe that Dirk may have information about their missing son Steve, who was detained at the same time as Alex, and tortured by Dirk's colleague, Pieter Muller. Because Pieter has not applied for amnesty at this stage of the novel, it initially falls on Alex and Sarah to try to extract this information.

The novel opens with a scene from Sarah's life in New York:

> Sarah glanced down, watching as her black suede ankle boots clipped up the subway stairs. She was smiling. No matter how often she sat in her prosecutor's seat waiting for a jury to deliver its verdict she would always find herself gripped by tension. Now the case was over, she felt almost light-hearted with relief... Not only had her victory buoyed her up, but on days like this she would experience anew the joy of being in New York (Slovo 2009b: 1).

As an example of reparative rather than punitive justice, the TRC proceedings will withhold precisely those features that Sarah has come to enjoy as a prosecutor. Here, there will be no sense of 'victory' or of the case being 'over'. As one character reflects: '[Sarah had] forgotten what this place was like. She'd forgotten that a story with a beginning, a middle and its own neat ending... was something New York might offer, but not South Africa' (Slovo 2009b: 336). Thus, the novel's opening lines – which appear to promise a courtroom procedural – prove misleading and the form of the narrative unravels into a more layered and equivocal meditation on the after-effects of violence.

Slovo draws on her own experience of the TRC. Her mother, Ruth First, was an anti-apartheid activist who was assassinated by letter bomb in 1982, while working in Mozambique. The men who orchestrated her killing applied for and were granted amnesty in 1998. *Red Dust* highlights the flaws of the reconciliation model of transitional justice and, unsurprisingly, emphasises the cost the process exacts from the victims and their families, who are forced to relive their trauma in public proceedings.

Slovo is best known as a crime novelist and the novel's use of suspense and scope align it with the thriller genre. The action builds towards a violent confrontation and the course of the investigation is marked by frustration and distrust of a flawed system. The crescendo of rough justice near the novel's end suggests the volatility of the past and the TRC's shortcomings in helping South Africa to process it. The text alludes to the criminal justice model, the reconciliation model and to violent retribution, but ultimately all three approaches are found wanting. In 'Novel Truths: Literature and Truth Commissions', Paul Gready writes,

> Cultural production has challenged the silences of apartheid and the TRC alike, and harbored its own silences. It has reflected upon ambiguity and complexity, interrogating gray areas of experience (for example, people may have been both victims and perpetrators). In the process it has redrawn the contours of South African culture and reconfigured the locus of truth telling. In part this potential is rooted in the fact that art and culture operate in different generic terrain, often asking questions rather than seeking answers (2009: 164).

In keeping with Gready's formulation, *Red Dust* 'ask[s] questions rather than seeking answers'. The novel questions the value of each approach to justice, but ultimately does not settle on a single approach. Instead, it uses the thriller mode to emphasise the difficulty and danger implicit in redressing national trauma. In his discussion of the thriller genre, David Glover writes that the form is 'concerned with creating obstacles, proliferating setbacks, traps, inconveniences, dead-ends and discomposure' (2003: 131). In *Red Dust*, many of these 'setbacks' result from the flaws implicit in existing models of redress, most notably the TRC. While much previous scholarship has focused on Sarah as a symbol of guilty white femininity, this chapter reads her narrative arc as an evocation (and dismantling) of crime fiction's generic expectations.

'Little perpetrator[s]'

In its portrayal of Smitsrivier, *Red Dust* treads a fine line between realism and the use of a microcosm to suggest a broader national reality. On the one hand, it represents a national crisis through a limited cast of characters, as the issue of reconciliation between races is dramatised through figures such as Dirk, Pieter, Alex and James Sizela – Steve's father. As Dorothy Driver writes: 'Slovo uses a classically Freudian model of family or pseudofamily relations in order to reflect on power relations in the social community' (2007: 108). However, the emphasis on family dynamics is not only a device to reflect the country at large, but also suggests that the trauma of apartheid has infiltrated every corner of domestic and family life. Gready identifies 'a number of recent South African novels that examine violence that is folded into intimate, interpersonal, everyday relationships' (2009: 170). *Red Dust* suggests that the betrayal and violations of apartheid were not only inter-communal, but also threatened to tear families and communities apart from within.

In the course of the novel, the characters uncover a series of revelations about apartheid-era murders and torture, but these seldom come to light through official channels. Significantly, almost none of the action-changing revelations are made in front of the TRC committee. Shameem Black writes: 'The omniscient form of the thriller, and its refusal of ambiguous knowledge about what happened in the past, allows for a form of knowability denied to the TRC. In this sense, Slovo's fiction asserts itself as the competitor of the truth commission' (2011: 55). Indeed, *Red Dust*'s challenge to the TRC is not one that insists on the unknowability or non-existence of truth: the novel provides an explanation for the reader, but it is not made available to the complete cast of characters or to the public records established by the TRC.

Instead, the revelations occur elsewhere in and around Smitsrivier: Alex Mpondo finds evidence that Steve Sizela withstood torture by finding a dead letter box by the river, still untouched by police. Pieter Muller's amnesty application characterises Steve's death as a suicide, but he later confesses in his own home, unmediated by officials and in earshot of his housebound wife. Steve's body is not identified through any legal or forensic procedure: we know it is him because his mother recognizes 'a watch' and 'a pair of sneakers' that have been buried with him, and '[begins] to wail' (Slovo 2009b: 264). That the real work of discovery is undertaken in and around the town underlines the inextricability of apartheid from bonds of friendship, family and marriage. By contrast, the action in the town hall tends to have a formal, staged quality, removed as it is from the patterns of everyday life.

Smitsrivier is a rundown town – 'the kind of *dorpie* [little town] the world had passed by' (Slovo 2009b: 239) – but we are aware from the start that terrible violence has occurred there. The town's history is bloody, as is evident from the gross human rights violations that are brought before the TRC. The TRC report defines gross human rights violations as 'the violation of human rights through – (a) the killing, abduction, torture or severe ill treatment of any person; or (b) any attempt, conspiracy, incitement, instigation, command or procurement to commit an act referred to in paragraph (a)' (TRC 1999: 60). In *Red Dust*, the most notable of these offences is the killing of Steve Sizela, but Slovo also depicts a slew of other violations that do not fall under the TRC's mandate.

Often these relate to the tacit reinforcement of the many injustices implicit in the apartheid social structure. The TRC's final report notes its failure to address these as a shortcoming of its model: 'This focus on the outrageous has drawn the nation's attention away from the more commonplace violations. The result is that ordinary South Africans do not see themselves as represented by those the Commission defines as perpetrators, failing to recognise the "little perpetrator" in each one of us' (1999: 1).

In Slovo's novel, the TRC's emphasis on 'the outrageous' (TRC 1999: 1) also enables whole communities to disassociate themselves from their histories of collusion. When the proceedings begin, the white community abruptly disassociates itself from people like Dirk Hendricks and Pieter Muller. Sarah's old schoolmate, a white barman named Andre, says: 'Muller's nothing. He's on his own now' (Slovo 2009b: 161). This is despite the fact that Pieter has always been looked upon as a 'pillar of the community' (334). Andre himself is depicted as a violent racist, who takes to the streets with a gun when protests spread out from the township, claiming that Smitsrivier's black population is 'running amok' (161). His attitudes are indistinguishable from Pieter Muller's, the only difference being the degree of ascendency each man has achieved in relation to the apartheid state. The community has created both men in its own image, but Pieter was granted a greater degree of power, hence his appearance before the TRC. Andre escapes perpetrator status because he is a barman and not a policeman, rather than because he is, in any sense, a better man.

Mahmood Mamdani argues that the TRC's focus on individual perpetrators paradoxically enabled group absolution for those who were not deemed to be involved in gross human rights violations: 'The TRC extended impunity to most perpetrators of apartheid ... the amnesty intended to be *individual* turned into a *group* amnesty. For any perpetrator who was not so identified was a perpetrator who enjoyed impunity' (2002: 35). Slovo's novel upholds this idea by demonstrating Dirk and Pieter as products of their social group, portraying them as 'pillar[s] of the community' (Slovo 2009b: 334) who are recast as scapegoats despite the popular support they have always enjoyed.

The TRC of the novel is focused on the actions of the two white men, but Slovo's emphasis on everyday cruelties in Smitsrivier transcends racial and gender divides. In the course of the novel, the town proves to be rife with 'little perpetrators'. One notable example is Pieter Muller's wife, Marie. Throughout their marriage she has avoided the subject of his work, becoming a collaborator through omission and silence. After Pieter goads James into killing him, Alex interprets Marie's failure to speak as a form of domination and control. He reflects:

> She'd stood by and watched, without interrupting, as James had twisted in the agony of what Pieter had told him and then she had taken up the gun, and stopped James from being James, from telling the truth. She had kept James as her sort had always tried to keep him: securely in his place (Slovo 2009b: 313).

Marie insists that her cover-up is an attempt to preserve Pieter's memory, but the act also robs James of his agency and identity. Following the shooting, James retires as headmaster of the local school, convinced that he is now too morally tainted to offer his students a role model: 'He could no longer foster those principles of probity, morality, integrity that were essential for the proper development of any individual. Not after what he had done' (Slovo 2009b: 307).

Marie's social status troubles the boundaries between strength and weakness: she is so physically frail that she is housebound, but at the end of the novel she realises that she has been complicit in apartheid by investing in the idea of a separate domestic realm, taking refuge in traditional gender roles to avoid seeing the truth. Of Marie, Slovo writes:

> She'd never eavesdropped on her husband, had never even thought of doing so. Pieter was a private man who guarded his secrets well. She had always respected that in him: throughout the many years they'd shared, she had never pried. Just as her mother had ruled over the household, leaving her husband free to negotiate the world, so Marie had done. She had liked it that way; she and Pieter had both liked it (Slovo 2009b: 297).

In overhearing the confrontation between her husband and James, Marie realises the stupidity of attempting to legislate between the 'household' and the 'world'. She denounces herself as 'stupid' and 'culpable' (Slovo 2009b: 299), but long before this scene there is evidence that the walls of the Muller home have never been enough to keep politics at bay. In one scene, Marie darns Pieter's suit following his summons to court, acknowledging that he has been subpoenaed without directly broaching the subject with him: 'This was not part of their communication. Never once in all the years of their marriage had she ever asked him about his work' (112). The illusion of separateness is finally demolished by the police officer who attends to Pieter's death. He says: 'Their domestic worker is already busy washing away the blood' (306). This domestic worker, Bessy, has been a largely silent presence in the household, while nursing Marie through an unspecified chronic illness. She is deeply involved in the Muller's home life, but for the most part is treated as an obedient shadow and lives in small quarters outside the main house. The policeman's words emphasise the irony of Marie's claim to have lived a life removed from politics, demonstrating as it does the presence of apartheid in her own home.

James Sizela, too, is a supposedly 'apolitical' character, who is nonetheless haunted by what he has done. When asked if James supported apartheid, Alex says:

> Not supported, no. But tolerated. James takes his Bible literally: he believes in rendering unto Caesar what is Caesar's. Upholding the law and obeying authority is his *sine qua non*. He tried to drum this into all his pupils, me included, and so when Steve joined the comrades, James had no way of understanding the move (Slovo 2009b: 244).

Although he has been comparatively powerless in relation to the apartheid state, James has been unyielding and harsh in his roles as father and teacher. When Sarah interrupts James in his classroom, she finds the older man in the middle of reciting from Shakespeare's *Richard III*. Sarah listens to 'a voice that was not his but the tyrant king's on the eve of Bosworth field, ringing out into that desolate space, an unaccustomed cry of shame for what he'd done, a man about to meet his fate' (Slovo 2009b: 177). The passage from which he quotes is as follows:

> My conscience hath a thousand several tongues,
> And every tongue brings in a several tale
> And every tale condemns me for a villain.
> Perjury, perjury, in the high'st degree! (Shakespeare 2000: 344)

In reading the classroom scene, it is tempting to associate the words 'tyrant king' with Pieter Muller, who killed James's son, but it soon becomes apparent that the reference to Richard's crisis of conscience foreshadows something else entirely. The 'cry of shame' one might expect to be uttered by a perpetrator at the TRC will come not from Pieter, but ultimately from James.

When the two men meet away from the proceedings, Pieter openly confesses to killing Steve, but threatens to expose James at the TRC. The testimony that James cannot bear to be publicly told does not relate to any crime, but to the way he brought up his son. The most damning testimony, for James, is Pieter's assertion that Steve felt his father had let him down and wept about it under torture. Pieter accuses him of being an 'unforgiving father' (Slovo 2009b: 301) who 'turned his back' on Steve, claiming: 'He kept on saying that if only you'd listened to him, if only you'd talked to him, he would never have got into this mess.'

James is forced to face the fact that he has been a tyrant in his own home, with his acid correctness and emphasis on respectability politics. Pieter reminds him of a time when, outraged by Steve's decision to attend a political meeting rather than church, James refused to speak to him for two weeks. Again, the offence is a negative one, a domestic sin of omission. James has betrayed Steve by refusing to talk and refusing to listen. For this kind of cruelty, there is no amnesty to be had.

Glover writes that part of the thriller genre's intensity derives from its depiction of heightened states, including 'a descent into pathological extremes of consciousness, the inner world of the psychopath or monster' (2003: 131). However, in *Red Dust*, Slovo often sacrifices intensity in order to depict the daily lives of the inhabitants of Smitsrivier. Even the perpetrators appear remarkable only in their very ordinariness. This refusal to pathologise or sensationalise human rights abuses and Slovo's depiction of the banality of evil is discussed below.

Defining motive

From the beginning of *Red Dust*, the reader is aware of Steve Sizela's likely fate. We are told: 'Although they had no concrete proof of this, most people in town – certainly most black people – believed that Steve was dead and that Muller was responsible' (Slovo 2009b: 16-17). Therefore, the mystery at the centre of the novel is not what happened to Steve, but why he was killed and where he was buried. In his discussion of the thriller genre, Glover writes: 'Often the thriller is preoccupied with the enormity of what is known and cannot be proved and this leads to an urgent desire for rough justice, an impatience with official procedures' (2003: 131). In the novel, the TRC process frustrates the search for answers, chiefly because the amnesty hearings reward claims of political intention. On the stand, Dirk's emphasis is on police procedure, rather than the competitive machismo that existed between him and Muller, and thus his unofficial role in Steve's killing never comes to light.

In her portrayal of the TRC proceedings, Slovo suggests a tendency for perpetrators to aggrandise their motives, attributing political depth to casual acts of cruelty. The TRC aimed to distinguish between 'politically motivated' behaviour and isolated acts of violence, with amnesty being offered only for the former type of violation. Anurima Bhargava argues that the reward offered for proof of political motivation – amnesty – ultimately incentivised the distortion and oversimplification of motives by perpetrators: 'An emphasis on orders underplays the motives of perpetrators and clouds the inquiry into why these crimes were committed. ... An accurate picture cannot be established when perpetrators have incentives to align their motives with the programmatic objectives to which they claim affiliation' (2002: 1331). By and large, Slovo's novel upholds this view.

In her article on *Red Dust*, Driver argues: 'For the TRC, listening to "motives and perspectives" as part of what it chose to call "personal or narrative truth" was a crucial addition to any discovery of forensic truth' (2007: 113). The novel places a different value on each type of truth that the commission pursues. The 'forensic truths' that emerge from the process prove to be valuable, while the 'motives and perspectives' on display are either misleading or impossible to discern. As Driver suggests: 'Motives and perspectives play a devious or self-deceiving role in the conversion of truths to lies and vice versa' (114). The fallibility of subjective testimony is not only the result of malicious deception: at the end of the novel, Sarah 'lies' to Alex about the timing of Steve's death in an attempt to release him from guilt. She does not realise her claim is true and that Dirk's claim that Alex sent Steve to his death is the lie. This episode shows the unstable relationship between truth and belief that attends the non-forensic 'narrative truth'.

In *Red Dust*, the most critical piece of forensic truth centres on the whereabouts of Steve's body. Prior to the revelation, his family had endured years of limbo, in which they waited for Steve to come home, 'hoping against hope' (Slovo 2009b: 45) that he had simply disappeared into exile abroad. The exhumation is the first confirmation of his death and allows his family to begin to mourn him. However, the question of *why* Alex and Steve were tortured – central to Dirk's attempt to win amnesty – is much less easily answered. The answer, when it arrives – not through any official channel, but through the reader's glimpse into Dirk's thoughts – is chilling in its pettiness.

In her article 'Revealing Is Healing', in which she discusses her own experience of the TRC, Slovo writes:

> How did the TRC hearing in which I participated affect me? Personally, if anything, it increased my feelings of hatred. Beforehand, I felt what happened to my mother was purely political. But after observing Ruth's killers' amnesty application I came to see that it was also personal: that they were murderers and that they were motivated by personal hatred as all murderers are (2007).

The novel's complex treatment of motive also resists the idea that motives can ever be 'purely political'. The torture of Steve and Alex can be read as politically motivated in the sense that the two men were African National Congress (ANC) operatives, detained for their political activities. It was their politics that initially placed them at the mercy of Dirk Hendricks and Pieter Muller, and a prevailing culture of violence that allowed the brutality against them to go unpunished. However, Slovo does not allow that Dirk and Pieter were only acting to further the interests of the state. Instead, she gradually reveals Dirk's antipathy for Alex as his cross-examination progresses and the reader is given glimpses of his thoughts that suggest he has been driven by 'personal hatred' and a taste for brutality.

While trying to talk Sarah around to the benefits of the TRC, Ben Hoffman claims that 'Alex and Dirk Hendricks have something very basic in common. They are both, in their own way, patriots . . . As is Pieter Muller' (Slovo 2009b: 150). On the stand, Dirk invokes the defence of patriotism, claiming: 'I was a loyal policeman. We were taught that the enemy was all around, that we must fight communism and its terrorists with all our might. This is what I did . . . I did it for the good of South

Africa' (131). However, in the final analysis, the killing of Steve Sizela is revealed, not as an act of due obedience, but as an unforeseen end to a violent game. It emerges that Steve's death was the outcome of a bet, in which Dirk and Pieter competed to see which of them could 'break' their prisoner first. Pieter went too far and Steve died under torture. When he is taunting James Sizela, Muller says: 'Steve's death was an oversight ... I did it by mistake. It was my hand that knocked his head against the wall, that knocked his brains out' (301). This piece of information is corroborated by Dirk and reveals the two policemen, not only as 'loyal' agents of a violent regime, but also as cavalier sadists. Characterising their actions as 'politically motivated' does not capture the lightness with which the lives of resistance fighters, and black lives in general, were treated.

In *Eichmann in Jerusalem: A Report on the Banality of Evil*, in which she details the 1961 trial of the infamous Nazi, Hannah Arendt writes:

> When I speak of the banality of evil, I do so only on the strictly factual level, pointing to a phenomenon which stared one in the face at the trial. Eichmann was not Iago and not Macbeth, and nothing would have been farther from his mind than to determine with Richard III 'to prove a villain' (1994: 287).

The Shakespearean characters evoked by Arendt – Richard III, Macbeth and Iago – are self-aware in their motives. Eichmann, she argues, was not. She argues: 'It was sheer thoughtlessness – something by no means identical with stupidity – that predisposed him to become one of the greatest criminals of that period' (1994: 134). The perpetrators in *Red Dust*, too, enact their brutality in the spirit of 'thoughtlessness', rather than considered intention. Even during the period of the TRC, Dirk persists in viewing the incident in the light of a workplace grudge. He reflects:

> And anyway. It was Pieter's fault. If Pieter had taken the trouble to dispose of his own bloody problems, all this would have turned out different. How could Pieter have let it happen in the first place? Why had he, usually so meticulous, suddenly been so careless? Foolish Pieter: killing a suspect by mistake (Slovo 2009b: 333).

In Slovo's text, this 'thoughtlessness' is inextricably tied to a double form of dehumanisation: because he is black and has been deemed a terrorist, Steve's death is seen as a 'bloody problem' rather than the extinguishing of a human life. As previously discussed, it is James who replicates Richard III's 'unaccustomed cry of shame for what he'd done' (Slovo 2009b: 177) in the climactic scene, while Pieter – by far the worse villain – looks on unmoved. James suffers agonies over Steve's death because he is able to fully apprehend the loss of his son. As Judith Butler writes in *Frames of War: When Is Life Grievable?*: 'Specific lives cannot be apprehended as injured or lost if they are not first apprehended as living' (2010: 5). Pieter, we learn, attended a church meeting soon after killing Steve, with no apparent sense of the irony of his actions, suggesting that he did not consider his actions murder, if indeed he considered them at all.

In Smitsrivier, the victims and the bereaved seek answers commensurate with the scale of their loss, but often the motive proves to be trivial from the perpetrator's perspective. As far as Dirk and Pieter are concerned, Steve's death was simply the outcome of a drunken wager. In introducing the idea of the bet, Slovo implies that the endpoint of dehumanisation is violence so nonchalant that it is essentially meaningless. Even as Dirk tries to frame himself as an innocent dupe of the apartheid system, his memories of being a torturer reveal the violence he enacted as being inextricable from his own motives. He recalls how Alex's eyelashes used to 'irritate him' to the point that he once considered 'cutting them off' (Slovo 2009b: 197).

In her memoir, *Every Secret Thing: My Family, My Country*, Slovo suggests the startling incongruity between the victims' experience of the impact of violence and that of the perpetrators. About interviewing Craig Williamson, one of the men responsible for her mother's murder by letter bomb, she writes:

> It was all too clinical for me, this tale of passing hands. I interrupted to ask whether they celebrated when they saw the package.
>
> 'It must sound terrible and strange . . .' Craig Williamson told me, '. . . it was almost casual . . . it wasn't as though somebody was responsible for this kind of thing . . . we had a particularly good technical guy . . . it was almost luck of the draw' (2009a).

In *Red Dust*, Steve's death is the result of a similar terrible lottery. Even Dirk's decision to implicate Pieter in Steve's killing turns out to be an impulse towards petty vengeance, rather than an act of conscience. It emerges that, annoyed by being made to bury Steve's body, Dirk planted evidence that confirmed that Pieter had been his torturer.

Slovo's eschewal of sensationalism in her depiction of evil can be considered a departure from genre. The reader follows Alex's failed attempt to assemble a chain of political cause and effect, but Slovo does not provide a fascinating portrait of pathology to compensate for the lack of political intrigue – a device that traditionally attends the depiction of motiveless violence in the thriller genre. The beginning of *Red Dust* promises a compelling villain in the form of Pieter Muller. Dirk's prison van is diverted from the road on a dark night and he is momentarily released from the back, only to come face to face with his old colleague. The image of Pieter is ominous. We are told: 'Any other man would have come up to Dirk and shaken his hand or clapped him on the back. But Pieter was not any man. Always controlled, always in charge, he merely walked a little closer before stopping to say: "Dirk"' (Slovo 2009b: 25). However, Slovo dismantles this image rather than building upon it.

In 'Noir and the Psycho Thriller', Philip Simpson discusses thrillers in which crime is depicted as a result of psychological extremes, rather than concrete motives:

> The 'psycho thriller' is a subgenre of the versatile thriller genre in which crime is represented as an outward manifestation of the internal workings of the pathological individual psyche ... The lead character in a psycho thriller is often engaged in a death struggle with the destructive, violent impulses of his or her own mind, or entangled in a contest of wits with a more-or-less equally matched opponent (2010: 187).

Neither Dirk nor Pieter 'struggles' against their 'violent impulses': their discomfort comes solely from their change in social circumstances. Similarly, although there are several scenes in which Sarah faces Dirk across a table, trying to manipulate him into revelation, their dynamic never develops into a true 'contest of wits', much less a meeting of minds. In *Red Dust*, meaningful confrontation is always elusive because the perpetrators cannot truly conceive of what they have done and the damage they have caused. The TRC fails to bridge the two points of view and a full verbal disclosure is never made, either during or outside the hearings.

In 'Thinking and Moral Considerations: A Lecture', Arendt describes Richard III's crisis of conscience – the very scene from which James Sizela recites – as 'an encounter of the self with its self' (1971: 443). The TRC proceedings represent an orchestrated encounter with conscience, in the sense that they force perpetrators to confront their victims and the consequences of their actions. However, Slovo implies that the apprehension of another's humanity, which is an act of imagining as much as seeing, cannot be enforced from without. It is therefore shown that confession does not imply the assumption of responsibility in cases where perpetrators cannot appreciate the humanity of those they have violated.

Truth and performance

In 'Performance, Transitional Justice, and the Law: South Africa's Truth and Reconciliation Commission', Catherine M. Cole argues: 'Not only were the [TRC] hearings performed before spectators, they also transpired on stages – the raised platforms and churches throughout the country where the TRC toured like a travelling road show' (2007: 179).

Even though the Smitsrivier town hall is lacking in grandeur, Slovo, like Cole, reaches for theatrical terms in her portrayal of the TRC proceedings. Before he is called to testify, Dirk Hendricks silently says: 'Showtime' (Slovo 2009b: 79). Sarah, preparing to appear as counsel, notes 'that tingle at her fingertips, the performance about to begin' (71). Within the text, the TRC is described in terms of both spectacle and novelty: it is said to be 'heading into town' (6) and is referred to by its local detractors as a 'circus' (83), a term identical to that used by the former prime minister of South Africa, P.W. Botha, to describe the real life proceedings (Cole 2007: 176).

On the first day of the hearings, Sarah observes the manner in which the set-up in the town hall mimics the promises of the new dispensation:

> That dusty, dead-end Smitsrivier should be witness to the likes of this! This dance of the past, this baroque blending of court ceremonial, street party and revivalist meeting. That a white policeman should have to come and explain his actions was astonishing enough, yet what felt really incredible was that the

faces out there in that sea of an audience were mostly black: here in this town hall where blacks had only ever been allowed to sweep up after the white audience had long gone home. Every rule by which all Smitsrivier had once lived out its life seemed to have been vanquished (Slovo 2009b: 82).

The 'baroque' demonstration of a new social order makes a dramatic statement, but it soon becomes clear that the old rules are far from being 'vanquished'. When Alex breaks down in the hearing, we are told: 'He pushed through the curtains and into the wings. Backstage was a dismal, crowded place. He scrabbled past old props and broken furniture' (Slovo 2009b: 202). Although the hall has presumably been used for community meetings in the past, the reader's attention is drawn instead to the forgotten relics of some kind of play. The disparity between 'on stage' and 'backstage' is significant: like the 'old props', it is clear that certain inconveniences have been moved just out of sight. Upon leaving the stage, Alex bolts from the hall and locks himself in a toilet stall. It is only afterwards that he realises that 'despite the abolition of segregated facilities he had made his way unerringly to this remnant of the past, to this, he smiled as he named it as of old, this *kaffir* [derogatory term for an African person] toilet' (202). This episode illustrates that segregation is still alive and well behind the scenes and in the psyches of Smitsrivier's inhabitants, despite the ostentatious changes out front.

In the novel, the suggestion of performance is not only a feature of the venue, but is also woven into the proceedings themselves. In Slovo's rendering, the structure of the hearings enables perpetrators to distort and weaponise the truth. Because the amnesty hearings allowed for far more narrative detail than would be considered relevant in a courtroom, perpetrators were given more opportunity to discuss their lives. Having already claimed responsibility for their actions in writing, they were literally tasked with explaining themselves on the stand. In doing this, Dirk has ample time to paint a picture of himself for the commission, even claiming post-traumatic stress disorder in a bid to appear more sympathetic.

Dirk's behaviour on the stand is based on the real testimony of police captain Jeffrey Benzien, who applied for amnesty at the TRC (Driver 2007: 108). Antjie Krog identifies Benzien's hearing as a historic moment: 'The amnesty hearing of police captain Jeffrey Benzien seizes the heart of truth and reconciliation – the victim face to face with the perpetrator – and tears it out into the light' (2004: 374). Dirk's manner and the answers he gives the commission follow Benzien's very closely, but Slovo's rendering imagines much of what the actual hearing suppresses.

In video footage of Benzien's TRC hearing, Tony Yengeni, one of his torture victims, says:

> What kind of man that uses a method like this one of the wet bag to people, to other human beings repeatedly and listening to those moans and cries and groans and taking each of those people very near to their deaths – what kind of man are you? What kind of man is that?[1]

Slovo's novel takes on the project of imagining the answer to this question. As Black writes, the 'omniscient form' (2011: 55) of the novel allows Slovo to contrast a perpetrator's bland answers with a revealing interior monologue, thereby suggesting an unspoken dimension to his testimony. The novel 'asserts itself as the competitor of the truth commission' by showing the multitude of resentments and complexities that can be contained behind an outward mask of compliance.

Dirk's unspoken thoughts reveal him as a spiteful and sadistic man, but this side of him is seldom revealed on the stand. For the most part, he comes across as bland and not particularly bright, as he dutifully delivers the lines that will allow him to walk free. When asked whether he has pared down the truth in his amnesty application, Dirk responds:

> 'I was in jail when I filled out the form,' this tamed, unfamiliar Dirk Hendricks insisted. 'Nobody told me how to do it. I was trained as a policeman only to write down the basic points and that's what I did here. I wrote what I thought was needed. If it wasn't enough, I'm sorry.' Repeating it, that meaningless utterance, 'I'm sorry,' this time accompanying it by the briefest of smiles and a renewed lowering of the head, a continuation of

---

1. Jeffrey Benzien's signature method of torture involved bringing victims to near asphyxiation by placing a wet bag over their heads. The quote is from a special report on the Truth Commission on SABC: http://sabctrc.saha.org.za/tvseries/episode57/section2/transcript8.htm?tab=victims.

his courtroom artifice, a construction for the purpose of getting amnesty which his satisfied lawyer punctuated by reaching across and clicking off the microphone (Slovo 2009b: 184).

The scene takes place from Alex's point of view and he characterises Dirk's body language – his 'brief' smile and the 'lowering of the head' – as a deceptive and expedient charade. As we learn more about Dirk's thought processes, we realise that Alex is correct in his assessment of Dirk's character and behaviour.

In *Performing South Africa's Truth Commission: Stages of Transition*, Cole points out:

> Significantly, the commission did not require perpetrators to express contrition or remorse. Rather the priority of the TRC was truth . . . there was no incentive or encouragement for those who appeared before the amnesty committee to 'perform' in the sense of projecting any particular demeanor, emotion or attitude (2010: 14).

However, as previously discussed, *Red Dust* is highly critical of the Commission's incentivising of political affiliation. Dirk's amnesty is not directly contingent upon a convincing performance of remorse, but it does demand that he show himself as the 'right' kind of perpetrator. For this reason, he masks his personal resentment and antipathy, portraying himself as a drone of a violent state, rather than a violent individual in himself. When he claims ignorance of how to fill in the amnesty forms, he projects an image of a humble, under-educated policeman with little initiative of his own.

In *A Human Being Died That Night: Forgiving Apartheid's Chief Killer*, Pumla Gobodo-Madikizela argues that the reconciliation model has the capacity to bring about catharsis through verbal apology:

> Beneath the surface of the TRC hearings, beneath the level of mere verbal exchange, something else was going on that constituted a powerful transfer of inner realities between killer and victims' relatives. In these situations, the killer's words are, in a sense, performative utterances, almost palpably potent instruments that accomplish the reorganization of the survivor's

inner reality even as they come out, regardless of how flat, shifty or uninspired they may sound. It is not the mannerisms the killer might use in speaking them that makes his words so powerful; it is the very fact that he is saying them at all. The words are what the victim wants to hear, to touch. *The words* themselves (2013).

In *Red Dust*, however, the concept of falsehood encompasses far more than what is implied by '*the words* themselves'. Here, the idea of 'performative utterances' is redolent of duplicity, even when characters are technically speaking truthfully. As Driver makes clear, *Red Dust* 'address[es], inter alia, the showy performance of contrition on the part of an amnesty-seeking perpetrator that tears out the heart of the notion of sincerity, to say nothing of truth' (2007: 108). Because Alex has an intimate understanding of his torturer, he cannot accept the persona that Dirk presents at the hearing, which – as Gobodo-Madikizela might have it – is a 'flat, shifty [and] uninspired' one (2013). Listening to Dirk's answers, Alex becomes outraged by his studied lack of inflection: 'The man Alex had known, the real Dirk Hendricks, had never spoken with such unrelenting monotony' (Slovo 2009b: 183). Dirk's 'courtroom artifice' (184) is aimed at getting amnesty, but in Alex's mind his 'showy performance' (Driver 2007: 108) of humility undermines his claims of responsibility.

Slovo juxtaposes Dirk's 'courtroom artifice' with moments of genuine revelation. However, it falls to the victim to use his 'intimate' (Slovo 2009a: 150) knowledge of his torturer to provide them. Whenever he manages to show the room the 'real' Dirk Hendricks, Alex is the one who suffers for it. Initially, he successfully draws 'flashes' of authenticity from Dirk by forcing him to discuss the details of his torture:

> Dirk Hendricks's tongue licked out, a snake's lick, before it hurriedly withdrew, a lustful, greedy, anticipating move. Watching, Sarah saw another man breaking free of the prisoner's chrysalis. She saw the narrowing of his eyes and the draining away of their colour. His lips tightened: no longer the Cupid's bow. His head lifted, his back straightened: he looked somehow more substantial and also much more dangerous. The shift was extraordinary. This was no longer the man who'd sat compliant on the stage ever since the onset of the hearing . . . That one was

gone – replaced by some other being that Alex had conjured up – a dangerous being (Slovo 2009b: 190-1).

This 'shift' echoes a turning point in the Benzien hearing, during which Yengeni instructed Benzien to demonstrate his preferred method of torture. Footage of the hearing shows a chilling change in Benzien's demeanour. Up to this point, his imposing size has been effaced by his position behind a table and by the suit he is wearing. During questioning, the bland, formal tone of his answers belies their content, preventing the viewer from forming a mental image of the incidents he is recounting. Throughout his testimony, he addresses his victims as 'Sir', in studied deference to the change in the country's power dynamics. When Ashley Forbes, another of his victims, says, 'Can I also ask that when I was arrested, do you remember saying to me that you are able to treat me like an animal or like a human being and that how you treated me, depended on whether I co-operated or not?' Benzien replies with formal detachment, saying: 'I can't remember it correctly Sir, but I will concede, I may have said it.'[2]

Yengeni's request momentarily forces Benzien to shed his placid persona. Like Dirk, Benzien is suddenly revealed as 'more substantial and also much more dangerous' (Slovo 2009b: 190) than he has previously appeared. In the torture re-enactment, he crouches over an inert black man and demonstrates suffocating him with a wet bag, restraining the man with the weight of his body. As Krog writes: 'The sight of this bluntly built white man squatting on the back of a black victim, who lies face down on the floor, and pulling a blue bag over his head will remain one of the most loaded and disturbing images in the life of the Truth Commission' (2004: 374). Indeed, the image is shocking, not only in its brutality, but also in its stark contrast to Benzien's earlier self-presentation. As in *Red Dust*, the victim has 'summon[ed] up his torturer' (Slovo 2009b: 193) for the Commission to see. However, the blunt reality of the re-enactment is a double-edged sword. At this point in the recording, Yengeni begins to stumble over his words, losing his composure as he is faced with the image of what has been done to him.

---

2. http://sabctrc.saha.org.za/tvseries/episode57/section2/transcript9.htm?t=%2B forbes+%2Bashley+%E2%80%98%2Byusuf%E2%80%99&tab=tv.

Red Dust dwells on this element of the Truth Commission, suggesting that in order for the truth to be aired, victims were forced to relive their own fear and humiliation. In 'The Enchantment of a False Freedom', Ato Quayson points out:

> *Red Dust* is particularly poignant for suggesting that, for the former victim to accuse his torturer properly and bring him to admit, a terrifying re-enactment of the scene of the torture is called for, in which the former victim, now apparently free, has to undergo the trauma of recall in order to invoke his torturer in his particularity as torturer (2005: 335-6).

Indeed, leading Dirk through an explanation of his torture by asphyxiation, Alex experiences a flashback:

> Now that Alex had called up the bag there was no escaping it. He felt the tug of it, its heavy fabric closing in, filling his mouth, his nostrils, smothering him. He shivered. Dark. Too dark. He lowered his head. He could feel the silence, building up around him, bringing with it dread. He looked round wildly (Slovo 2009b: 190).

Alex may understand Dirk well enough to 'summon' up his other side, but Dirk, equally, is able to expose this lesser-known, terrified version of Alex. When Alex enters the town hall, Dirk notes 'how different he looked. So different, in fact, that if Dirk hadn't known he would be there, he wouldn't have recognized him . . . What else had he expected? Mpondo was no longer a prisoner. He was an MP. No wonder he looked different' (Slovo 2009b: 78). As Alex leads Dirk through questioning, he loses his assurance and Dirk begins to direct the conversation, chipping away at Alex's public demeanour. The proceedings recast Alex in a role he thought he had left behind – one that was created for him by Dirk. When he eventually turns his back on the proceedings, Alex frames it as a repudiation of this role, stating: 'I won't be his victim again' (316).

The price Alex pays is not only a product of having to remember the trauma he has experienced, but also of Dirk's weaponisation of the truth. During cross-examination, Dirk reveals that Alex broke down under questioning and told him the location of an ANC arms cache. In doing so, he deliberately exposes Alex to the threat of censure from his community. Indeed, the effect of this revelation is immediately palpable within the town hall: 'The collective was united: like a wounded animal it gave up a soft burrowing hum that hovered above the hall until very gradually it died away. Nothing now – only silence – as the crowd let sink in what Alex, their hero, had done' (Slovo 2009b: 192). By focusing on Dirk's fresh victimisation of Alex, *Red Dust* suggests the unfairness of proceedings that essentially punished victims for their participation by laying bare their own histories for public scrutiny.

Red Dust characterises Dirk's exposure of Alex's response to torture as a deliberate act of malice, a charge that was also levelled against Benzien. Krog suggests that, following the wet bag demonstration, Benzien deliberately engaged in retaliatory shaming as he revealed, unasked, the fact that Yengeni had identified his comrades after being tortured: 'Back at the table, Benzien quietly turns on him and with one accurate blow shatters Yengeni's political profile right across the country. "Do you remember, Mr Yengeni, that within thirty minutes you betrayed Jennifer Schreiner? Do you remember pointing out Bongani Jonas to us on the highway?"' (2004: 374). Krog further describes Benzien's loaded reminiscences about his 'friendship' with activist Ashley Forbes, in which he claimed: 'I think that the two of us, after weeks of confinement, really became quite close.' In the novel, Dirk resorts to both of these tactics, subtly threatening his questioner with destruction under the guise of good faith.

Again, much of Dirk's testimony is literally 'true', but contextually misleading. In the footage of the Benzien hearing, Benzien reminds Ashley Forbes of a trip they took to the countryside, recalling Forbes eating Kentucky Fried Chicken and playing in the snow next to the road while a married couple snapped pictures of him. However, he is vague about the details of torture and assault. When activist Gary Kruser takes his turn to question him, he challenges Benzien's professed failure of recall, saying: 'You seem to remember very flimsy things, like the Kentucky and whatnot' (SABC 1996a). In a harrowing follow-up interview Forbes fills in the details that Benzien has 'forgotten' or omitted, such as the fact that their day trips were part of a process of psychological torture, which included severe violence, 'to the point where ... after three months I tried to commit suicide' (SABC 1996b). Forbes continues:

And then he takes you for a drive and he's all dressed nicely and so forth and he says, 'Come, let's go, go have something to eat' and he takes me to a shop or some place and have something, you know, he says Kentucky or steak or something and he says, 'No you've done well and everything's okay' and then maybe at two or I don't know what time in the morning he'll take you back to the cell again. And the next day at about five, six, he'll come again (SABC 1996b).

Here, it becomes apparent that the trips Benzien has put forward as evidence of his own kindness were not a respite from cruelty, but part of his attempts to break his suspects. However, by invoking the memory, Benzien at once suggests Forbes's collusion with his captors and casts himself in a comparatively benevolent role. Dirk uses the same approach, referencing a trip to the country in which Alex ran around 'like a child' (Slovo 2009b: 193) and reminding Alex of a joke they had shared. In doing so, he reinforces their old power dynamics, taunting Alex by reminding him of a time when he 'would have done anything for Dirk Hendricks' (192). Slovo characterises Dirk's tone as 'gleeful', which casts the entire story of the day trip as an attempt to humiliate Alex by suggesting him as a servile collaborator and reminding him that there are far more damning revelations to come.

The TRC report notes the dangers attending public disclosure, but discusses them only in relation to perpetrators. The report asserts that amnesty was not synonymous with impunity, in part because it forced applicants to claim culpability in a public forum, leaving them open to social consequences. The report reads:

Apart from the most exceptional circumstances, the application is dealt with in a public hearing. The applicant must therefore make his admissions in the full glare of publicity... Often this is the first time that an applicant's family and community learn that an apparently decent man was, for instance, a callous torturer or a member of a ruthless death squad that assassinated many opponents of the previous regime. There is, therefore, a price to be paid. Public disclosure results in public shaming, and sometimes a marriage may be a sad casualty as well (TRC 1999: 8-9).

In *Red Dust* victims such as Alex must relive the past in the same 'glare of publicity' and are therefore vulnerable to identical 'public shaming' when their response to torture emerges. In implicating Dirk, Alex has to 'unleash his own disgrace' (Slovo 2009b: 192), losing his status as a 'hero' in the eyes of the community. He knows that if the questioning of Dirk Hendricks proceeds, his own betrayal of Steve will eventually come to light. In the end, the 'price to be paid' proves to be too high for him to continue with the process, and he decides to break his association with Hendricks by declining to question him further. He says: 'I can't risk Dirk Hendricks's narrative, his version of history, becoming mine. And he's bound to get his amnesty, so why should I put myself through this? I can't sleep. I can't eat. I can't go on. I'm sorry' (228).

When Sarah protests at the idea of Dirk being able to walk free, Ben replies: 'No, he won't. He has lost his wife and his children: to lose the hope of such intimacy is a far greater punishment than any jail sentence' (Slovo 2009b: 319). However, the idea of the TRC process as both trial and punishment again suggests consequences for all involved. James kills Pieter partly because he cannot bear to lose the dignity of his position in the community or for his wife to find out how deeply he had hurt their son. In fact, it is the threat to his marriage that finally spurs James to shoot him. Pieter's last words are: 'I'm going to tell the truth to the Truth Commission . . . I'll describe your son and the pain he underwent. I'll tell them what he told me about you as well. I'll make you listen, not only you, but his mother as well' (302). This demonstrates that the TRC's assertion quoted above – that 'sometimes a marriage may be a sad casualty as well' – may apply to victims as well as perpetrators. James has already lost his son and he fears that if he pursues the process, he will lose his wife as well. Like Alex, he has the opportunity to bring to light behaviour far more abhorrent than his own, but ultimately cannot bear to submit his shame to public scrutiny.

In 'Cracked Vases and Untidy Seams: Narrative Structure and Closure in the Truth and Reconciliation Commission and South African Fiction', Meg Samuelson discusses fictional narratives depicting the TRC and says: 'Their endings along with the very texture of the narratives reveal how they position themselves in relation to the TRC process and its desired end-result of reconciliation and nation-building' (2003: 66). *Red Dust* ends on an ambivalent note and the question of whether the victims' ordeal at the Commission has been worthwhile extends far beyond the scope of the novel. This ambivalence is partly a feature of genre. In the thriller genre, a villain is often corralled and punished, but unlike in Golden Age crime writing, the reader is continually made aware that the guilty party is part of a pervasive pattern of social violence. Thus, along with the relief that comes with apprehending the criminal, the texts also tend to leave readers with a lingering sense of disquiet. The context of social transition adds an additional layer to this ambivalence. In this case, it stems from the fact that the effects of the proceedings are intended to produce long-term, systemic change.

Sarah finds it difficult to accept that the hearings have been valuable when she sees the damage they have wrought in Smitsrivier. When she raises this protest, Ben says: 'You've got it all wrong . . . The reconciliation the Commission talks about is not between individuals' (Slovo 2009b: 318). This implies that the TRC has value as a national ritual. In Ben's view, the very publicness of the proceedings will help to bring about national catharsis, even as it exerts terrible pressure on the individuals involved. In 'Revealing Is Healing', Slovo herself expresses this hope, even as she criticises many other elements of the proceedings. Of the public broadcasts, she writes:

> There were those who told me of driving with the radio on, and of being so affected by what they heard that they had to stop their cars and vomit. But there were also those who turned off their radios, and their televisions, and spoke of other things. And yet even for them, I do not doubt that the drip, drip of the TRC was powerful: the fact that apartheid's thin veneer of civilisation was gradually being peeled away, could not be completely ignored (Slovo 2007).

During the period in which the novel is set, it was still impossible to decide what good the TRC had achieved, but even though Dirk will walk free there is a sense that not all is lost. The Commission is intended as a beginning, rather than an ending, and the form of the narrative imitates this in its resistance to a firm conclusion.

Homecoming

The narrative takes place from several different perspectives, but it begins and ends from Sarah's point of view. In the course of the novel, she is made to confront her own childhood in Smitsrivier and to weigh her decision to leave. From the start, she suspects that Ben has an ulterior motive when he asks her to return for the TRC, but resolves not to be drawn in:

> She would not allow herself to be dragged into a contemplation of her past. Leaving small-town Smitsrivier had been her childhood goal and she had managed it as completely as she could ever have wished. She was here to do a job of work because Ben had asked her to come and because she owed him too much to contemplate refusal. That's all (Slovo 2009b: 12).

It emerges that this attitude of detachment is precisely what Ben, himself a lawyer, is hoping to challenge in Sarah. Despite her technical brilliance at practising the law, he suspects her of lacking humanity. After her initial interview with Alex Mpondo, in which she challenges his version of events to prepare him for questioning, Ben accuses her of being a 'hunter' (Slovo 2009b: 67) and an 'unfeeling monster' (68). Sarah protests: 'Isn't this why you brought me all the way from New York: because you needed my objective eye?' (67). In fact, Ben wants to test Sarah's capacity for compassion, rather than objectivity. He says: 'Let's see now if you're still capable of crossing the divide from prosecutor into people's champion' (43).

Sarah is an excellent lawyer and her failings and missteps in Smitsrivier do not result from any lapse in technical brilliance, but are implied as a failure of the judicial model itself. Sarah objects to the TRC on the grounds that it is not enough to satisfy the 'perfectly understandable human desire' for justice (Slovo 2009b: 39). Ben says: 'Can't you see how your emphasis on the law is a prosecutor's obsession that would lead to the most terrible injustice?' (42). The narrative does not reward Ben's strong belief in the value of the TRC process, but neither does it champion Sarah's initial 'emphasis on the law', which aims to isolate and extract criminality, rather than addressing the legacy of a violent system. This is highlighted at the end of the novel, when Ben, Alex and Sarah all collude in allowing James to walk free after his murder of Pieter Muller. Because of the tangled and violent history that the two men share, Sarah is forced to agree that conventional ideas of crime and punishment should not apply. She further demonstrates how far she has strayed from her 'prosecutor's obsession' (42) by reflecting that 'perhaps James would come out of this better' (329). While the novel does not advocate a specific method of long-term redress, it makes it clear that context and history will have to be taken into account.

Sarah's transformation over the course of the narrative is largely enacted through her relationship with Alex. In the beginning, her judicial outlook insists on a binary relationship between truth and falsehood that does not factor in the ways in which trauma is processed and remembered. This is evident in her first interview with Alex, in which he misremembers the last time he saw Steve. His version of events is impossible, according to the floor plan of the police station that Sarah produces from her handbag. She confronts him with the disparity and when he doesn't respond, she says: 'Answer me, Alex. What did you really see?' (Slovo 2009b: 64). Her demand suggests that Alex is lying, but his story ends up being at least partially true. The fragment of memory is accurate, but has been stored out of context because Alex was not aware that, as a prisoner, he had been drugged and moved to a second location outside the main town. It is only through flashbacks and sense memories that he comes to recall the experience of being transported in the boot of Dirk Hendricks's car with Steve at his side.

At the end of the novel, it is Sarah who resorts to a lie. She says: 'Hendricks told me . . . he told me that Steve was dead long before you ever named him' (Slovo 2009b: 331). Alex's intimate knowledge of Dirk means that he cannot be so easily fooled: 'The fact that she'd assumed Alex would believe what she'd told him, showed just how long she'd been away' (336). Their exchange proves that Sarah still lacks Alex's local knowledge of Smitsrivier, but also that she has come to value compassion more highly than the universal application of truth. In their final scene together, she is more intent on consoling him than with establishing a record of what has occurred: 'She thought that this reassuring of Alex was much more important than the truth could ever be' (331). In the same scene, she acknowledges that her feelings for Alex have changed from 'suspicion and attraction' to 'tenderness' (328). She embraces him after they have been talking about his period in detention, transcending the attorney-client divide, the colour bar and the life-work boundary in one efficient gesture.

Sarah's return is metaphorically loaded. Her original incarnation is best understood as an evocation of a particular genre: the Sarah we meet at the beginning of the novel is single, childless, hard-drinking and expensively shod. Her New York success story suggests the triumph of the individual: there, she embodies a kind of empowerment often characteristic of the female investigator in a certain kind of popular culture. In *Hardboiled and High Heeled: The Woman Detective in Popular Culture*, Linda Mizejewski writes:

> So is this the feminist heroine for the turn of the twenty-first century? The refusal of wife/mother roles certainly aligns them with the non-traditional women's stories. But other aspects of these characters could as well align them with conventional and even right-wing thinking. The successful loner, the gritty nonconformist, the stubborn individualist who's licensed to carry a gun – these are figures more likely to be found in the NRA [National Rifle Association] than in NOW [National Organization for Women] ... The [Sue] Grafton and [Patricia] Cornwell series in some ways exemplify the 1970s toughchic school of feminism, in which women succeed on male turf without changing the rules of the game (2004: 36).

Our first glimpse of Sarah suggests that she is one of these 'toughchic' heroines. Ben's wife Anna says: 'She has so much going for her. She's beautiful, she's intelligent, she has friends, a good standard of living, she's a good lawyer' (Slovo 2009b: 118). The unmaking of this figure does not represent a criticism of the hardboiled crime genre, or even of the American justice system per se, but rather suggests the individualist litigator as being out of place in the context of the TRC, with its emphasis on community engagement and the value of subjective testimony. When Sarah first appears she is 'buoyed' up by 'black suede ankle boots' and 'victory' (1), but the text does not dwell on the fact that both of these have presumably been earned through the business of conviction and incarceration. Instead – like Sarah's designer shoes, which are 'ruined' (35) by the red dust of Smitsrivier – her beliefs are shown to be suitable for New York, but are rendered 'completely inappropriate' (36) by her sudden 'continental shift' (8). In South Africa her 'toughness' manifests as insensitivity and her 'individualism' as arrogance.

The unravelling of the 'toughchic' persona is not limited to Sarah's views on truth and justice, but is also a disassembling of the entire identikit sketched in the first few pages. This includes Sarah's 'refusal of wife/ mother roles' (Mizejewski 2004: 36) and her estrangement from both family and community. At the beginning of the book, Sarah treasures her upscale apartment precisely because she shares it with nobody else: 'She loved its solitude and its uncluttered elegance ... this was home' (Slovo 2009b: 2). However, once Sarah arrives in Smitsrivier she becomes sensitive to what she perceives as Ben's disapproval of her single lifestyle. She begins to see it when he names a John Coltrane ballad out of context ('You don't know what love is' [120]) and she interprets another of his comments as possibly 'making a judgement about her and her lack of either husband or children' (319).

Ben's criticisms about her 'heartless' litigation methods are part of a greater judgement about her incapacity for, or avoidance of, intimacy. He says: 'I failed her. I encouraged her to go and I didn't make sure that she came back. And now she no longer belongs here. Or anywhere perhaps' (Slovo 2009b: 118). Ben surmises that Sarah's tendency to be ruthless in her work is part of her fundamental inability to connect with other people on a human level. The narrative upholds this idea: Sarah's change in attitude leads her, not only nearer to Alex's way of thinking, but into his arms as well. Similarly, although she intends to return to New York, Sarah prolongs her stay in Smitsrivier in order to spend time with Ben before he dies, assuming a daughterly role by his side.

Slovo's characterisation of Sarah is problematic at times. As a character, she lacks psychological depth and yet her experience of return is linked with much graver variations on the theme. This is best exemplified by the title of the novel. As previously discussed, the dust of Smitsrivier ruins Sarah's shoes, suggesting her past and undermining her attempts at self-reinvention. However, the tenacity of the dirt is used in other places to suggest the violent stains of South African history. Dirk observes that, after burying Steve, 'the dirt had got everywhere, in his skin and in his clothes; he remembered how much Katie had complained about the way the red dust had clogged up the washing machine' (Slovo 2009b: 334). In Dirk's case, the image of the red stains can be read as one of the text's many references to Shakespeare's *Macbeth* and suggests the impossibility of washing away the violence of the past. This meaning sits oddly with Sarah's attempts to forget her old self, just as the conundrum of restorative justice makes an awkward companion to the question of whether Sarah will ever 'know what love is' (120).

When Sarah initially receives Ben's phone call, she thinks: 'There is no going back. Not after all this time' (Slovo 2009b: 3), but it is unclear what is at stake in her return. Her family has emigrated from South Africa and Ben is the only person in Smitsrivier with whom she has kept in touch. The memories the town brings back for her are of awkwardness and discomfort rather than trauma: as Ben's misfit protégée, she received a far more progressive education than most white children in Smitsrivier and thus grew up as something of an outsider.

Georgina Horrell writes: 'The parallels between "Sarah" and Gillian – character and novelist – are implicit . . . Slovo deftly sets up a picture of a woman who had left the agonies, contradictions and conflicts of South African white womanhood behind, in order to immerse herself in a metropolitan environment apparently less fraught' (2004: 770). However, Horrell's analysis falsely conflates self-imposed exile with political exile and she does not account for her use of 'agonies' to describe Sarah's experience.

At most, the examples that Horrell offers – for one, Sarah's feeling of anxiety and guilt when black men avert their eyes from her in the street – suggest awkwardness. There is nothing in Sarah's background to align her with those who, like Slovo, were raised in families committed to a liberation struggle, a position that, in many cases, may properly be described as agonising. One suggests the trauma of formative enmeshment in politics, the other a vague feeling of survivor's guilt for having avoided becoming thus enmeshed. We learn that, as a teenager, Sarah was arrested for breaking segregation laws by drinking at an illegal shebeen, but she acknowledges this as 'a stupid risk [taken] merely for rebellion's sake' (Slovo 2009b: 34), rather than a committed act of resistance. Furthermore, Ben secured her release 'within minutes' of his arrival at the police station, meaning the consequences of the action proved negligible.

Metaphorically, the significance of Sarah's return is sound: her symbolic homelessness exists as a warning about the dangers of leaving behind the past without so much as a backward glance. However, nothing in the novel really accounts for the idea that Sarah does not belong anywhere and her journey 'home' symbolises more than it entails. In the main, she exists as a kind of conduit, whose musings on the subject of the past open the door for the theme to be discussed from a broader and more political point of view. Driver writes:

The novel's deployment of a white woman from New York as its central character is aligned with the book trade dictum . . . that American audiences can be involved in an action only through American eyes. With its major focaliser being at least part American, the book . . . threatens to be less foreign (2007: 106).

This is a fair (if rather cynical) interpretation of Sarah's role in the novel: she operates as both a symbol of return and a cultural mediator within the text, her insider/outsider position enabling her to both supply local knowledge and to demand it on the reader's behalf. However, Sarah's sense of dislocation in Smitsrivier is not merely indicative of the novel's 'aspirant bestseller status' (Driver 2007: 107). The 'foreignness' that Sarah interprets for readers is not only the disparity between New York and Smitsrivier, but also the disparity between the TRC and existing models of justice. In setting up Sarah's characterisation, Slovo uses crime fiction shorthand to suggest conventional modes of justice and then subjects Sarah and her beliefs to the pressures of a different milieu. Apartheid, the novel implies, is not a case to be solved by a tenacious loner, but requires a different kind of protagonist altogether.

Conclusion

In the course of *Red Dust*, three different responses to apartheid are played out, but no single approach emerges as a clear way forward. The TRC proves, in many ways, inadequate, but so do the clear legal principles that Sarah initially seeks to import. James's violent revenge eliminates Pieter from society, but his own relief is mingled with agony and regret. However, if the novel does not end with reconciliation, its denouement suggests, at the very least, forward motion.

When Alex first appears in the novel, he keeps lifting his foot 'further off the accelerator' (Slovo 2009b: 29) as he drives towards Smitsrivier, deferring his arrival. At the end of the book, he 'pressed down on the accelerator and the landscape accelerated, its muted colours joining into one vast sage blur, passing him by. He let it go. Keeping his foot on the gas, he thought of nothing in particular: he just drove' (337). As he drives away, Alex reflects: 'He had looked Dirk Hendricks in the eye. That was a start' (338). It is implied that South Africa may be able to achieve what Alex calls 'a general moving on' (336), although it is unclear whether this will occur because of the Truth Commission, or in spite of it. Without rewarding a specific form of engagement, the novel nonetheless upholds the idea that the past must be 'looked in the eye' before any progress can be made. Sarah's return and her journey from detachment to compassion is used to illustrate the need for an engaged and empathic model of redress, although a comprehensive vision of what might have been is not realised in the narrative. In this way, the very structure of the text is allowed to echo the complexity of the subject matter, eschewing easy answers and emphasising the complex issues that attend the project of healing.

5

Hijacked Narrative
Nuruddin Farah's *Crossbones*

Nuruddin Farah's *Crossbones* is set in Somalia and was first published in 2011. It operates both as a stand-alone novel and as the conclusion to Farah's Past Imperfect trilogy. The books in the trilogy have several characters in common, but are set in different political eras. The trilogy traces the fall of the military dictator General Siad Barre (*Links* [first published in 1978]), the rise of power among local warlords, or 'strongmen' (*Knots* [first published in 2006]), and the emergence of piracy and militant Islam in the form of Al-Shabaab (*Crossbones*). Each of the texts details a different protagonist's return to Somalia, but *Crossbones* stands out for its subversive use of genre. It is also unique in terms of structure: *Crossbones* is a denser and more fragmented work than its predecessors. The novel engages with the media image that has been created of Somalia, countering it with a chaotic, unresolved narrative.[1]

The novel initially appears to conform to the narrative techniques of crime fiction, but ultimately shatters them by reneging on the promises of its opening chapters. While crime fiction typically builds towards revelatory catharsis, Farah's novel is structurally and thematically preoccupied with dissolution, rather than resolution. In order to emphasise the elusiveness and complexity of life in a collapsed state, Farah begins the novel with a clear line of inquiry: we learn that the novel's two 'detective' figures, Malik and Ahl, have returned to Somalia to solve the 'riddle' (Farah 2012: 41) of a teenage boy's disappearance. However, once Malik and Ahl actually arrive in the country, every attempt they make to impose narrative on their surroundings seems to result in greater frustration and

---

1. Part of this chapter was published in 2017 as Kamil Naicker, 'Going to Pieces: Narrative Disintegration in Nuruddin Farah's *Crossbones*', *Social Dynamics* 43 (1): 8–18.

uncertainty. The promise of closure is broken down, as are the detective figures themselves: the two protagonists undergo a process of physical and mental disintegration as they attempt to piece together a version of the truth.

Although justice and catharsis are depicted as emotionally necessary and desirable, Farah always places them out of reach, emphasising their virtual impossibility in the Somali context. At the start of the novel Jeebleh notes, sadly:

> The great tragedy about civil wars, famines and other disasters in the world's poor regions . . . is that the rubble seldom divulges the secret sorrows it contains. The technology, the forensics to determine what is what, scientifically, is not available; the dead are rarely identified or exhumed. Often no one knows how many have perished in the mudslide or the tsunami. One never gets to hear the last words that passed their lips, or what, in the end, caused their death: a falling beam, a failing heart, a spear of bullet-shattered glass? Or sheer exhaustion with living in such horrid circumstances day in and day out? (Farah 2012: 26)

Similarly, Malik, reflecting on a friend's murder, says: 'I often think how, in fiction, death serves a purpose. I wish I knew the objective of such a real-life death' (Farah 2012: 285). In *Crossbones*, death is both senseless and commonplace: it does not provide a catalyst for action, nor does it further the character development of those left behind. Rather, it is simply the humdrum, inevitable result of the 'horrid circumstances' (26) the civil war has imposed upon Somalia's inhabitants.

The apparent randomness of the violence in Somalia is amplified by the fact that it is largely enacted remotely. Cambara (the protagonist of *Knots*, who also appears in *Crossbones*) says: 'For me . . . there is no difference between the imam remote-controlling the suicide bomber and the guy orchestrating the Tomahawk launch from the safety of his Colorado base' (Farah 2012: 355). In modern warfare, perpetrators and their motives are so far removed from their acts of deadly force that the violence itself often appears both pointless and anonymous. During the Ethiopian invasion, Malik is having drinks with friends when an explosion sounds outside: 'Just then a single rocket falls close by. The house trembles slightly, the windowpanes shaking in their frames, the bulbs of the chandelier lightly knocking against one another with a tinkling sound that, to Malik, distantly recalls one of his daughter's wind-up toys' (285). The reference to the wind-up toy suggests a moral weightlessness: the very mechanisms of the pre-programmed rockets and drones put perpetrators at a remove from the consequences of their actions, creating the illusion of toy warfare, while those in the firing line die unexamined deaths.

The form of the narrative in *Crossbones* – fragmented, 'unofficial' and progressively breaking down – is a deliberate attempt to reflect the scope and complexity of the Somali situation, in which cause, motive and effect are often difficult to discern. Rather than containing his subject matter within a recognisable form of narrative, Farah pushes the crime genre to its limits by reneging upon every generic expectation of the form, thereby suggesting the inability of historically Western forms of narrative to capture the reality of postcolonial, post-collapse Somalia. Not only have villain/victim categorisations been broken down by years of intimate conflict in the civil war, but enterprises such as 'Somali piracy' are part of a vast, tangled web of international financial interests. Farah does not seek to redress every popular misconception with a countering 'truth', but the chaotic, apparently incomplete structure of the novel is itself a call for fresh terms of engagement. By writing a 'crime novel' that evokes more questions than answers, Farah suggests the facility of all forms of narrative that claim to unilaterally 'capture' the Somali reality.

Rumour and revelation

Crossbones is set in 2006 and depicts the final days of the Union of Islamic Courts (UIC) and Ethiopia's invasion of Somalia. The novel begins with two characters' attempts to construct their own metanarratives about the region. Malik, a foreign correspondent, has come to Mogadishu to write about the 'homeland' he has never seen. He also intends to help his brother Ahl, who is searching for his underage stepson, Taxliil. Taxliil has been recruited by Al-Shabaab operatives in Minneapolis and has run away to join their ranks in Somalia. His disappearance is presented as the novel's central mystery:

> The next time misfortune called, Taxliil was ready to follow. She took him back to Somalia, his route an enigma, the source of the funds that paid for his air ticket a mystery, his handlers a

puzzle, the talent spotters who recruited him a riddle. When Ahl decided that he would go to Somalia, [Ahl's wife] Yusur asked him why he would risk his own life in pursuit of the hopeless case of a young boy who had disappeared to God knows where. Ahl replied that he wished to reduce the number of unknown factors (Farah 2012: 41).

To return to Tzvetan Todorov's statement quoted in the introduction: 'For there to be a transgression, the norm must be apparent . . . Genres are precisely those relay-points by which the work assumes a relation with the universe of literature' (1975: 8). Farah's framing of Taxliil's disappearance as 'a mystery', 'a puzzle', 'a riddle' – all things that demand solving – signals the major tenets of the crime genre, evoking generic expectations in the reader. Having set up Taxliil as the narrative's ostensible quarry, Farah then diverts from the norm by allowing Taxliil's story to recede and remain largely unknown. The narrative therefore moves further and further away from cohesion, not only in the case of Taxliil, but also through Malik's repeated failed attempts to capture the region through reportage.

Farah repeatedly undermines the traditional function of the literary detective by thwarting his two protagonists in their quest to pin down Somalia in terms of a single narrative. In 'The Fingerprint of the Foreigner: Colonizing the Criminal Body in 1890s Detective Fiction and Criminal Anthropology', Ronald R. Thomas argues: 'The work the literary detective performs is an act of narrative usurpation in which he converts stories told by subjects about themselves into alibis proffered by suspects' (1994: 656). Although Thomas explicitly refers to Golden Age crime, his formulation holds true for the majority of detective stories in which the narrative tends towards revelation. Even lacking the traditional confrontation between 'criminal' and detective, the detective's eventual summation becomes the official explanation for all that has gone before. In the traditional narratives, the detective ultimately restores order through the 'act of narrative usurpation', exerting authority by superimposing a single version of events over the many versions of truth that the suspects proffer.

Farah's repudiation of narrative authority carries meaning beyond the context of genre: it is also used to critique the behaviour of the international media. By making one of his literary detectives a journalist,

Farah implicitly suggests 'narrative usurpation' as a facet of modern journalism. Malik's job is to collect information ('clues') and to distil many stories into a cogent article. However, Malik struggles to filter the information that bombards him from every side. He also finds it difficult to reconcile what he has read about Somalia with what he experiences in the country itself. In *Getting Somalia Wrong? Faith, War and Hope in a Shattered State*, Mary Harper discusses the country's reputation abroad, which is one of undiluted horror:

> Media reports talk of a country surrounded by 'pirate-infested waters' and of the capital, Mogadishu, as 'the most dangerous place in the world'. The word 'Mogadishu' has entered some people's vocabulary as a way of describing a place or situation that is truly terrible. Mogadishu was the title of a British play which premiered in 2011; it was not about Somalia, but a troubled inner-city secondary school in England. While covering the riots that hit some parts of England in August 2011, a BBC reporter described the Tottenham district of London as looking like Mogadishu (2012: 1).

Farah repeatedly addresses such treatments in *Crossbones*: early on, one of the supporting characters, Jeebleh, remembers his foreign wife's 'refrain about Somalia, "That unfortunate country, cursed with those dreadful clanspeople, forever killing one another and everyone around them"' (Farah 2012: 11). Malik also frequently contrasts the intelligence he garners from local sources with what he has read about in *The Guardian*, or heard on Al-Jazeera and the BBC (366). On his arrival in Somalia, he finds the work of the reporters there inadequate, which he blames on local journalists being intrepid but undertrained. However, Malik and Ahl barely have more success in decoding their surroundings. In *Crossbones*, the truth proves to be complex, subjective and volatile, as is reflected in the nickname Farah gives one of the Al-Shabaab operatives: he is known as 'Al-Xaqq – "the Truth"' and is 'an explosives genius' (5).

In *Crossbones* unofficial narratives are given the same weight (or perhaps weightlessness) as those that issue from recognised authorities. In 'The Short Story from Poe to Chesterton', Martin A. Kayman remarks on the historical relationship between crime fiction and journalism: 'The insistence that the story is dealing with facts... constitutes in a narratological sense, the fundamental structure of the more classic puzzle-solving "detective" genre' (2003: 42). Indeed, Farah's decision to provide an array of competing truths makes *Crossbones* appear structurally incomplete: because of the many loose ends, it reads like a cross section of a far vaster network of stories, rather than a cohesive tale in itself.

In the mystery genre, it is axiomatic that the reader must be exposed to each clue that informs the eventual revelation (Van Dine 1928). This is a narrative technique that has remained popular well beyond the Golden Age mystery because it allows the reader to theorise a solution in tandem with the literary detective. However, in *Crossbones*, Farah sets up Taxliil's disappearance as a clue-puzzle ('a riddle' [Farah 2012: 41]) and then reneges on the literary 'contract' this implies. Despite Ahl's early promise to 'reduce the number of unknown factors', the reader remains almost completely unaware of the machinations involved in Taxliil's recruitment and eventual escape from Al-Shabaab. Even Malik and Ahl, the detective figures, appear to be hazy on the details. Ahl deems news about Taxliil a 'miracle' (280) and for all the reader is told, his abrupt return may as well be a case of divine intervention.

In an interview with *The Guardian Online*, Farah asserts that Somalia is 'full of stories. We say, "one sick person; a hundred doctors". Somalia is a sick country and everyone has an opinion. Mine is one version; in a civil war, there are millions' (Jaggi 2012). *Crossbones* implies this kind of polyphony by suggesting that a multitude of unheard conversations informs the brothers' investigation. In the opening pages, we are given Jeebleh's view of intelligence gathering in Somalia:

> In the absence of verifiable reports in Somalia, given its statelessness, all one has to do is to circulate a *kutiri-kuteen* hearsay not traceable to any particular person, and you can be sure that once the word hits the street it will grow its own legs and will, in its wanderings, recruit more and more hearers, with each new hearer adding their bit to the roaming tale until it gains more speed and runs faster than truth (Farah 2012: 14).

As David Samper writes in 'Cannibalizing Kids: Rumor and Resistance in Latin America', societies often have recourse to rumour in 'ambiguous situations' (2002: 5), such as when there is no longer a central authority to dispatch news, reliable or otherwise. Often the rumour is 'true' in spirit, but false in its literal expression. Ahl has great success in using rumour and hearsay to locate Taxliil: arriving in Puntland, he is besieged by offers of help from locals who believe him to be a journalist. His main ally appears to be Fidno, a negotiator for a group of pirates. Fidno instigates a chain of whispers in order to locate Ahl's stepson, but in return he wants the opportunity to amplify his version of Somalia to the world. Malik's access to the world stage becomes valuable currency, as sources offer their help in exchange for interviews. That Malik's interview skills are so in demand emphasises the idea of Somalia's many silenced narratives. Farah does not represent them all, but by leaving the main narrative of *Crossbones* gapingly unresolved, he implicitly locates it as only one of the many that are clamouring to be heard.

When Taxliil finally appears, his version of events proves to be as unreliable as any rumour. He vacillates between stories, even though his re-entry into the United States depends upon his producing a convincing counter-narrative to the allegation that he is a terrorist. His re-emergence is so abrupt that there can be no narrative catharsis. Even Ahl, finally reunited with him, finds his behaviour bizarre and anti-climactic: 'Taxliil has a way of throwing another wrench into the works every time Ahl manages to wrest one free. He finds all this exhausting, and he feels himself in danger of cracking up, never mind his stepson' (Farah 2012: 341). Indeed, Taxliil appears so conflicted that at the end of the novel Jeebleh, a Dante scholar, implies that the boy's period of 'purgatory' in Djibouti will be beneficial, allowing him to process and come to terms with what has happened to him (380). That this process can only take place in foreign custody, outside of the 'inferno' of Somalia, suggests that Taxliil's own narrative can only be compiled in a third location, removed from the pressures of each of the countries from which he has come.

Degeneration and the detectives

Farah further undermines the idea of narrative authority by depicting the progressive fragmentation of the 'detectives' themselves: as the text's investigator figures, Ahl and Malik are used to explore the disparity between the region's reputation and its realities. Their father is Somali, their mother Malaysian-Chinese, and they have grown up in Yemen. F. Fiona Moolla argues that Malik and Ahl's mixed origins are part of

Farah's efforts to explore the condition of the 'self-made man' who is no longer bound by Somali clan affiliation:

> Mixed origins and tenuous paternal authority constitute Malik and Ahl as ideal protagonists unchained from filiation, in terms of which non-modern identity was determined; and from those forms of affiliation, in terms of which modern national identity is determined. They are thus, using Joe Slaughter's terms . . . "tautologically and teleologically" free to construct their own identity (2014: 179).

Moolla somewhat overstates the 'freedom' of these characters who, despite their mixed heritage, are always mindful that their journey to Somalia carries the weight of an ancestral return – on arrival, Malik says, 'It feels bizarre that I am back in a place to which I have never been before' (Farah 2012: 72). The brothers' multicultural background can therefore be more productively read as part of their role as microcosms of the national situation. The very word 'Somali', Farah demonstrates, is far more complex than it seems.

Farah describes Somalia as 'a region more varied in hyphenated identities than even the United States' (2012: 57). Indeed, as Harper suggests, 'it is one of the great Somali contradictions that, in diametric opposition to the dream of a "Greater Somalia", are clan and other divisions that have led to extreme fragmentation within the country itself' (2012: 34). In addition to this internal 'fragmentation', Farah depicts the country as influenced by innumerable political cross currents. During the 'Scramble for Africa', foreign powers were attracted by Somalia's strategic position on the coast (Harper 2012: 46) and Farah makes it clear that the attraction endures to this day. Towards the end of his stay, Malik wearily asks a source whether it is true that 'every single Somali politician has a different paymaster outside this country from whom he receives instructions, and whose interests he serves' (Farah 2012: 244). Ahl and Malik are used to embody 'modern national identity' (Moolla 2014: 179) to the extent that their fates become inextricably bound to that of the country. However, rather than being free to 'construct their own identity', the brothers gradually lose all semblance of self-image and control, and collapse in imitation of the state. By the end of the novel, both are located in 'limbo' (183): Ahl has begun a long detainment with

Taxliil in Djibouti, the outcome of which is uncertain, and Malik lies in a Kenyan hospital, his life hanging in the balance.

The use of overt national allegory is evident in Farah's body of work. In his 1970 novel *From a Crooked Rib*, Farah uses the protagonist, Ebla, to compare the plight of Somali women to the repeated colonisation of the country itself. In *Crossbones*, the brothers' characterisation degenerates over the course of the narrative, as both characters undergo a gradual loss of identity. Ahl and Malik undergo a process of dissolution, paradoxically illustrating the futility of trying to 'characterise' a collapsed state in a hopelessly entangled globalised world. Towards the end of the novel, Ahl thinks to himself: '"I am everything that is around me"... Who was the poet, Wallace Stevens or Robert Frost? What is around him but the misery of a nation down in the dumps?' (Farah 2012: 274).

The idea of 'national character' underpins many of the media stereotypes that abound in relation to Somalia. Lyndon C.S. Way refers to the tendency for 'homogenization' in press reporting on piracy (2013: 29) and this tendency to generalisation and essentialism is present in reports on the country as a whole. In *The World's Most Dangerous Place: Inside the Outlaw State of Somalia*, British journalist James Fergusson repeatedly uses explanations such as 'classic Somali behaviour' (2013: 301) to describe things he has observed in the region, or even in the Somali diaspora. Of a less than forthcoming source, he writes:

> There was no sense of logic to the way he bent the truth. I was reminded of Richard Burton's frustrated observation that 'these people seem to lie involuntarily: the habit of untruth with them becomes a second nature. They deceive without object for deceit, and the only way of obtaining from them correct information is to inquire, receive the answer, and determine it to be diametrically opposed to fact' (Fergusson 2013: 171).

Fergusson's uncritical (and un-ironic) quoting of a colonial explorer is far from the only instance of orientalism in his book. References to 'Somali souls' (Fergusson 2013: 222), 'the nomad psyche' (270) and even 'bad Somali teeth' (313) abound. Farah himself makes an appearance in the book: Fergusson meets him for dinner in Minneapolis, during which Fergusson offers the opinion that 'the Somalis' capacity for violence [is] innate' (366). Although Fergusson merely records Farah as being 'impatient' with this suggestion, *Crossbones* refutes the idea assiduously and repeatedly.

The use of two protagonists rather than one further emphasises the idea of 'national character' as a flawed and elusive concept. The fact that Ahl is stationed in Puntland, and Malik in Mogadishu, underlines the disunity of what is popularly perceived to be a single, homogenous country. As Harper points out:

> By viewing the whole country through the lens of the capital, Mogadishu, many descriptions of Somalia project an image of a nation in a permanent state of war with itself. However, large areas are quite peaceful, with their own administrations, legal systems and economies . . . [An] area of relative stability is the neighbouring north-eastern region of Puntland, which has set up its own semi-autonomous administration, although it was for some time a major pirate stronghold (2012: 9).

Puntland is depicted as a 'pirate stronghold' in the novel, but Farah disassembles these connotations by portraying a place of relative order and peace. It is perhaps for this reason that Ahl, lulled into a sense of security, sends Malik into a dangerous situation in Mogadishu, misreading (potentially fatally) the mood of the city. By placing the two regions in terms of a sometimes-contentious sibling relationship, Farah is further able to deconstruct the homogenous reputation that Somalia has acquired abroad.

In many ways, Malik's investigation proves more difficult than Ahl's. Ahl, after all, seeks only Taxliil, while Malik is attempting to construct a narrative of Somalia itself. Rather than imposing order on his violent surroundings, Malik finds his journalistic abilities compromised: despite many hours in his 'work room' (a phrase which, unlike 'office' or 'study', suggests writing as a process of conscious construction), he is unable to piece together a satisfying narrative. On a fragment of paper, he writes: '*Somalis are a people in a fix; a nation with a trapped nerve; a country in a terrible mess. The entire nation is caught up in a spiralling degeneracy that a near stranger like me cannot make full sense of. It is all a fib, that is what it is, just a fib*' (Farah 2012: 297).

On first arriving, Malik, a seasoned reporter 'appears certain he needs no telling what he must or mustn't do' (Farah 2012: 14). However, this confidence and composure begins to unravel as soon as he gets to his lodgings in Mogadishu. Immediately, he is beset by nightmares and mysterious itching. This is far from his first foray into a danger zone: he has worked in 'the Congo, Afghanistan [and] Iraq', among other 'hot spots', but something about Somalia undoes him:

> Jeebleh feels the sense of stress spreading, with Malik biting his lower lip, too angry to speak. Jeebleh thinks how stresses produce inexplicable results and he wonders how the stresses they are all under, the strain that is bound to invade them – Malik, Ahl and himself – will affect them. What will they be like when they crack up? What will Malik be like when the nervous tension makes him go to pieces? He watches with worry as Malik steps away and stands before the mirror on the wall in the living room and takes a good look at his reflection. Jeebleh senses that even to himself Malik must look older in a matter of moments, rugged and more wrinkled, his face careworn (Farah 2012: 32).

The fear of 'cracking up' or 'going to pieces' is not depicted as a general reaction to the stresses of a war zone, but is particular to the brothers' return to Somalia. At this point, nothing more dramatic has happened than the confiscation of Malik's computer by the UIC, but something corrosive is plainly at work. In the United States, Ahl works as the director of an institute 'tasked with researching matters Somali' (Farah 2012: 33), but he too finds himself unprepared for what he finds in Somalia. As Farah says in his interview with Maya Jaggi: 'How can you reconstruct a country that's self-destructing continuously?' (Jaggi 2012).

The more their assumptions about Somalia are challenged, the more the 'detectives'' personal identities erode. Malik, ordinarily a cautious man, finds himself driving to town in order to taunt a dangerous militant known as 'Big Beard'. Ahl, confronting the 'television technician' who repeatedly searches his hotel room, feels that 'the din is making him lose touch with his senses, or worse, his reason' (Farah 2012: 98). Malik's process of disintegration is completed when Ahl sends him to interview Fidno and Malik is grievously wounded by a roadside bomb, or 'fragmentation grenade' (333).

Ahl's decline also manifests physically: however, it is less dramatic than his brother's, which is, perhaps, a reflection of the situation in

Puntland versus the explosive violence of Mogadishu. Over the course of the narrative, it becomes clear that Ahl is in the grip of a degenerative disease and is gradually losing control of his 'out of kilter' body (Farah 2012: 34). It is implied that his illness began to manifest at the time of Taxliil's disappearance:

> Ahlulkhair, known to family and close friends as Ahl, older brother to Malik and the director of a Minneapolis-based centre tasked with researching matters Somali, calls in sick, the first time he has done so in his long career as an educator. The truth is, the growing trend among Somali youths to join the self-declared religionist radical fringe, Shabaab, has thrown him off balance (Farah 2012: 33).

Malik and Ahl's physical and emotional dissolution represents their inability to exert mastery over their surroundings: there can be no narrative closure because, in Somalia, there are no easy solutions. In Thomas's formulation, the strength of the literary detective lies in his ability to impose names on others and to articulate his version of the truth (1994: 656). By the end of the novel, Malik, though alive, 'is still in no state to speak, much less comprehend what is going on' (Farah 2012: 379). Ahl attempts to impose a false name on his stepson in order to take him back home, but Taxliil refuses even to open his new passport and gives their identities away in Djibouti. That neither of the brothers appears as a speaking character in the final scenes underlines the extravagant failure of authority and articulation.

Tyranny and narrative

Farah further separates the idea of narrative usurpation and genuine justice by portraying the text's 'detectives' as being forced to operate outside the law. By the time Taxliil arrives in Somalia, the legal system has already failed him. Both the FBI (Federal Bureau of Investigation) and the UIC have their own interest in his case, but their motives are separate from Ahl and Malik's moral imperative to rescue him. Thomas writes: 'In detective fiction ... the property rights to someone's story are transferred to the official or unofficial agent of society who is empowered to see and identify the body of the criminal, speaking for the whole society in assigning a story to that figure' (1994: 660). In *Crossbones*, instead of the narrative tending towards this kind of unmasking and the apportioning of blame, it is implied that this 'transfer' has already occurred, with devastating consequences. Taxliil has been branded an outlaw, just as Somalia has acquired the reputation of being an outlaw state.

The fact that the novel is set post-revelation shows the manifold complications and inaccuracies that arise when a single version of events takes precedence over nuance. Instead of 'unmasking' him as a criminal, Malik and Ahl intend to liberate Taxliil from the identity in which he has been imprisoned. Ironically, this identity was originally suggested to Taxliil during an FBI interrogation. We learn that Taxliil was made a suspect after his Kurdish-American schoolmate returned to Iraq as a suicide bomber. Farah describes the family's interrogation, the morning after the news of Samir's death breaks:

> Taxliil was made to endure longer hours of interrogation with repeated threats . . . The officer asked [Taxliil's mother] Yusur if Ahl was likely to recruit Taxliil as a suicide bomber. They suggested she get it off her chest; they were friends, and they meant her well. Who were *his* friends? Whom did he contact, and how did he do it?
>
> Eventually, all three were released by the FBI. Even so, they were told to inform the agency of any suspicious activities. If they failed to do so, they would be reclassified (2012: 40-1).

The language Farah uses here resonates with a greater theme in the novel as a whole: the threat of 'reclassification' is not just intelligence jargon for being placed under suspicion, but also represents a form of narrative confiscation. When the FBI casts Taxliil as a terrorist, they inadvertently move him to solidarity with Al-Shabaab. Their recasting also works retrospectively, changing his image of Samir. Taxliil and Samir are described by Farah as best friends, in the most wholesome of terms: 'They played sports and computer games together; swapped clothes; swam and took long walks on weekends. They spurred each other to achieve their ambitions. Neither admitted to knowing what the word *impossible* meant. Doing well wasn't good enough; they did better than anyone else' (Farah 2012: 40). Taxliil's interrogation puts an end to this youthful iteration of the American Dream and recasts Samir as a brother in arms. Embracing Islam becomes a way for Taxliil to reject the United States and to claim fellowship with the friend he has lost.

On one level, Farah's emphasis on the FBI's role in Taxliil's radicalisation can be read as a reflection of the relationship between Somalia and the United States. Harper argues that the United States' initial characterisation of Somalia as an international terrorist threat 'inadvertently advertised the country as a promising new battle front for jihadists from across the world' (2012: 4), thereby nurturing the region's capacity for recruitment. On another level, the suggestion of a self-fulfilling prophecy speaks to the unique experience of those recruited from the diaspora, for whom joining Al-Shabaab is an attempt at self-actualisation as much as a political statement. Taxliil rejects an American identity and pursues a 'Somali' one. However, once he submits to the will of Al-Shabaab, he finds himself in over his head. His minders conflate 'Somali-ness' with blind obedience to radical Islam, in another example of narrative usurpation.

The novel engages extensively with the idea of radical Islam as a strategic superimposition, rather than an entrenched part of national identity in Somalia. At the period at which the protagonists arrive in the country, the UIC is still in a position of power and enforces its own form of social control, despite the collapsed state. Harper contends:

> The most significant contribution of the courts was the way in which they ensured basic law and order, including the enforcement of contracts, which made it possible to have commercial and civil life. One of the functions of Islam is that it provides an off-the-shelf, culturally validated code for many aspects of social, economic and political life, which allows for a form of public order and administration in the absence of a state (2012: 82).

The expression 'off-the-shelf' suggests a pre-existing code for ethical conduct, one that is seamlessly understandable and accepted in the local culture. In *Crossbones*, Farah disputes this idea. In the novel he suggests that the UIC is manipulating ideas of Somali culture in order to bolster its own interpretation of Islam and thereby lend authority to its own laws. Much of the novel is preoccupied with the idea of staged authenticity in the ranks of the UIC and Al-Shabaab. One of Taxliil's minders (aptly nicknamed History) is used to reflect this:

> 'Our instructor had a northern accent, and yelled at us a lot, and wouldn't tolerate any back talk; he was quite a taskmaster.' Then half-laughing and half-serious he tries to imitate his instructor. 'We are not part of history. We are *making* history, *living* history! We are not liberators, fellows,' he would chant. 'We are martyrs, through the expression of our fury, through our ambition in action, to lead this nation away from self-ruin.' Then he'd resume his chorus. 'We are not part of history. We are *making* history, *living* history!' (Farah 2012: 346)

Taxliil's instructor superbly embodies the idea of tyrannical narrative: in the world of the novel, nothing is more dangerous than a version of history that will not tolerate any 'back talk'.

The form of Islam the UIC and Al-Shabaab extol is shown by Farah as, at best, an imported tradition, and at worst an invented one. Invented tradition, as described by Eric Hobsbawm, is defined as

> a set of practices, normally governed by overtly or tacitly accepted rules and of a ritual or symbolic nature, which seek to inculcate certain values and norms of behaviour by repetition, which automatically implies continuity with the past. In fact, where possible, they normally attempt to establish continuity with a suitable historic past (Hobsbawm and Ranger 2000: 1).

In *Crossbones*, Farah emphasises the ritual and symbolism with which Somalia's 'Islamic revival' is invested, but implies that the 'suitable historic past' that is being evoked has been strategically curated as a way of consolidating power. By terming their laws 'the Islamic code of conduct' (Farah 2012: 347), the UIC ensures that any dissent from its laws is blasphemy and that anyone voicing dissent may be termed 'a traitor to Islam' (323). Bile, another character who, like Jeebleh, has experienced Somalia's former political incarnations, says: 'I am displeased . . . when someone spouts the obsequious fallacy that all Somalis are Muslim, especially if this is meant to offer legitimacy to a clique of religionists determined to impose their will on this nation' (120). The idea of

Somalia as, first and foremost, 'a Muslim country' is used to justify all manner of decisions, including the instigation of war with Ethiopia. The UIC announces that they 'will defeat the invaders the moment they set foot on our soil, a Muslim soil' (154), claiming an identity that situates the conflict as a form of holy war, thereby enforcing its support.

The disparity between old and new is most evident in the subplot featuring Young Thing, an adolescent recruit of Al-Shabaab who is on a mission to 'consecrate' a safe house for his handlers. His story demonstrates both the brutality of the organisation and the uneasy place its practices occupy in relation to Somali tradition. Young Thing goes to the wrong residence and encounters an elderly man named Dhoorre, whom he will eventually be forced to shoot. When his handlers catch up with him, Young Thing allows Dhoorre to hide from them in the bathroom. Farah contrasts Dhoorre's devotion to Islam with that of the group that has stormed his home by showing the old man in a private moment of devotion:

> Dhoorre, who is in the bathroom with the door bolted, eavesdrops on their conversation. When he hears all three men leave the house, he takes a hurried birdbath by letting the water drip into his cupped hands in the manner of somebody performing an ablution in an arid zone where water is scarce. In Islam, it is incumbent on a Muslim performing ablution to use even the sand if there is no water. Allah will look favourably on one if one is 'clean' at the moment of death. He looks at his face in the mirror and confirms that he badly needs a shave – it's a pity that the blade is dull and he has no replacements.
>
> Just then there is a sudden escalation of noise as TruthTeller returns, grumbling about the weight of the machine-gun and bazooka parts (Farah 2012: 62).

Here, Farah emphasises the jarring incongruity between Dhoorre's enactment of a solitary, desert-culture practice and the modern weaponry wielded by the Islamic militants just outside the door. The scene marks Dhoorre out as a devout Muslim to whom Al-Shabaab's actions appear alien. When the old man entreats them not to punish Young Thing for his mistake, he says: 'Islam is peace, the promise of justice' (Farah 2012: 66), but the militants' professed loyalty to a curated past does not extend to the living history in front of them.

Farah suggests that while militant Islam and youth do continue a tradition in the region, it is in fact a political tradition, rather than a religious one. He writes:

> Jeebleh thinks that there is undeniable similarity between Caloosha [his childhood tormentor] and Big Beard's methods, which both claim are in service to higher causes; the late Caloosha asserted his socialist ideals in the same way that Big Beard takes the sanctity of Islam as his mantra, asserts it is the beacon lighting his way to divine authority (Farah 2012: 108).

Caloosha, who also appears in *Links*, is defined by his incapacity for genuine loyalty. He is suspected of killing his stepfather, is instrumental in having his half-brother imprisoned by General Barre and is guilty of the rape and abduction of the underage girl he takes as a 'wife'. Caloosha adopts different belief systems with opportunistic haste, adapting to the clan-based warlord system immediately after General Barre's fall, despite years of lip service to Barre's dogma of Scientific Socialism. Jeebleh says, disgustedly: 'Your loyalties are peripatetic' (Farah 2003: 103). Similarly, when the UIC is dismantled, the tyrannical Big Beard immediately shaves off his defining facial hair, and begins to wear a suit (247). Despite his changed appearance, his demeanour is exactly the same and he is unabashed by his seamless change in allegiance.

While Farah is convincing in his location of Islam in relation to Somali history, he does not adequately account for it as a revived, globalised form of militarism. However, by separating symbols of broad, global affiliation from local political motivations, he succeeds in complicating the discourse surrounding Somali Islam, if only by showing its apparent simplicity and authenticity as a carefully curated phenomenon.

Piracy

As the title of Farah's novel indicates, one of its chief preoccupations is with media depictions of piracy in Somali waters. Farah depicts Somali 'piracy' as blurring the line between legality and criminality, terrorism and resistance, but emphasises that the very word 'pirate' carries an insoluble stigma. The word 'crossbones', as Moolla (2014) notes, references the Jolly Roger flag that was once flown by pirate vessels. Peter T. Leeson points out:

Although the specific images on Jolly Rogers varied, the purpose was the same in each case. As one witness described it in the pages of the *White-hall Evening Post*, 'the black Flag with a Death's Head in it . . . is their Signal to intimate, that they will neither give nor take Quarter' (*White-hall Evening Post* October 18–October 21, 1718). By communicating 'pirate' to merchantmen, the Jolly Roger helped merchantmen understand they were under attack by piratical belligerents who could and would devastate them if they resisted, as opposed to 'legitimate' belligerents who were likely to be more restrained in how they responded to resistance (2010: 507).

Just as ancient pirates displayed the flags to signify their own 'outlaw' status, so the word 'piracy' has been applied to the Somali phenomenon to imply its unequivocal criminality. The word also conjures up the idea of a fight between enlightened modernity and benighted savagery, while the repeated emphasis on the phenomenon as exclusively Somali both imposes distance and absolves other parties involved in the trade. Farah's novel deconstructs this image of piracy and demonstrates the perils of representing a complex political phenomenon with a single, ominous signifier.

Way refers to 'homogenization' as a core component of media depictions of piracy:

It seems questionable to apply such personal and social traits [drug use, alcoholism, age and motivation] to all those involved in Somali piracy considering the various backgrounds, tribal affiliations and expertise involved in pirate operations. Such homogenization, however, does draw upon discourses of Orientalism that represent the 'other' negatively, justifying the need for military intervention (2013: 29)

Rather than reversing media binaries to form a solid counter-narrative, Farah critiques piracy in more ambivalent terms. By insisting on the diversity that media reports elide, he avoids both condemnation and romanticisation of the phenomenon, placing the pirates in an ambiguous third category between 'villainy' and 'victimhood'. As Nigel Cawthorne argues, Somali 'pirates' themselves have always framed their behaviour as a legitimate defensive manoeuvre, if not an act of outright heroism. In discussing the hijacking of the Ukrainian *MV Faina* in 2008, Cawthorne says: 'The Somali hijackers did not consider themselves pirates or sea bandits. "We consider sea bandits those who illegally fish in our seas and dump waste in our seas and carry weapons in our seas," he said. "We are simply patrolling our seas. Think of us like a coastguard"' (2009: 564). Fidno, the pirate negotiator in *Crossbones*, describes the pirates as 'conscientious avengers fighting to save our waters from total plunder' (Farah 2012: 211).

Farah does not entirely embrace the idea of piracy as an idealistic act of defence. Throughout the novel, multiple characters endorse the idea of piracy as a direct response to Western theft of African resources. The presence of the foreign vessels is interpreted as a kind of neocolonialism, and piracy as an act of resistance. However, although Farah uses this explanation to contextualise the phenomenon in historical terms, he makes little attempt to argue for the morality of the enterprise. Rather, he emphasises the impossibility of clinging to legality in the context of a collapsed state, and stresses that accusations of 'piracy' are less about intrinsically criminal behaviour than they are about the lack of a recognised flag under which to patrol the seas. His interrogation of the term 'pirate' highlights the complex relationship between legality, morality and legitimacy in Somalia.

The first time Ahl hears the term 'privateer', he is 'uncertain' of how well it captures the Somali phenomenon:

> He understands privateers as vessels armed and licensed to attack the ships of enemy nations and confiscate their property. Historically, many European sovereigns issued such licences and they left it up to the licensed captains to determine the nature of the punishment to be meted out to the vessels they apprehended. A percentage of their catch went to the captain and crew, and the remainder to the licence-issuing sovereign (Farah 2012: 211).

Ahl does not suggest behaviour as a means of assessing whether or not something qualifies as piracy. The distinction is founded entirely on whether or not the vessels have state affiliation: legitimacy is conferred by 'the licence-issuing sovereign', rather than by their conduct at sea. As denizens of a collapsed state, it becomes impossible to have this kind of legitimacy conferred. By default, Somali pirates are 'outlaws', even though they 'operate for the most part in their own seas' (Farah 2012: 214).

Farah also avoids making a unilateral moral judgement by stressing that piracy has evolved into a sophisticated and stratified system, with motives that vary widely from tier to tier. Furthermore, he identifies exploitation and inequality within the pirate hierarchy itself. This is in contrast to certain media depictions, which sweepingly describe Somali pirates as being 'very, very rich' (Gettleman 2008). In an article in *The New York Times*, Jeffrey Gettleman paints a lavish picture of piracy and its rewards:

> In Somalia, it seems, crime does pay. Actually, it is one of the few industries that does.
>
> 'All you need is three guys and a little boat, and the next day you're millionaires,' said Abdullahi Omar Qawden, a former captain in Somalia's long-defunct navy.
>
> People in Garoowe, a town south of Boosaaso, describe a certain high-rolling pirate swagger. Flush with cash, the pirates drive the biggest cars, run many of the town's businesses – like hotels – and throw the best parties, residents say. Fatuma Abdul Kadir said she went to a pirate wedding in July that lasted two days, with nonstop dancing and goat meat, and a band flown in from neighboring Djibouti.
>
> 'It was wonderful,' said Ms. Fatuma, 21. 'I'm now dating a pirate' (2008).

In *Crossbones*, Farah suggests that while some may be 'making a killing', others in the trade are far from being millionaires. Malik, learning that Bile's nephew is a pirate but still struggles financially, says: 'You mean there are no lavish weddings being staged, no formidable mansions being built in Eyle, Hobyo and Xarardheere? The entire region is not flush with funds and full of luxury goods?' (Farah 2012: 73). Furthermore, Farah quashes the broad, glamourous notion of 'high-rolling pirate swagger' (Gettleman 2008) by presenting a starkly different image of those involved in the lower tiers of the trade. Our first glimpse of active piracy comes from a set of photographs:

Young men – in boats, in ships, manning guns, holding men, faces covered with balaclavas. Young men eating, sleeping, fooling around with one another, speaking on their mobile phones, some of them dressed in the jackets of which they dispossessed their hostages, of whom there are also photos . . . The haul is big. But the young men wielding the AK-47s, the collapsible machine guns, are skinny, hungry-looking, many appearing as ill prepared for what life may throw at them as Paris Hilton might be going into the ring with Mike Tyson. Are these youths pirates? And if they are not pirates, then who are they, what are they? (Farah 2012: 102)

Fidno, the pirates' negotiator, could not be more different from the young men pictured here. While he laments the loss of ransom money to foreign parties, he is very evidently motivated by profit, rather than survival. Fidno has a touch of the 'high-rolling pirate swagger' suggested by the *New York Times* article: Malik observes that 'he looks like a character out of a crime novel: deviously handsome in a Humphrey Bogart way, with a smile so captivating you have to fight to get your heart back; eyes alive with promise – a promise that will leave you cursing the day you met him' (Farah 2012: 361). However, his motives cannot be compared to those of the 'skinny, hungry' youths who undertake the most dangerous part of the work. Fidno has previously worked as a medical doctor in Berlin and Abu Dhabi, but in both cases was reported for malpractice. Following this, a wealthy uncle set him up as a financier in Mogadishu.

Ultimately, Taxliil is shown to have more in common with the pirate youths than Fidno does. At the end of the novel, he describes his time with Al-Shabaab in utterly childish terms, saying: '"Life was harsh. No TV. No fun. No games"' (Farah 2012: 348). In these final scenes, he is very much an overwhelmed child, rather than the 'terrorist' he has been labelled. That his unpreparedness mirrors that which Ahl perceives in the photograph of the pirates suggests that they, too, may simply be impressionable youngsters in thrall to exploitative recruiters.

Fidno is not cast as an idealist, then, but as someone involved in a sophisticated business enterprise. Although Farah refers ironically to the clichéd 'crossbones' in his title, the text in itself goes to great lengths to undermine the linguistic time warp in which Somali piracy has been placed:

> 'As Somali "privateers" – we are not pirates, we insist – we avail ourselves of a network of informers of different nationalities and disparate professions: ship brokers, security officials with access to information about ship movements, bankers, accountants; a run of the entire gamut to do with shipping. We communicate with London on secure satellite phones; receive info from someone at the Suez Canal with the schedules of the ships, the nature of the cargo, the name of the owners and their final destination. Dubai. London. Sana'a. The world is at our fingertips' (Farah 2012: 364).

Piracy is depicted as a merely another branch of global, postcolonial capitalism. Farah once again emphasises Somalia's interconnectedness by referencing London, Dubai and Sana'a. In doing so, he implicitly complicates the notion of 'Somali piracy' by referencing the international network behind it. It is implied that those who make the most money in the trade are the foreign backers, rather than local 'financiers', but the entire hierarchy is riddled with inequality and plays on the desperation of Somalia's poorest citizens. Negotiators such as Fidno have access to sophisticated technology, even if their underlings are so poor that 'jackets' and 'mobile phones' (Farah 2012: 102) seem like worthwhile plunder.

The 'high-seas' promise of the title is ultimately left unfulfilled. The young men in the photographs never appear in person and we are never precisely assured of 'who' and 'what' they are. In narrative terms, the effect is anti-climactic, but the pirates' very invisibility effectively demolishes the stereotypes by which they are known. By declining to portray the pirates, Farah suggests they are figments made up of the projections and fears of others. It is implied that no text can adequately encompass the broad group of people involved in piracy as long as they are categorised by affiliation alone. This erosion of caricature contributes to an open-ended, 'unfinished' narrative, which privileges nuance over cohesion. In its treatment of piracy, *Crossbones* eschews broad strokes, while suggesting that humanity is in the details.

Conclusion

At 385 pages, *Crossbones* is a sprawling work, which seeks to explore many aspects of life in post-collapse Somalia and the complications implicit in returning to one's ancestral home. In casting such a wide net, Farah sacrifices many elements of the traditionally structured novel and of the crime novel, in particular. The pace of the narrative is choppy and unpredictable, and apparently significant happenings are frequently permitted to sink out of sight. However, the very lack of narrative cohesion provides a strong sense of conditions on the ground, rather than echoing the superimposed view from above, for which Farah criticises the international media. Its form encompasses unfathomable tragedy, but leaves room for hope as well: though its characters are left in a state of purgatory, the novel's lack of resolution also allows for the possibility that all is not yet lost.

This is reflected in the final lines, which Cambara speaks in a phone call from the Kenyan hospital: '"Goodbye for now," she says. "Malik is waking"' (Farah 2012: 382).

Conclusion

If traditional crime fiction is 'a literature of containment' (Plain 2001: 3), 'restoration' (James 2013) and 'triumph' (Auden 2016), then the subgenre explored in this book can best be described as a literature of elusiveness, ambivalence and loss. Each of the detective figures sets out in the pursuit of wholeness, aiming to piece together the puzzle of the investigation and the riddles of their own identity. As they journey 'home', the detectives must contend with the lack of a strong justice system, the dearth of information in the context of social breakdown, the elusiveness of belonging and the limits of various forms of testimony.

Genre, expectation and structural breakdown
While the novels discussed in the previous chapters have much in common, they differ in illuminating ways. Each of the five books demonstrates the inadequacy of crime fiction conventions in the context of the worlds they project, but employs markedly different techniques. Referring to Patricia Merrivale and Susan Elizabeth Sweeney's definition of the metaphysical detective story, John Scaggs writes: 'The intention of the metaphysical detective story is to overload generic expectations in order to undermine them' (2005: 152). 'Overload' is an apt description of Kazuo Ishiguro's narrative technique in *When We Were Orphans*. The unreliable narrator is unable to discard his generic delusions until the full force of the Second Sino-Japanese War overpowers them. In the Shanghai of the novel, there are too many villains, too many victims and too many global links – in fact, too much world altogether – to fit within the narrow bounds of Christopher Banks's generic dream. His increasingly bizarre attempts to frame the outbreak of the Second World War in generic terms illustrate the narrowness and frailty of Golden Age conventions.

Nuruddin Farah, too, overloads his text with a multitude of partial villains and victims in order to show the futility of dialectical notions of guilt and innocence in post-collapse Somalia. However, unlike Ishiguro,

Farah also deliberately *under*-writes parts of his novel. By keeping both his detectives and his readers in the dark about much that has occurred, Farah suggests that contemporary Somalia defies comprehensive or linear explanation. In withholding so many answers, the text performs a kind of emotional mimesis. The detective figure Malik reflects on another character's death by saying: 'I often think how, in fiction, death serves a purpose. I wish I knew the objective of such a death' (Farah 2012: 285). The text's refusal to assign meaning or purpose to much of what it depicts provides the reader with a faint echo of this frustration. Thus, part of Farah's world-making project is enacted through the withholding of information, leaving the reader in a state of bafflement that mirrors the anxiety and disorientation of life in an active war zone. There is no reassuring commentary from above about what has befallen the characters. Rather, the narrative is imperfectly patched together from speculation and rumours, a number of which are never confirmed, or even referred to a second time.

In *The Long Night of White Chickens*, Francisco Goldman produces a comparable mimetic effect, but unlike Farah he achieves this through a process of narrative multiplication, rather than dissolution. In *Crossbones*, many things go unexplained, while in *The Long Night of White Chickens* every event has several explanations, each as likely and as unprovable as the last. The style of Goldman's prose imitates this process of multiplication and uncertainty. Unlike *Crossbones*, in which gaping gaps are left in Taxliil's (subjective and suspect) account of his time with Al-Shabaab, Flor's murder remains unsolved because the detectives uncover too many motives, too many murderers and too many secret sides to Flor's life. Again, 'overload' describes the technique, but the outcome is quite different to that in *When We Were Orphans*.

In Ishiguro's novel, the central mystery does have a 'solution', albeit one that is too ambivalent and complex to be revealed until the text's generic premise has entirely broken down. In *The Long Night of White Chickens*, there is no 'sense of an ending' (Kermode 1967), but merely of an investigation deferred. The labyrinthine form of the narrative is such that Roger's homecoming could theoretically be repeated ad infinitum, without ever leading to a breakthrough. This suggests that Guatemala's repressive regime renders the 'riddle of social injustice' (Goldman 2007: 395) impenetrable and also that the multiplication of suspects is the only possibility in a country with 'so much and so many kinds of murder'.

In *Anil's Ghost* the narrative is redirected, rather than overloaded. As Sailor's identity is gradually filled in, Anil recognises the inadequacy of forensic terminology in describing what has been lost. However, the novel is comparable to *When We Were Orphans* in the sense that its ostensible subject shifts towards the end of the novel. Ishiguro's novel purports to be about a very specific set of disappearances, but is gradually revealed as a story about colonialism, the opium trade and the causes of the Second World War. *Anil's Ghost* is initially framed in terms of the search for Sailor's identity, but towards the end of the novel the focus (and the meaning of the title) suddenly alters to reflect Sarath. The revelation of Sailor's name becomes hollow and with Gamini's eulogy over his brother's body we are given the type of history that forensic information is incapable of rendering. Michael Ondaatje's novel can also be compared to Farah's *Crossbones* in the sense that it produces certain silences, but implies that these stories are being enacted outside the scope of the novel. Through Sarath's murder, we realise that Ruwan Kumara's life and death must have been every bit as deeply felt by his community, but we are not given any picture of this because we share the limited view of the investigative team. Like the human rights organisation that photographs victims of political murders, displaying their injuries but 'covering the faces' (Ondaatje 2011a: 209), Anil's reconstruction of Sailor renders him only partially known. Thus Ondaatje demonstrates the incompleteness of Anil's conception of truth and the implausibility of the idea that traditional investigation can provide a comprehensive account of the war. The violence enacted in the civil war is both too diffuse (as the vignettes of carnage show) and too deeply, individually traumatic to be alleviated by the blithe maxims ('the truth shall set you free') that Anil brings to the scene of the crime.

Gillian Slovo's novel also emphasises the elusiveness of truth and the questionable morality of certain types of revelation: indeed, the slogan of the Truth and Reconciliation Commission (TRC) is 'the truth will set you free', an affirmation that is questioned by many of the characters. As in *Anil's Ghost*, the social context means that revelation and justice are not synonymous. In *Red Dust*, there is a further break between individual retributive justice and mass restorative justice, meaning that the pursuit of one may impede the progress of the other. The complexity of these distinctions means that no firm resolution is possible. Even if individual characters appear to get their just deserts, there remains the chance that this will sow national discord further down the line. The conclusion can therefore only be an ambivalent and open-ended one, as the characters wonder whether or not their pain has been in the cause of the greater good.

In all five cases, the form of the novel widens rather than narrows, meaning that the significance of the individual recedes, a technique that underlines the complexity of systemic violence. Because revelation is not synonymous with justice in these contexts, the novels' conclusions tend to omit either or both, so that each narrative evokes disquiet, rather than reassurance.

This disquiet often results in a difficult reading experience. Jonathan Coe's generally positive review of Goldman's novel notes that the book is occasionally 'indecipherable' and 'awkward' (1993). Hirsh Sawhney, reviewing *Crossbones* for *The New York Times* writes: 'The real problems in this novel are inconsistent plotting, repetitiveness and a verbose third-person narration that results in muddled psychological portraits' (2011). Michiko Kakutani describes *When We Were Orphans* as 'a messy hybrid of a book' (2000), one that is 'ragged, if occasionally brilliant'. These novels do not follow straight lines: they are 'messy', 'muddled', 'ragged' and 'awkward', to varying degrees.

However, as in the original crime genre, there is a strong overlap between reading experience and ideology. In *Form and Ideology in Crime Fiction*, Stephen Knight argues:

> The content of the text, its omissions and selections, is important. Plot iself is a way of ordering events; its outcome distributes triumph and defeat, praise and blame to the characters in a way that accords with the audience's belief in dominant cultural values – which themselves interlock with the social structure. So texts create and justify what has come to be called hegemony, the inseparable bundle of political, cultural and economic sanctions which maintain a particular social system to the advantage of certain members of the whole community (1980: 4).

In offering discord rather than accord, these novels suggest a challenge to established systems of meaning. By declining to distribute 'triumph and defeat, praise and blame' in a way that rewards dominant ways of thinking, they implicitly offer resistance through their seemingly unrewarding narratives. The banishing of wish fulfilment or comfort from the reading experience also represents an insistence on a more complex and disturbing world view. The most 'muddled' of the texts explored in this book are also those that most successfully project a world of global entanglements and anxieties, framing their postcolonial settings in greater spacial and historical context.

Interestingly, the novels with comparatively smooth transitions and endings (*Anil's Ghost* and *Red Dust*) are those that avoid highlighting certain global connections, suggesting that palatability and worldliness may sometimes be mutually exclusive. Ondaatje and Slovo project worlds in which crime cannot be contained, but these worlds are postcolonial countries that appear as anarchic pockets in an otherwise stable world. Thus, like the conventional crime novel, they '[make] safe' (Plain 2001: 3), if only by curtailing their scope. Here, we see the dangers and seductions of the narrowing of form – the novels that focus on the postcolony without casting a critical eye on the role of the West are most compact and accessible, while the others become unwieldy in their complexity and detail.

Intimacy, civil war and world-making

All the novels begin with an apparent line of inquiry, but soon segue into narratives that are more preoccupied with world-making than they are with building a particular case. Often, the narrative scope broadens out to show the limitations of perceiving crime as an anomaly in a context where violence is ubiquitous. By suggesting the central crime as one of many, the writers effectively highlight the relentless emotional cost of life in an extremely violent society. In *On the Postcolony*, Achille Mbembe points out:

> The colony is primarily a place where an experience of violence is lived, where violence is built into structures and institutions ... The violence insinuates itself into the economy, domestic life, language, consciousness. It does more than penetrate every space: it pursues the colonized even in sleep and dream. It produces a culture; it is a cultural praxis (2001: 174).

The milieus depicted in the novels discussed in this book are deeply affected by this lingering 'cultural praxis'. By departing from the idea of crime as an aberration, each text suggests its setting as a place where violence is deeply and, perhaps even indelibly, inscribed. Although each author differs in the extent to which they signpost the colonial past, the legacy of colonialism manifests in all of the novels, in the form of racial discrimination, sectarian violence, economic exploitation and indigenous disenfranchisement. Often, these injustices are enshrined in law, or tacitly condoned by the ruling administration, making the notion of crime ever more difficult to define.

In *Crossbones*, Farah suggests that violence is an endemic part of life by depicting a slew of deaths that offer no apparent contribution to the plot. Farah's descriptors mean that these deaths are not sensationalised and the fact that they are unremarkable suggests that Somalia is a place where 'life . . . is built on quicksand. Alive one minute, dead the next, and buried in the blink of an eye, no post-mortem, not even an entry in a ledger' (Farah 2012: 247). Other writers strike a different balance between the thrilling and mundane, but in each case it is made evident that the central 'crime' is part of a systemic pattern, rather than a rogue transgression from the norm.

The novels further work to shatter villain/victim oppositions by emphasising the impossibility of neutral observation or arbitration. W.H. Auden writes: 'The interest in the study of a murderer is the observation, by the innocent many, of the sufferings of the guilty one. The interest in the detective story is the dialectic of innocence and guilt' (2016). In these novels, this dialectic is broken down to reflect the dynamics of civil discord and transitional unrest. This means that the 'innocent many' cease to exist and the detective himself is unable to observe the guilty from a neutral perspective.

By the end of the novels, many of the returnees carry a sense of culpability. Instead of bringing salvation or justice, they have themselves become part of a morally ambiguous situation. In *Anil's Ghost*, Anil remembers a line from Alexandre Dumas's *The Man in the Iron Mask*: 'We are often criminals in the eyes of the earth, not only for having committed crimes, but because we know that crimes have been committed' (Ondaatje 2011a: 50). The quotation comes to her before she has endangered her colleagues, immediately after she and Sarath have found Sailor's bones. This suggests that her very knowledge implicates her, rather than placing her in the observational position traditionally occupied by the literary investigator. In contexts where there is no recourse to justice and revelation is dangerous, the truth can weigh heavily instead of providing a path to the restoration of order. Because both revelation and suppression carry moral and physical risks, the detective may become one in a long line of accessories to a crime, rather than an agent of justice.

None of the novels identifies a single perpetrator, suggesting that the violence in each geopolitical context is collaborative and complex. In *Anil's Ghost*, Sailor is revealed to have been killed by the government, but this only occurred because 'a *billa* – someone from the community with a gunnysack over his head, slits cut out for his eyes' identified him as a rebel sympathiser: 'A *billa* was a monster, a ghost, to scare away children in games, and it had picked out Ruwan Kumara and he had been taken away' (Ondaatje 2011a: 265). The anonymous traitor is, once again, a neighbour or a friend and not a stranger or a member of an invading army. Monstrosity does not stalk the community from outside of it, but can be slipped on as easily as a gunnysack by any one of its members. The idea of intimate and collaborative violence is further highlighted by a story Sarath tells Anil. Recalling his experience of seeing a man being 'disappeared' and transported away on a bicycle, he says:

> When they took off, the blindfolded man had to somehow hang on. One hand on the handlebars, but the other he had to put around the neck of his captor. It was this necessary intimacy that was disturbing . . . the blindfolded man had to balance his body in tune with his possible killer (Ondaatje 2011a: 150).

In many of the novels, the intimacy of civil war is invoked through the motif of romantic and familial betrayal, indicating that the fabric of the private sphere has been destroyed by the 'complete breakdown of the social contract' (Addison and Mansoob Murshed 2001: 1). Goldman's depiction of Flor's lovers, all of whom may be implicated in her death, is perhaps the clearest example of this. Gamini of *Anil's Ghost* has been in love with his brother's wife and both men are shattered by guilt and regret after she commits suicide. This suggests that the crimes of civil war contain an emotional complexity that defies notions of friendship and enmity. This is evident in Slovo's depiction of Smitsrivier, as the town's small size emphasises the inescapability of politics. It becomes clear that James has been a collaborator of sorts by teaching his students to conform to the status quo and by punishing his own son for becoming involved in political resistance. Similarly, Marie Muller discovers that she has been 'culpable' (Slovo 2009b: 299) in apartheid brutality, despite the fact that for years she has been largely confined to her house.

At times, the texts' world-making project becomes problematic. As in the case of *Anil's Ghost*, the authors' decision to contrast the detective's point of departure with the otherness of their place of origin may become overtly sensationalist when combined with features of genre. In avoiding explanation of the conflict, Ondaatje also avoids implicating the West in what has befallen its former colony. Although he raises important questions about the ethics of international intervention through the figure of Anil, Ondaatje also avoids examining the mechanics of a violent state by using thriller conventions (making the threat to the protagonist appear 'immeasurable and boundless' [Glover 2003: 130]) to depict the government as a single terrible entity. Combined with his decision to set much of the action in 'humanless' (Ondaatje 2011a: 186) parts of the countryside, this means that the question of what makes individuals turn to violence is not directly addressed.

Even when it is executed in a way that eschews sensationalism (Farah, for example, reneges on so many of the crime genre's expectations that even suspense is often sacrificed), the device of the returnee suggests a particular readership. Each of the novelists writes in English and none lives in the context they are depicting, although the reasons for this range from childhood emigration to political exile (Ishiguro is of Japanese origin, but his father grew up in Shanghai during the interwar period [Hunnewell 2008]). Thus, their novels represent international interventions in themselves and can be regarded as being primarily pitched towards readers who are unfamiliar with the local contexts. It is not only the rules of genre that are established and departed from, but also the Western contexts the protagonists leave behind. Their relatively stable, middle-class lives in the West are often sketched only briefly, while their return is always rendered in great detail, establishing their place of origin as the lesser known 'other'. In part, this is a result of the crime genre as a form having emerged under imperial conditions, but framing the step out of genre as an international journey also firmly establishes the culture of departure as the unremarkable norm. *Red Dust*'s Smitsrivier is described as 'New York's polar opposite' (Slovo 2009b: 7). The publisher's foreword to the Random House edition of Ondaatje's novel reads: 'Anil's Ghost transports us to Sri Lanka', assuming that its readers ('us') are not already living there. As demonstrated in Chapter 5, the Somalia Farah 'builds' for his readers is not made from whole cloth, but is constructed in direct opposition to media stereotypes that have proliferated abroad, which the novel conscientiously demolishes.

Thus, this particular kind of crime fiction illustrates the intimacy, frustrations and confusion of civil war, but by framing the stories as double departures – from place and from genre – it does so within a comparative frame, assuming a baseline of generic and geographical knowledge in its readership. The texts represent a form of defamiliarisation by removing features of the crime novel that are so well established as to be taken for granted, such as the value of truth, the availability of justice and the justness of legal retribution. In the absence of these elements, the detectives, who in many cases are regarded as experts in their fields, find themselves experiencing the anxieties of life in a society that has become formless and unpredictable.

However, in some cases the trope of the double departure suggests a false equivalence between the staples of crime fiction and actual Western judicial systems. As discussed in Chapter 4, *Red Dust* uses New York to symbolise a certain type of hard-boiled justice, but does not comment on the United States' support of apartheid, or the racial biases of its own justice system. We are told that the protagonist had 'forgotten that the story with a beginning, a middle and its own neat ending . . . was something New York might offer, but not South Africa' (Slovo 2009b: 336). The use of place to sketch a particular generic milieu is an economical device, but can result in an uncritical comparison between countries, relying as it does on literary stereotypes. South Africa is depicted with a certain moral and political complexity, but Sarah's other home remains depoliticised because it is frozen in genre, making that world one-dimensional.

In terms of world-making, the most successful texts are those that enable their protagonists to investigate their places of departure as well as the point of return. These novels come closer to fulfilling Edward Said's conception of worldliness by emphasising global interconnectedness. In *What Is a World*, Pheng Cheah writes: 'For Said, a literary work's worldliness is its geographical infrastructure, its spatial situated-ness, the "historical affiliation" that connects cultural works from the imperial center to the colonial peripheries and the interdependencies that follow from these connections' (2016: 219). In *When We Were Orphans* and *The*

Long Night of White Chickens, the returnees' travels away force them to take a second look at the homes they have established elsewhere, highlighting 'interdependencies' and 'connections' previously unrecognised.

In both these novels, a second look reveals the insidious nature of neocolonialism, which leaves scars with its extractions, but provides wealth and stability for the colonising country. At the end of *When We Were Orphans*, Christopher, who strives to be the stereotypical Englishman, finds that he is economically complicit in terrible crimes abroad. The profits of violence and exploitation have been lurking under the civilised veneer of his 'inheritance' and his place in society all along. Similarly, in Goldman's novel, when Roger sets about trying to solve Flor's murder, he must reach much further back than her return to Guatemala. Although the explicit violence occurred there, it soon becomes evident that the damage began in a quiet family home in Namoset in the United States.

By suggesting the unreliability of their protagonists' initial perceptions, Ishiguro and Goldman establish the difference between the 'real' countries the detectives inhabit and the myths that paint them as just and peaceful societies. In *Crossbones*, the link between the United States and Somalia is also made evident, albeit in a more sporadic way. The two countries are narratively linked by the FBI's investigation of Taxliil and his Kurdish school friend's attempt to avenge the loss of his family in Iraq by becoming a suicide bomber. The United States is also present in the drones that fly over Mogadishu. At all times, the reader is made aware of Somalia's place in the global order, as Farah emphasises both its political and 'spatial situated-ness' (Cheah 2016: 219).

Each of these three texts reveals the postcolonial (and neocolonial) aspects of their settings, rather than focusing only on civil conflict, suggesting global as well as local complicity. Contrastingly, in *Anil's Ghost*, Sri Lanka's colonial history is lightly suggested, but never as a contributing factor to the civil war, meaning that Ondaatje's depiction of Sri Lanka is untethered by global historical context. This suggests Sri Lanka is an isolated pocket of violence, whereas the more thorough demolition of the guilty-innocent dialectic (as portrayed by Ishiguro, Goldman and Farah) ensures that the idea of 'the innocent many' (Auden 2016) is erased, not only in relation to those embroiled in civil war, but also with regard to those who invisibly benefit from other countries' instability.

Contrapuntal thinking, constellational thinking and the role of the returnee

In these five novels, we witness two different kinds of awakening on the part of the protagonists. One type of character evolution is emotional: in the course of the narratives, almost all the detectives move towards a more nuanced understanding of their own identity and the meaning of home. As previously discussed, this kind of understanding is well described by Said's formulation of contrapuntal thinking (2013). However, a cognitive shift is also evident in each protagonist's character evolution. In the course of their inquiries, the detectives are forced into a Socratic realisation of their own ignorance. In order to achieve wisdom, and to function as useful investigators, they must admit to the glaring limitations of their own knowledge.

Rather than a portraying a journey towards certainty, the returnees' narrative arcs tend towards the renunciation of their earliest convictions and a willingness to claim ignorance of much of the 'outsized reality' (García Márquez 1982) that surrounds them. In the process, they become more receptive to other ways of thinking and to accepting local contributions to their inquiries. In 'The Virtue of Socratic Ignorance', Alan R. Drengson argues: 'Our preoccupation with knowledge in both the abstract and the concrete often prevents us from realizing ignorance close at hand, and this failure prevents us from being aware of the open and unsettled character of much of human life' (1981: 237). Often, the mysteries at the heart of these novels remain 'open and unsettled', but the detective paradoxically emerges wiser for having acknowledged his or her own limitations.

In realising that they may be out of their depth, the investigators must often decide to limit the use of their personal power, rather than wielding it to its full extent. The returnee detective occupies the uneasy position of social arbiter of a society from which they are partially estranged. This partial estrangement is an effective literary device, enabling the characters to decode their surroundings for an international readership without ever claiming complete authority. However, within the world of the novels, the combination of non-belonging and social arbitration often becomes problematic, bordering as it does on neocolonialism. In discussing the idea of the United States as a new imperial power, Upamanyu Pablo Mukherjee says: 'The common rhetorical and representative strategies employed, at least in the West, to document the birth pangs of this new form of globalized power have been precisely those of order, deviance and punishment' (2003: 1). The West's history of global policing and international intervention often emerges as a conscious theme in these novels and each of the detectives faces questions about their fitness for the role they are undertaking, implicitly problematising both the role of the detective and the ethics of international intervention.

In 'The White-Savior Industrial Complex', Teju Cole discusses the figure of the Western rescuer in international media narratives about the developing world. In order to demonstrate the appeal of this archetype, Cole compares the scant media coverage of peaceful anti-corruption marches in Nigeria in 2012 with the kind of traction achieved by media campaigns such as 'Kony 2012'. Cole argues that the latter campaign, in which the United States charity Invisible Children raised millions of dollars towards the capture of Ugandan guerrilla leader Joseph Kony, succeeded in raising attention because of its simplistic narrative and its glorification of Western humanitarianism. Of the under-reported Nigerian story, Cole writes: 'After all, there is no simple demand to be made and – since corruption is endemic – no single villain to topple. There is certainly no "bridge character," [Nicholas] Kristof's euphemism for white saviors in Third World narratives who make the story more palatable to American viewers' (2013: 7).[1]

Cole argues that the idea of 'rescuing' developing countries betrays an inability to think 'constellational[ly]' (2013: 5) about power structures and systems of governance. He argues: 'There is much more to doing good work than "making a difference." There is the principle of first do no harm. There is the idea that those who are being helped ought to be consulted over the matters that concern them' (7). In invoking 'the principle of first do no harm', Cole suggests that such campaigns have the potential to cause damage even as they purport to offer aid. This is an anxiety that is clearly surfaced in many of the novels discussed in this book. We are made aware that, as Joseph R. Slaughter would have it, 'the

---

1. Cole refers to Nicholas Kristof's journalistic portrayals of Africa, in which Kristof often focuses on foreign aid workers. Defending this choice, Kristof writes: 'One way of getting people to read at least a few grafs is to have some kind of a foreign protagonist, some American who they can identify with as a bridge character. And so if this is a way I can get people to care about foreign countries, to read about them, ideally, to get a little bit more involved, then I plead guilty' (2010).

banalization of human rights means that violations are often committed in the Orwellian name of human rights themselves, cloaked in the palliative rhetoric of humanitarian intervention' (2007: 2). The terms of Cole's critique are useful in framing the role of the returnee in these five novels. Each novel both employs and resists the idea of the 'bridge character' as saviour by undermining the protagonist's attempts to unilaterally effect change. In each text, the protagonist must also renounce her or his own certainties and embrace the idea of constellational thinking.

Anil's Ghost is a useful case study in evaluating the ethically ambiguous role of the bridge character in these novels. As a literary device, Anil operates as a cultural mediator, one whose role is to make the story more 'palatable' (Cole 2013: 7) to an uninitiated readership and to ease them into local stories. This is suggested by the very title of the novel, which initially appears to foreground Anil's work with Sailor, but is finally revealed as a reference to Sarath. However, Ondaatje also embeds criticisms of the Western saviour ideal into the text, thus acknowledging it as a problematic trope. Gamini explicitly mocks stories about the 'Third World' which end as soon as the Western hero departs from the war zone (Ondaatje 2011a: 282). Sarath says to Anil: 'I want you to understand the archaeological surround of a fact. Or you'll be like one of those journalists who file reports about flies and scabs while staying at the Galle Face Hotel. That false empathy and blame' (Ondaatje 2011a: 40). Anil's fixation on a single fact ultimately sends Sarath to his death, while his understanding of Sri Lankan society saves her life. As demonstrated in Chapter 2, Ondaatje's portrayal of Anil is arguably problematic in many respects, but the narrative undoubtedly rewards the idea of a constellational approach to social arbitration.

Similarly, in the other novels, local characters attempt to promote constellational thinking, reproving the detectives for their high-handed behaviour and lack of community engagement. In *Red Dust*, Ben Hoffman says: 'But you must see . . . that nothing is as simple as you would have it. We are all interconnected here. You cannot pay attention only to the one side as if it stands separate from the other' (Slovo 2009b: 151). Qasiir in *Crossbones* unsuccessfully attempts to talk sense into Malik when he goes to confront the militant Big Beard, invoking his ancestral knowledge of the local community: 'There is no benefit in provoking Big Beard unnecessarily . . . Grandpa, who knew him all his life, always advised me to give him a wide berth' (Farah 2012: 245). In *When We Were Orphans*, the Japanese colonel Christopher meets attempts to correct his myopic understanding of the Second Sino-Japanese War, saying: '*The entire globe*, Mr Banks, the entire globe will before long be engaged in war. What you just saw in Chapei, it is but a small speck of dust compared to what the world must soon witness (Ishiguro 2000: 295).

The embrace of constellational thinking sometimes results in the deliberate abandonment of the investigation. Of the example set by early detective fiction, specifically Edgar Allen Poe's *The Murders in the Rue Morgue*, Knight maintains: 'The crime and the resolution are without history, without recurring roots. This powerful and frighteningly delusive notion is still with us, that desocialised, unhistorical understanding can, by deciphering isolated problems, resolve them' (1980: 44). The novels explored here support the idea that this notion is a 'delusive' one. To solve an individual case is often to remove the symptom, but not the 'root' cause, risking 'recurring' violence.

In *Red Dust*, for example, Sarah Barcant's character evolution is not complete until she accepts that Alex has decided to withdraw from the TRC hearing without questioning Dirk any further. This is professionally counter-intuitive, but indicates that Sarah has realised that some cases should not be pursued at any cost. The 'rational truth' (Slovo 2009b: 320) is that Alex is blameless in the matter of Steve's killing, but he is unable to emotionally extricate himself from the role he may have played by breaking down under torture, and he cannot risk his relationship with his community, which will endure long after the truth commission and Sarah herself have moved on.

Sometimes the protagonist's constellational awakening comes too late. The death of Sarath in *Anil's Ghost* is perhaps the most dramatic example of harm done through returnees' misreading of the local situation, but each returnee finds themselves violating 'the principle of first do no harm' (Cole 2013: 7) in the course of their investigation. Because they are operating in extremely violent societies, the detectives must face the fact that they risk triggering more violence with both their personal and their professional behaviour. Ahl of *Crossbones* is indirectly responsible for the death of Malik's stringer Qasiir as well as Malik's own injury in a roadside bombing, and afterwards he is 'choked' by his 'sense of guilt' (Farah 2012: 368). Sarah Barcant inadvertently re-traumatises her client by subjecting him to conventional pre-courtroom questioning, unable to see that his reticence goes much deeper than simple uncooperativeness. Ben Hoffman, berating her, describes the interview as 'a crucifixion' (Slovo 2009b: 65).

The liminal identities of the protagonists have benefits as well as limitations, however. In *Reflections on Exile*, Said writes:

> We take home and language for granted; they become nature, and their underlying assumptions recede into dogma and orthodoxy . . . Borders and barriers, which enclose us within the safety of familiar territory, can also become prisons, and are often defended beyond reason or necessity. Exiles cross borders, break barriers of thought and experience (2013).

The returnee detective performs precisely this role, opening up new possibilities that their local counterparts are not in a position to consider. The returnees' complex relationships with their countries of origin give them unique insight and impetus, even if they sometimes walk the line between boldness and arrogance. As an international journalist, Malik is uniquely placed to bargain for information about Taxliil because he can offer his sources access to the world stage. At the same time, he has a local's proficiency in Somali, opening the doors of communication and granting him partial insider status.

In *Anil's Ghost*, the inquiry is catalysed by Anil's refusal to accept the unwritten rules of the conflict zone. The investigation into Sailor's death is only able to take place because her argument for holding the government to account is persuasive enough to convince Sarath. Even after her reckless revelation condemns him, he makes sure that when she escapes, it is with their findings on Sailor, tacitly affirming their value. Anil's devotion to truth is never portrayed in a wholly negative light. She may be unversed in Sri Lanka's particular dangers and nuances, but she is also not blinkered by its conventions and prejudices, including the acceptance of closed doors and open secrets. David Farrier says: 'Anil's nomadism, as she does engage in the unburial of intimate testimony, represents a potential freedom from geographical as well as historical consternation' (2005: 85). Her attitude inspires Sarath to attempt the reconstruction, even though he understands the risks and limitations of the endeavour far better than Anil does.

In Slovo's *Red Dust*, Sarah is also not bound by many social conventions and lacks the racial prejudices common to the white community of

Smitsrivier. Because of this, she is able to simply walk through many of the invisible barriers left over from apartheid. Her cosmopolitanism also makes her chafe against the town's gender segregation. When she goes for a drink, she avoids the empty 'ladies bar', which is described as 'a small windowless space' (Slovo 2009b: 102) and instead seats herself in the main room, where she is free to observe the townspeople at her leisure. In doing so, she establishes herself in opposition to characters such as Marie Muller, who seek to avoid political involvement by keeping strictly to the female-coded domestic realm. It is in the bar that Sarah has her first encounter with Alex outside of a professional setting, and where their relationship begins its evolution from 'suspicion and attraction' to 'tenderness' (328). However, it is only her disregard for the prevailing social mores that makes this evolution possible and eventually enables her to establish a bond of trust with him. As can be seen in these examples, the liminality of the returnee figures enables them to transcend social codes, giving them a unique vantage point, even as their lack of local knowledge sometimes lets them down. They therefore approach their inquiries with relative freshness and freedom.

In turn, the investigation has beneficial effects for the protagonist. As well as moving towards a constellational view of their surroundings, they also renounce certainty in their conceptions of home and away, moving towards an outlook that Said terms 'contrapuntal thinking'. Although few of the returnees qualify for Said's definition of political exiles, which specifies banishment from their place of origin, their lifestyles contain strong similarities to the condition Said describes. In *Reflections on Exile*, Said says: 'Most people are principally aware of one culture, one setting, one home; exiles are aware of at least two, and thus plurality of vision gives rise to an awareness of simultaneous dimensions, an awareness that – to borrow a phrase from music – is *contrapuntal* (2013). The returnees achieve this 'plurality of vision' by reincorporating their places of origin into their identities, without renouncing the aspects of self they have acquired abroad.

For the most part, the returnees begin their narrative lives as somewhat damaged individuals. Of the experience of exile, Said continues:

> There is the sheer fact of isolation and displacement, which produces the kind of narcissistic masochism that resists all efforts at amelioration, acculturation and community. At this extreme

the exile can make a fetish of exile, a practice that distances him or her from all connections and commitments. To live as if everything around you were temporary and perhaps trivial is to fall prey to petulant cynicism as well as to querulous lovelessness (2013).

The detectives' lifestyles resemble Said's description of the alienation of exile. Their pre-return existences are variously described as 'sparse' (Ondaatje 2011a: 63), 'miserable' (Ishiguro 2000: 193), 'hardened' (Slovo 2009b: 118) and 'deadbeat' (Goldman 2007: 367). (In *Crossbones*, the damage caused by rootlessness is depicted through the figure of Taxliil, who attempts to subsume his contradictions in the dogma of Al-Shabaab.) As discussed in Chapter 4, the idea of the damaged investigator is partly a feature of genre: the lone detective is a recurring figure in the canon, as is the dysfunctional, Holmesian genius, in part because their lack of external investments allows a monomaniacal approach that raises the stakes of the investigation. Knight describes 'alienation' as a recurring characteristic of the classic literary detective (1980: 159). However, in these texts the returnee's damage is also inextricably linked to their status as emigrants.

Most of the texts (with the exception of *Crossbones*, in which the return is to an ancestral home) characterise the detectives as having initially left their 'home' countries without critically examining their reasons for doing so. Either these characters have been relocated as children (Christopher, Roger) or their emigration is portrayed as part of the rebellion of young adulthood (Sarah and Anil). The returnees' evolution in character implies that the damage of displacement can only be eased by coming to terms with the old milieu, enacting what Palipana of *Anil's Ghost* calls 'the paradox of retreat' (Ondaatje 2011a: 303). He says: 'You renounce society, but to do so you must first be a part of it, learn your decision from it.' Each of the protagonists must come to terms with the scene of their childhood – not as an idealised memory, but as a troubling and complex reality – before they can achieve a sense of wholeness in their personal lives. In attaining a nuanced and constellational understanding of what they have left behind, the protagonists are able to further their own evolution from distance to empathic engagement.

The motif of orphanhood is common to almost all the novels, with the lack of a welcoming older generation emphasising the rupture in continuity. In *Reflections on Exile*, Said comments: 'No matter how well they may do, exiles are always eccentrics who feel their difference (even as they frequently exploit it) as a kind of orphanhood' (2013). Like orphanhood, displacement proves an irreversible process for these characters: even though they are physically able to return, the protagonists are unable to pick up their former lives where they left off. Indeed, the absurdity of this idea is highlighted by Christopher's fixation on reclaiming (and repopulating) the household of his childhood. Instead, the returnees are forced to forge new relationships in an imperfect simulation of repair. Often these bonds are couched in familial terms, emphasising the idea of the provisional, self-defined home through the motif of the non-biological family.

Roger, for example, sets about repairing an old wrong when he joins forces with Moya. As schoolchildren, the two boys vowed to be 'like brothers' (Goldman 2007: 64), a covenant they were supposed to seal by scaling a fence and confronting a vicious dog. In the event, Roger betrayed Moya by allowing him to leap into danger on his own. Besides echoing the United States' public denunciation of Guatemala, this incident plays a formative role in Roger's self-perception. When he agrees to work with Moya, their investigation becomes a second attempt at establishing brotherhood and a way for Roger to prove that he is not the '*gringo de mierda*' ('gringo made of shit') (67) who abandoned Moya all those years ago. In the end he makes amends by rescuing Moya from the surveillance van that is tailing them, cementing their bond. While he acquires a second would-be sibling, the relationship cannot assuage the grief of Flor de Mayo's death.

Anil initially eschews most emotional connection, but eventually identifies herself as being 'like a sister' (Ondaatje 2011a: 282) to Sarath and Gamini. In the forest grove, she defers to Palipana as a father figure (of Palipana, Sarath says: 'We need parents when we're old too [42]). The idea of the imperfect and approximate reconstruction of family life is evident in *Red Dust* as well. At the beginning of the novel, Ben Hoffman says that Sarah is 'no longer the person I knew or the lawyer I trained' (Slovo 2009b: 67). However, at the end of the novel they are reconciled and Sarah commits herself to being with him during his illness, if not as his literal daughter then as his protégée and his intellectual heir. As discussed in Chapter 1, it takes Christopher until the end of *When We Were Orphans* to accept that he has had a family all along. While his adopted daughter does not compensate for his lost origins, she provides him with the hope of a future. In every case, the returnee gains something, without replacing what they have lost. The later relationships are valuable because they are so hard won. Separation is therefore portrayed as an injury for which one can find solace, but not necessarily an antidote and the bittersweet complexity of the texts' final chapters reflects this.

Afterword

All the novels discussed in this book avoid offering solutions to the problems they present. In withholding easy answers, they offer the reader a more complex and critical view of the circumstances they depict. In these settings, the act of narrowing down suspects and possibilities could have disastrous consequences. The detectives must embrace an ambivalent vantage point - one that is both contrapuntal and constellational - in order to establish an ethical relationship with their surroundings. This implies that true understanding - of violence, of the postcolony and of the idea of home - is a process of complication, rather than simplification.

In each narrative, simplification proves to be a dangerous method - it leads Christopher to cling to false hope, it leads Anil to pursue the truth at any cost, it denies the role of the international community in Guatemala's tragedy, it negates the role of trauma in memory and it allows figures such as the 'Somali pirate' to gain international infamy while history and context go unaddressed. However, each writer also acknowledges the appeal of a simplified world as well as its dangers. The comforting expectations of genre are first evoked and then abandoned in order to underline the difficulty and complexity of the constellational approach and the emotional toll it exacts. The reader is inaugurated into a world of ambiguity, broken promises and loss. In projecting these worlds, the novelists insist on the communal elements of violence and exploitation, sacrificing depictions of anomalous monstrosity in order to highlight the kind of atrocities that hide in plain sight.

The discomfort of the reading experience lies partly in the writers' eschewal of shorthand and suspense. Instead of providing ease of narrative flow, they disrupt and make difficult, raising more questions than answers. The realities these novels project resist capture, either by legal or narrative authority. In this way, they avoid one of the qualities that Auden attributes to detective fiction. In 'The Guilty Vicarage', he writes: 'I forget the story as soon as I have finished it, and have no wish to read it again' (Auden 2016). Interestingly, Auden lists this 'immediacy' as one of the genre's attributes, rather than one of its deficits. The quality of being forgettable is the result of the traditional crime novel's agenda of wish fulfilment: because the answers have all been delivered, there is nothing left to puzzle over.

By contrast, the novels described in this book often demand a second look, withholding wish fulfilment to the point that many of them have been criticised for their unreadability. However, in their very difficulty, these novels offer a challenge to popular ideas of truth and justice by allowing the reader to glimpse the devastation of certainty that attends social collapse and intimate conflict.

Select Bibliography

Addison, Tony and Syed Mansoob Murshed. 2001. 'From Conflict to Reconstruction: Reviving the Social Contract'. Discussion Paper 2001/048. Helsinki: UNU-WIDER. https://www.wider.unu.edu/publication/conflict-reconstruction.

Adorno, Theodor W. 2005. *Minima Moralia: Reflections on a Damaged Life*. London: Verso.

Anderson, Jean, Carolina Miranda and Barbara Pezzotti. 2012. *The Foreign in International Crime Fiction: Transcultural Representations*. New York: Continuum.

Appiah, Kwame Anthony. 1991. 'Out of Africa, Topologies of Nativism'. In *The Bounds of Race, Perspectives on Hegemony and Resistance*, edited by D. LaCapra, 134-63. Ithaca: Cornell University Press.

Arendt, Hannah. 1971. 'Thinking and Moral Considerations: A Lecture'. *Social Research* 38 (3): 417-46.

———. 1994. *Eichmann in Jerusalem: A Report on the Banality of Evil*. New York: Penguin.

Auden, W.H. 2016. 'The Guilty Vicarage: Notes on the Detective Story, by an Addict'. *Harper's Magazine*, 22 December. https://harpers.org/archive/1948/05/the-guilty-vicarage/. Originally published in *Harper's Magazine*, May 1948, 406-11.

Bhargava, Anurima. 2002. 'Defining Political Crimes: A Case Study of the South African Truth and Reconciliation Commission'. *Columbia Law Review* 102 (5): 1304-39.

Black, Shameem. 2011. 'Truth Commission Thrillers'. *Social Text* 29 (2): 47-66.

Booth, Martin. 1996. *Opium: A History*. New York: Simon and Schuster.

Boym, Svetlana. 2001. *The Future of Nostalgia*. New York: Basic Books.

———. 2007. 'Nostalgia and Its Discontents'. *The Hedgehog Review* 9 (2): 7-19.

Bronfen, Elisabeth. 1993. *Over Her Dead Body: Death, Femininity, and the Aesthetic*. Manchester: Manchester University Press.

Butler, Judith. 2010. *Frames of War: When Is Life Grievable?* New York: Verso.

Cawthorne, Nigel. 2009. *Pirates of the 21st Century: How Modern-Day Buccaneers Are Terrorising the World's Oceans*. London: John Blake.

Chandler, Daniel. 1997. 'An Introduction to Genre Theory'. https://faculty.washington.edu/farkas/HCDE510-Fall2012/Chandler_genre_theoryDFAnn.pdf.

Cheah, Pheng. 2016. *What Is a World? On Postcolonial Literature as World Literature*. Durham: Duke University Press.

Christie, Agatha. 2013. *The Lost Mine*. New York: Harper.
Christopher, Lissa. 2011. 'Interview with Gillian Slovo'. *Sydney Morning Herald*, 15 December. https://www.smh.com.au/entertainment/books/interview-gillian-slovo-20111215-1ovef.html.
Clausen, Christopher. 1984. 'Sherlock Holmes, Order, and the Late-Victorian Mind'. *The Georgia Review* 38 (1): 104-23.
Coe, Jonathan. 1993. 'What Else Is New?' *London Review of Books* 15 (5), 11 March. https://www.lrb.co.uk/the-paper/v15/n05/jonathan-coe/what-else-is-new.
Cole, Catherine M. 2007. 'Performance, Transitional Justice, and the Law: South Africa's Truth and Reconciliation Commission'. *Theatre Journal* 59 (2): 167-87.
———. 2010. *Performing South Africa's Truth Commission: Stages of Transition*. Bloomington: Indiana University Press.
Cole, Teju. 2013. 'The White-Savior Industrial Complex'. *The Atlantic Online*, 11 January. http://www.theatlantic.com/international/.../03/the-white-savior-industrial-complex/254843/.
Davis, Emily S. 2009. 'Investigating Truth, History, and Human Rights in Michael Ondaatje's *Anil's Ghost*'. In *Detective Fiction in a Postcolonial and Transnational World*, edited by Nels Pearson and Marc Singer, 15-30. Farnham: Ashgate.
Dawes, James. 2016. 'The Novel of Human Rights'. *American Literature* 88 (1): 127-57.
De Votta, Neil. 2000. 'Control Democracy, Institutional Decay, and the Quest for *Eelami*: Explaining Ethnic Conflict in Sri Lanka'. *Pacific Affairs* 73 (1): 55-76.
Derrickson, Teresa. 2004. 'Will the Un-Truth Set You Free? A Critical Look at Global Human Rights Discourse in Michael Ondaatje's *Anil's Ghost*'. *Literature Interpretation Theory* 15 (2): 131-52.
Dickens, Charles. 2005. *David Copperfield*. Dover: Mineola.
Döring, Tobias. 2006. 'Sherlock Holmes, He Dead: Disenchanting the English Detective in Kazuo Ishiguro's *When We Were Orphans*'. In *Postcolonial Postmortems: Crime Fiction from a Transcultural Perspective*, edited by Christine Matzke and Susanne Muehleisen, 59-86. Amsterdam: Rodopi.
Doyle, Arthur Conan. 2013. *The Adventures of Sherlock Holmes*. E-book. Not So Noble.
Drengson, Alan R. 1981. 'The Virtue of Socratic Ignorance'. *American Philosophical Quarterly* 18 (3): 237-42.
Driver, Dorothy. 2007. 'Gillian Slovo's *Red Dust* (2000) and the Ambigous Articulations of Gender'. *Scrutiny2* 12 (2): 107-22.
Evans, Mary. 2009. *The Imagination of Evil: Detective Fiction and the Modern World*. New York: Continuum.
Farah, Nuruddin. 1970. *From a Crooked Rib*. London: Heinemann.
———. 2003. *Links*. Cape Town: Kwela.
———. 2007. *Knots*. New York: Riverhead.
———. 2012. *Crossbones*. London: Granta.
Farrier, David. 2005. 'Gesturing towards the Local: Intimate Histories in Michael Ondaatje's *Anil's Ghost*'. *Journal of Postcolonial Writing* 41 (1): 83-93.

Fergusson, James. 2013. *The World's Most Dangerous Place: Inside the Outlaw State of Somalia*. London: Transworld.

Finney, Brian. 2002. 'Figuring the Real: Ishiguro's *When We Were Orphans*'. *Jouvert: A Journal of Postcolonial Studies* 7 (1). https://legacy.chass.ncsu.edu/jouvert/v7is1/ishigu.htm.

Foniokova, Zuzana. 2007. 'The Orphan's Dream Come True: Representation of Reality in Ishiguro's *When We Were Orphans*'. *South Bohemian Anglo-American Studies* 1 (1): 118–22.

Galeano, Eduardo. 1997. *Open Veins of Latin America: Five Centuries of the Pillage of a Continent*. New York: Monthly Review Press. Kindle edition.

García Márquez, Gabriel. 1982. 'Nobel Lecture', 8 December. https://www.nobelprize.org/prizes/literature/1982/marquez/lecture/.

Gettleman, Jeffrey. 2008. 'Somalia's Pirates Flourish in a Lawless Nation'. *The New York Times*, 30 October. https://www.nytimes.com/2008/10/31/world/africa/31pirates.html.

Glover, David. 2003. 'The Thriller'. *The Cambridge Companion to Crime Fiction*, edited by Martin Priestman, 135–54. Cambridge: Cambridge University Press.

Gobodo-Madikizela, Pumla. 2013. *A Human Being Died That Night: Forgiving Apartheid's Chief Killer*. London: Portobello Books. Kindle edition.

Goldman, Francisco. 2007. *The Long Night of White Chickens*. New York: Grove Atlantic.

———. 2010. *The Art of Political Murder: Who Killed Bishop Gerardi?* New Delhi: Atlantic.

Goldman, Marlene. 2004. 'Representations of Buddhism in Ondaatje's *Anil's Ghost*'. *CLCWeb: Comparative Literature and Culture* 6 (3). https://docs.lib.purdue.edu/clcweb/vol6/iss3/4/.

Grandin, Greg. 2000. *The Blood of Guatemala: A History of Race and Nation*. Durham: Duke University Press.

———. 2011. *The Last Colonial Massacre: Latin America in the Cold War*. Chicago: Chicago University Press.

Gready, Paul. 2009. 'Novel Truths: Literature and Truth Commissions'. *Comparative Literature Studies* 46 (1): 156–76.

Green, Rayna. 1975. 'The Pocahontas Perplex: The Image of Indian Women in American Culture'. *Massachusetts Review* 16 (4): 698–714.

Harper, Mary. 2012. *Getting Somalia Wrong? Faith, War and Hope in a Shattered State*. London: Zed Books.

Harris, Susan Cannon. 2003. 'Pathological Possibilities: Contagion and Empire in Doyle's Sherlock Holmes Stories'. *Victorian Literature and Culture* 31 (2): 447–66.

Hirsch, Marianne and Nancy K. Miller, eds. 2011. *Rites of Return: Diaspora Poetics and the Politics of Memory*. New York: Columbia University Press.

Hobsbawm, Eric J. and Terence Ranger, eds. 2000. *The Invention of Tradition*. Cambridge: Cambridge University Press.

Holquist, Michael. 1971. 'Whodunit and Other Questions: Metaphysical Detective Stories in Post-War Fiction'. *New Literary History* 3 (1): 135–56.

Horrell, Georgina. 2004. 'A Whiter Shade of Pale: White Femininity as Guilty Masquerade in "New" (White) South African Women's Writing'. *Journal of Southern African Studies* 30 (4): 765–76.

Horsley, Lee and Katharine Horsley. 2006. 'Body Language: Reading the Corpse in Forensic Crime Fiction'. *Paradoxa: Terrain Vagues* 20 (1): 7–32.

Hunnewell, Susannah. 2008. 'Kazuo Ishiguro, The Art of Fiction No. 196'. *The Paris Review* 84. http://www.theparisreview.org/interviews/5829/kazuo-ishiguro-the-art-of-fiction-no-196-kazuo-ishiguro.

Ishiguro, Kazuo. 1986. *An Artist of the Floating World*. London: Faber and Faber.

———. 2000. *When We Were Orphans*. London: Faber and Faber.

———. 2005. *A Pale View of Hills*. London: Faber and Faber.

———. 2009. *The Remains of the Day*. London: Faber and Faber.

Jaggi, Maya. 2012. 'Nuruddin Farah: A Life in Writing'. *The Guardian*, 21 September. http://www.theguardian.com/culture/2012/sep/21/nuruddin-salah-life-in-writing.

James, P.D. 2013. 'P.D. James: Who Killed the Golden Age of Crime?' *The Spectator*, 11 December. http://www.spectator.co.uk/2013/12/a-nice-gentle-murder.

JanMohamed, Abdul R. 1983. *Manichean Aesthetics: The Politics of Literature in Colonial Africa*. Amherst: University of Massachusetts Press.

Jonas, Susanne. 1996. 'Dangerous Liaisons: The U.S. in Guatemala'. *Foreign Policy* 103: 144–60.

Jung, C.G. 1954. *The Collected Works of C.G. Jung*. London: Routledge and Kegan Paul.

Kakutani, Michiko. 2000. 'The Case He Can't Solve: A Detective's Delusions'. *The New York Times*, 19 September. https://www.nytimes.com/2000/09/19/books/books-of-the-times-the-case-he-can-t-solve-a-detective-s-delusions.html.

Kanaganayakam, Chelva. 2006. 'In Defense of Anil's Ghost'. *ARIEL: A Review of International English Literature* 37 (1): 5–26.

Kapferer, Bruce. 1988. *Legends of People, Myths of State: Violence, Intolerance, and Political Culture in Sri Lanka and Australia*. Washington: Smithsonian Institute Press.

Kayman, Martin A. 2003. 'The Short Story from Poe to Chesterton'. In *The Cambridge Companion to Crime Fiction*, edited by Martin Priestman, 41–58. Cambridge: Cambridge University Press.

Kermode, Frank. 1967. *The Sense of an Ending: Studies in the Theory of Fiction*. Oxford: Oxford University Press.

Knepper, Wendy. 2006. 'Confession, Autopsy and the Postcolonial Postmortems of Anil's Ghost'. In *Postcolonial Postmortems: Crime Fiction from a Transcultural Perspective*, edited by Christine Matzke and Susanne Muehleisen, 35–58. Amsterdam: Rodopi.

Knight, Stephen. 1980. *Form and Ideology in Crime Fiction*. Bloomington: Indiana University Press.

———. 2003. 'The Golden Age'. In *The Cambridge Companion to Crime Fiction*, edited by Martin Priestman, 77-94. Cambridge: Cambridge University Press.

Kristof, Nicholas. 2010. 'Westerners on White Horses...'. *The New York Times*, 14 July. https://kristof.blogs.nytimes.com/2010/07/14/westerners-on-white-horses/.

Krog, Antjie. 2004. 'The Wet Bag and Other Phantoms'. In *Violence in War and Peace: An Anthology*, edited by Nancy Scheper-Hughes and Philippe I. Bourgois, 372-7. Oxford: Blackwell.

Leeson, Peter T. 2010. 'Pirational Choice: The Economics of Infamous Pirate Practices'. *Journal of Economic Behavior & Organization* 76 (3): 497-510.

Loomba, Ania. 2015. *Colonialism/Postcolonialism*. London: Routledge.

Machinal, Hélène. 2009. '*When We Were Orphans*: Narration and Detection in the Case of Christopher Banks'. In *Kazuo Ishiguro: Contemporary Critical Perspectives*, edited by Sebastian Groes and Sean Matthews, 79-90. New York: Continuum.

Mamdani, Mahmood. 2002. 'Amnesty or Impunity? A Preliminary Critique of the Report of the Truth and Reconciliation Commission of South Africa (TRC)'. *Diacritics* 32 (3): 33-59.

Marcus, Laura. 2003. 'Detection and Literary Fiction'. In *The Cambridge Companion to Crime Fiction*, edited by Martin Priestman, 245-68. Cambridge: Cambridge University Press.

Marinkova, Milena. 2011. *Michael Ondaatje: Haptic Aesthetics and Micropolitical Writing*. New York: Continuum

Martínez, Susana S. 2008. 'Guatemala as a National Crime Scene: Femicide and Impunity in Contemporary U.S. Detective Novels'. *Journal of Interdisciplinary Feminist Thought* 3 (1): 1-23.

Mbembe, Achille. 2001. *On the Postcolony*. Berkeley: University of California Press.

McClintock, Anne. 1993. 'Family Feuds: Gender, Nationalism and the Family'. *Feminist Review* 44: 61-80.

Merivale, Patricia and Susan Elizabeth Sweeney. 1999. *Detecting Texts: The Metaphysical Detective Story from Poe to Postmodernism*. Philadelphia: University of Pennsylvania Press.

Mitter, Rana. 2014. *China's War with Japan, 1937-1945: The Struggle for Survival*. New York: Penguin.

Mizejewski, Linda. 2004. *Hardboiled and High Heeled: The Woman Detective in Popular Culture*. New York: Routledge.

Moolla, F. Fiona. 2014. *Reading Nuruddin Farah: The Individual, the Novel & the Idea of Home*. Woodbridge: James Currey.

Mukherjee, Upamanyu Pablo. 2003. *Crime and Empire: The Colony in Nineteenth-Century Fictions of Crime*. Oxford: Oxford University Press.

———. 2013. '"Out-of-the-Way Asiatic Disease": Contagion, Malingering, and Sherlock's England'. In *Literature of an Independent England: Revisions of England,*

Englishness and English Literature, edited by Claire Westall and Michael Gardiner, 77-90. Basingstoke: Palgrave Macmillan.

Naicker, Kamil. 2017. 'Going to Pieces: Narrative Disintegration in Nuruddin Farah's *Crossbones*'. *Social Dynamics* 43 (1): 8-18.

Nun Halloran, Vivian. 2007. 'Health Professionals, Truth, and Testimony: Witnessing in Human Rights-Themed Entertainment'. *The Journal of the Midwest Modern Language Association* 40 (2): 97-114.

Ondaatje, Michael. 1982. *Running in the Family*. New York: Vintage.

———. 1999. *Handwriting: Poems*. New York: A.A. Knopf.

———. 2011a. *Anil's Ghost*. New York: Random House.

———. 2011b. *The Cat's Table*. London: Jonathan Cape.

Orford, Margie. 2013. 'The Grammar of Violence, Writing Crime as Fiction'. *Current Writing* 25 (2): 220-9.

Pamuk, Orhan. 2011. *The Black Book*. London: Faber and Faber.

Peña, Daniel. 2015. 'The Rumpus Interview with Francisco Goldman'. *The Rumpus*, 16 October. http://therumpus.net/2015/10/the-rumpus-interview-with-francisco-goldman/.

Plain, Gill. 2001. *Twentieth-Century Crime Fiction: Gender, Sexuality and the Body*. Chicago: Fitzroy Dearborn.

Priestman, Martin. 2003. 'Introduction: Crime Fiction and Detective Fiction'. In *The Cambridge Companion to Crime Fiction*, edited by Martin Priestman, 1-6. Cambridge: Cambridge University Press.

Quayson, Ato. 2005. 'The Enchantment of a False Freedom'. *Interventions: International Journal of Post Colonial Studies* 7 (3): 333-7.

Rogers, John D. 1994. 'Post-Orientalism and the Interpretation of Premodern and Modern Political Identities: The Case of Sri Lanka'. *Journal of Asian Studies* 53 (1): 10-23.

SABC (South African Broadcasting Corporation). 1996a. 'Truth and Reconciliation Commission Amnesty Hearing: Jeffrey Benzien'. Episode 57, SABC2.

———. 1996b. 'Truth and Reconciliation Commission: Special Report'. Episode 57, SABC2.

Said, Edward W. 1978. *Orientalism*. London: Routledge and Kegan Paul.

———. 2013. *Reflections on Exile and Other Literary and Cultural Essays*. London: Granta Books. Kindle edition.

Samper, David. 2002. 'Cannibalizing Kids: Rumor and Resistance in Latin America'. *Journal of Folklore Research* 39 (1): 1-32.

Samuelson, Meg. 2003. 'Cracked Vases and Untidy Seams: Narrative Structure and Closure in the Truth and Reconciliation Commission and South African Fiction'. *Current Writing* 15 (2): 63-76.

Sanghera, Sandeep. 2004. 'Touching the Language of Citizenship in Ondaatje's *Anil's Ghost*'. *CLCWeb: Comparative Literature and Culture* 6 (3): 1-7. https://doi.org/10.7771/1481-4374.1241.

Sawhney, Hirsh. 2011. 'A Novel of Pirates, Zealots and the Somalia Crisis'. *The New York Times*, 11 September. https://www.nytimes.com/2011/09/11/books/review/crossbones-by-nuruddin-farah-book-review.html.

Scaggs, John. 2005. *Crime Fiction*. London: Routledge.

Scanlan, Margaret. 2004. '*Anil's Ghost* and Terrorism's Time'. *Studies in the Novel* 36 (3): 302–17.

Scheper-Hughes, Nancy. 2010. 'Face to Face with Abidoral Queiroz: Death Squads and Democracy in Northeast Brazil'. In *Roots, Rites and Sites of Resistance: The Banality of Good*, edited by L. Cheliotis, 151–77. London: Pan Macmillan.

Segal, Eyal. 2010. 'Closure in Detective Fiction'. *Poetics Today* 31 (2): 153–215.

Shakespeare, William. 2000. *The Tragedy of King Richard III*. Edited by John Jowett. Oxford: Oxford University Press.

Siddiqi, Yumna. 2008. *Anxieties of Empire and the Fiction of Intrigue*. New York: Columbia University Press.

Siderits, Mark. 2007. 'Buddhist Reductionism and the Structure of Buddhist Ethics'. In *Indian Ethics: Classical Traditions and Contemporary Challenges*, edited by Purushottama Bilimoria, Joseph Prahbu and Renuka M. Sharma, 283–96. Aldershot: Ashgate.

Siegal, Erin. 2011. *Finding Fernanda: Two Mothers, One Child, and a Cross-Border Search for Truth*. Boston: Beacon.

Simpson, Philip. 2010. 'Noir and the Psycho Thriller'. In *A Companion to Crime Fiction*, edited by Charles J. Rzepka and Lee Horsley, 187–97. Oxford: Wiley-Blackwell.

Slaughter, Joseph R. 2007. *Human Rights, Inc: The World Novel, Narrative Form, and International Law*. New York: Fordham University Press.

Slovo, Gillian. 2007. 'Revealing Is Healing'. *New Humanist*, 31 May. https://newhumanist.org.uk/articles/585/revealing-is-healing.

———. 2009a. *Every Secret Thing: My Family, My Country*. New York: Hachette. Kindle edition.

———. 2009b. *Red Dust*. New York: Hachette.

Stoker, Bram. 2011. *Dracula*. Oxford: Oxford University Press.

Stratton, Florence. 2002. *Contemporary African Literature and the Politics of Gender*. E-book. Taylor and Francis.

Symons, Julian. 1992. *Bloody Murder: From the Detective Story to the Crime Novel*. New York: Mysterious Press.

Tambiah, Stanley Jeyaraja. 1992. *Buddhism Betrayed? Religion, Politics, and Violence in Sri Lanka*. Chicago: University of Chicago Press.

Thomas, Ronald R. 1994. 'The Fingerprint of the Foreigner: Colonizing the Criminal Body in 1890s Detective Fiction and Criminal Anthropology'. *ELH* 61 (3): 655–683.

Todorov, Tzvetan. 1975. *The Fantastic: A Structural Approach to a Literary Genre*. Ithaca: Cornell University Press.

———. 1977. *The Poetics of Prose*. Ithaca: Cornell University Press.

TRC (Truth and Reconciliation Commission). 1999. *Truth and Reconciliation Commission of South Africa Report, Volume I*. https://www.justice.gov.za/trc/report/finalreport/Volume%201.pdf.

Van Dine, S.S. 1928. 'Twenty Rules for Writing Detective Stories'. *The American Magazine*, September. http://www.thrillingdetective.com/trivia/triv288.html.

Walker, William O. 1991. *Opium and Foreign Policy: The Anglo-American Search for Order in Asia, 1912–1954*. Chapel Hill: University of North Carolina Press.

Way, Lyndon C.S. 2013. 'Orientalism in Online News: BBC Stories of Somali Piracy'. *Journal of African Media Studies* 5 (1): 19–33.

White, Luise. 2000. *Speaking with Vampires: Rumor and History in Colonial Africa*. Berkeley: University of California Press.

Wijesinha, R. 2003. 'The Continuing Colonial Mindset'. *Daily News* (Sri Lanka), 26 February. http://www.dailynews.lk/2003/02/26/fea02.html.

Willis, Jan. 2009. 'Dharma Diversity: The Many Forms and Faces of Buddhism in America'. Paper presented at the Lenz Foundation for American Buddhism Leadership Conference, Boulder, Naropa University. https://www.fredericklenzfoundation.org/sites/default/files/Jan-Willis-Dharma-Diversity.pdf.

Index

Abuelita (character in *The Long Night of White Chickens*) 80
Adler, Irene (character in 'A Scandal in Bohemia') 37
adoption 78, 89, 90, 93, 94, 95
Ahl (Ahlulkhair, character in *Crossbones*) 129-30, 132, 133, 134, 135-7, 138, 139-40, 141, 147, 149, 165
Akira (character in *When We Were Orphans*) 21, 27, 32, 38-9
Al-Shabaab 13, 131, 134, 140, 141, 142, 143, 144, 149
Al-Xaqq (the Truth, character in *Crossbones*) 133, 144
Ananda (character in *Anil's Ghost*) 44, 50, 51, 59, 60, 61
André (character in *Red Dust*) 102
Anil's Ghost (Michael Ondaatje, 2000) 40-67
  and Buddhism 59, 60-4
  and Cartesian split 52, 53
  and crime fiction genre 9-10, 40-1, 45-6, 49-50, 54-6, 63, 66-7, 154, 156, 159-60
  and fear 44, 47, 52, 55
  and forensic pathology 12, 41, 43, 44, 47, 49-50, 52-4, 55
  and identity 40, 41, 42, 43-5, 47-8, 51-2, 63, 64, 65-6, 67, 162, 169
  and Sri Lankan Civil War 11-12, 40-2, 43, 44, 46, 48, 51, 53, 54, 55-8, 61, 62, 63, 64, 66, 154, 159, 161
  and tactility 50-2, 67

see also Ananda; Diyasena, Gamini; Diyasena, Sarath; Lalitha; Manuel; Palipana; Sailor; Tissera, Anil
Árbenz, Jacobo 79, 80
Armas, Castillo 80
The Art of Political Murder (Francisco Goldman, 2010) 86, 92
An Artist of the Floating World (Kazuo Ishiguro, 1986) 35-6
Auden, W.H. 1, 2, 3, 4, 23, 152, 157, 161, 170-1

Banks, Christopher (character in *When We Were Orphans*) 14, 15-19, 20-5, 26, 27-8, 29, 31, 32-3, 34, 35, 36, 37, 38-9, 152, 161, 165, 168, 169-70
  father of 25, 31
  mother of 23-4, 25, 27, 30, 31, 34
Banks, Jennifer (character in *When We Were Orphans*) 25, 37, 169-70
Barcant, Sarah (character in *Red Dust*) 13, 98-9, 100, 104, 106, 107, 110, 111, 115, 120, 121-7, 128, 165-7, 168, 169
Barre, Siad 129, 145
Benzien, Jeffrey 112-13, 116, 118-19
Bessy (character in *Red Dust*) 104
Big Beard (character in *Crossbones*) 145, 164
Bile (character in *Crossbones*) 142-3
Botha, P.W. 111
Buddhism 59, 60-4

181

Caloosha (character in *Crossbones* and *Links*) 145
Cambara (character in *Crossbones* and *Knots*) 130, 151
Cat's Table (Michael Ondaatje, 2011) 42
Central Intelligence Agency (CIA, USA) 79, 89
China 11
civil war 4-5, 6, 7, 130, 158
Cold War 80, 87
Colombo (Sri Lanka) 41-2
colonial ideology and practice 4, 36, 39, 95; *see also* imperialism; neocolonialism
Conan Doyle, Arthur 29
crime fiction
  and the British Empire 3, 8
  as distraction 1, 170-1
  and double narrative 69
  forensic 52, 54
  genre subversion 2-3, 6-8, 10-11, 14, 132, 155-6, 157, 170, 171
  Golden Age 9, 15, 19, 22, 23, 29, 30, 31, 38, 121
  hegemonic 155
  and journalism 133-4
  and justice and ethics 1, 2, 157-8, 171
  metaphysical 68, 87, 152
  and the other 3-4, 6, 62
  post-modern 85-6
  and women 70-1
  see also detectives
Crossbones (Nuruddin Farah, 2011) 129-51
  and crime fiction genre 129, 131, 132-3, 134, 140-1, 150-1, 152-3, 154, 155, 159, 160
  and identity 162
  and justice 130, 144
  and national allegory 137
  and neocolonialism 161
  and piracy 131, 145, 146, 147-50
  and Somali conflict 13, 130-1, 153, 157
  and Somali Islam 145
  and Union of Islamic Courts (UIC) 142-4, 145
  see also Ahl; Al-Xaqq; Big Beard; Bile; Caloosha; Cambara; Dhoorre; Fidno; Jeebleh; Malik; Qasiir; Samir; Taxliil; Young Thing; Yusur

Darlington, *Lord* (character in *The Remains of the Day*) 36
De Mayo Puac, Flor (character in *The Long Night of White Chickens*) 12, 68-70, 71, 72, 73, 74-6, 77-8, 79, 80, 81-2, 83-4, 87, 88, 89, 90, 91, 92, 93, 94, 95, 96, 97, 153, 158, 161, 169
  father of 75
detectives
  female 124
  literary 17, 132, 140, 168
  returnee 1, 6, 7, 8-9, 13, 162-3, 164-7, 168, 169, 170
  traditional 34-5
  see also crime fiction
Dhoorre (character in *Crossbones*) 144
Diyasena, Gamini (character in *Anil's Ghost*) 45, 48, 49, 51, 52-4, 63, 64, 154, 158, 164, 169
Diyasena, Sarath (character in *Anil's Ghost*) 40, 41-2, 44, 46, 47, 50-1, 52-4, 55, 56, 57, 58, 59, 60, 65, 67, 154, 157, 158, 164, 165, 166, 169
Dracula (Bram Stoker, 1897) 96
dreaming 21

Ebla (character in *From a Crooked Rib*) 137

Eichmann, Adolf 108
El Sed (character in *The Long Night of White Chickens*) *see* De Mayo Puca, Flor, father of
The English Patient (Michael Ondaatje, 1992) 59
Englishness 15, 24, 26, 32, 33, 34
evil 2, 3, 4, 15, 16, 23, 27, 29, 31, 33, 58, 108, 110
exile 19, 24, 166, 167-8, 169; *see also* return and returnees

Faina (ship) 147
fear 26, 29, 31, 44, 47, 52, 55
Federal Bureau of Investigation (FBI, USA) 140, 141, 142, 161
female bodies 70-1, 72-3, 76
Fidno (character in *Crossbones*) 135, 139, 147, 149, 150
First, Ruth 99, 107, 109
Forbes, Ashley 116, 118-19
From a Crooked Rib (Nuruddin Farah, 1970) 137

Garcia Márquez, Gabriel 87-8
genre theory and expectations 3, 10, 11, 152, 170
Golden Age writing *see* crime fiction, Golden Age
Graetz, Ira (character in *The Long Night of White Chickens*) 80, 83, 89-90
Graetz, Mirabel (character in *The Long Night of White Chickens*) 80, 83
Graetz, Roger (character in *The Long Night of White Chickens*) 69, 70, 71, 72, 73, 74, 75, 76, 77-8, 79, 80, 81-2, 83-4, 85, 87, 89-90, 91, 94, 96-7, 153, 161, 168, 169
Great Expectations (Charles Dickens, 1861) 26
Grove of Ascetics (Sri Lanka) 59, 62, 64

Guatemala
 adoption law 94
 civil war 12, 47, 68, 69-70, 71-2, 81, 85, 86-7
 femicide 73-4
 history and politics 78-81, 92, 94-5

Hemmings, Sarah (character in *When We Were Orphans*) 36, 37
Hendricks, Dirk (character in *Red Dust*) 98, 100, 102, 106, 107-8, 109, 110, 111, 112, 113-14, 115-16, 117-18, 119, 123, 125, 127, 165
Hendricks, Katie (character in *Red Dust*) 125
Hoffman, Anna (character in *Red Dust*) 124
Hoffman, Ben (character in *Red Dust*) 98, 107, 120, 121, 122, 125, 126, 164, 166, 169
Holmes, Sherlock 10, 16, 18, 31, 37, 38
human rights 64, 81, 163-4; *see also* Truth and Reconciliation Commission
humanitarian aid 163-4

imperialism 162-3; *see also* colonial ideology and practice
India 36
International Settlement (Shanghai) *see* Shanghai
invented tradition 143
Invisible Children (charity) 163
Ishiguro, Kazuo 159

Japan 11, 29
Jeebleh (character in *Crossbones*) 130, 133, 134, 135, 139, 145
Johnstone, James 30
Jonas, Bongani 118
justice 1, 2, 99, 100, 127, 128, 130, 144, 154, 157-8, 171

Knots (Nuruddin Farah, 2006) 129
Kony, Joseph 163
Kruser, Gary 118
Kumara, Ruwan (character in *Anil's Ghost*) *see* Sailor
Kung, *Inspector* (character in *When We Were Orphans*) 38

Lalitha (character in *Anil's Ghost*) 50, 51
Latin America 87-8, 94
Liberation Tigers of Tamil Eelam (LTTE) 59
Links (Nuruddin Farah, 1978) 129
London 24, 37-8
The Long Night of White Chickens (Francisco Goldman, 1992) 68-97
  and adoption 78, 89, 90, 93, 94, 95
  and crime fiction genre 68, 69, 71, 77, 81, 82, 84, 85, 86, 87, 88, 89, 97, 153, 155, 159, 160
  and femicide 73-4
  and Guatemalan Civil War 12, 68, 69-70, 71-2, 74, 81, 85, 86-7, 93, 95, 96, 97, 153
  and identity 69, 83-4, 86, 97, 162, 169
  and neocolonialism 81, 95, 161, 170
  and truth 89-91, 93, 95-6
  see also Abuelita; De Mayo Puac, Flor; El Sed; Graetz, Ira; Graetz, Mirabel; Graetz, Roger; Los Quetzalitos; Martinez, Luis Moya; McCourt, Sylvia; Quix, Lucas Caycam; Tony
Los Quetzalitos (orphanage in *The Long Night of White Chickens*) 68, 78, 82, 89, 92, 93-4, 96
The Lost Mine (Agatha Christie, 1923) 3, 29-30

Malik (character in *Crossbones*) 129-31, 132, 133, 134, 135-6, 137,
138-9, 140, 141, 148, 149, 151, 153, 164, 165, 166
Manuel (character in *Anil's Ghost*) 46
Marikana massacre (South Africa) 5
Martinez, Luis Moya (character in *The Long Night of White Chickens*) 69, 75, 77, 82, 84, 85, 87, 88, 90, 92-3, 96, 97, 169
McCourt, Sylvia (character in *The Long Night of White Chickens*) 92-3
Medhurst, Cecil (character in *When We Were Orphans*) 36, 37
memory 22-3
Mogadishu (Somalia) 133, 138, 140, 161
Mpondo, Alex (character in *Red Dust*) 98, 100, 101, 104, 106, 107, 109, 110, 112, 114, 115, 116, 117-18, 119, 120, 122, 123, 125, 127, 165-6, 167
Muller, Marie (character in *Red Dust*) 103-4, 159, 167
Muller, Pieter (character in *Red Dust*) 98, 100, 101, 102, 103, 104, 105, 106, 107, 108, 109, 110, 120, 122, 127
The Murders in the Rue Morgue (Edgar Allen Poe, 1841) 165

nationalism 76-7
neocolonialism 81, 95, 161, 170; *see also* colonial ideology and practice
Nigeria 163
nostalgia 19, 23, 77

Ono, Masuji (character in *An Artist of the Floating World*) 35-6
opium trade 25-6, 29-31, 33
Orford, Margie 5
Orient 33
Oronsay (ship) 43-4
orphanhood 26-7, 168-9

A Pale View of Hills (Kazuo Ishiguro, 2005) 35
Palipana (character in *Anil's Ghost*) 43, 59-60, 61, 62, 63, 168, 169
Past Imperfect trilogy (Nuruddin Farah, 1978-2011) 129
Pearson, *Mr* (character in the *The Lost Mine*) 30
Philip, *Uncle* (character in *When We Were Orphans*) 31, 32, 38
piracy 13, 131, 137, 138, 145-50, 170
Puntland (Somalia) 135, 138, 140

Qasiir (character in *Crossbones*) 164, 165
Quix, Lucas Caycam (character in *The Long Night of White Chickens*) 78, 93

Red Dust (Gillian Slovo, 2000) 98-128
 and crime fiction genre 10, 12-13, 99, 100, 101, 127, 156, 159, 160
 and family metaphor 100-1
 and identity 162, 169
 and justice 99, 100, 127, 128, 154
 and TRC process 13, 99, 100, 101, 106, 110-12, 113-14, 115-18, 119, 120-1, 122, 124, 127, 154-5, 165
 see also André; Barcant, Sarah; Bessy; Hendricks, Dirk; Hendricks, Katie; Hoffman, Anna; Hoffman, Ben; Mpondo, Alex; Muller, Marie; Muller, Pieter; Sizela, James; Sizela, Steve; Smitsrivier
The Remains of the Day (Kazuo Ishiguro, 2009) 35
return and returnees 9, 83, 157, 159, 162, 165, 166, 167, 168, 169; *see also* exile
Roylott, *Dr* (character in 'The Speckled Band') 29, 30, 33
rumour 95, 96, 134-5

Sailor (character in *Anil's Ghost*) 41, 42, 43, 44, 46, 47, 49-50, 52, 53, 54, 55, 56, 58-9, 60, 61, 154, 157, 158, 164, 166
Samir (character in *Crossbones*) 141, 142
'A Scandal in Bohemia' (Arthur Conan Doyle, 1891) 37
Schreiner, Jennifer 118
Second World War 28-9, 35-6
Shanghai (China) 11, 19, 20-1, 23, 24, 25, 26, 27-8, 29, 31, 32, 35, 36, 37, 38, 39, 152
Sino-Japanese War (1937-1945) 14, 20-1, 26, 27-8, 35, 36
Sizela, James (character in *Red Dust*) 100, 103, 104, 105, 108, 109, 111, 120, 122, 123, 127, 158-9
Sizela, Steve (character in *Red Dust*) 98, 101, 102, 104, 105, 106-7, 108, 109, 110, 120, 123, 125, 159
Slovo, Gillian 99, 126
Smitsrivier (in *Red Dust*) 100, 101, 102-3, 105, 111-12, 121, 122, 124, 125, 126, 158, 159, 167
Somalia
 civil conflict 13, 133, 134, 139
 clan divisions 136
 national character 137-8, 142, 143-4
 and piracy 13, 131, 137, 138, 145-7, 148, 170
 and terrorism 142
Sri Lanka
 civil war 11-12, 40-2, 43, 59
 colonial rule 42
 as ethnocracy 59
 and medicine 45
Stevens (character in *The Remains of the Day*) 36

Taxliil (character in *Crossbones*) 131-2, 134, 135, 137, 138, 140, 141-2, 149, 153, 161, 166, 168

Temple of the Tooth (Kandy, Sri Lanka) 59
thrillers 4, 56, 57, 66, 100, 101, 105-6, 110, 121
Tissera, Anil (character in *Anil's Ghost*) 11-12, 40-6, 47-52, 53, 54, 55, 57, 58-60, 62, 63, 64-6, 67, 154, 157, 158, 159, 164, 166, 168, 169, 170
Tony (character in *The Long Night of White Chickens*) 76
truth 89-91, 93, 95-6, 100, 106, 123
Truth and Reconciliation Commission (TRC, South Africa) 10, 13, 98, 99-100, 101-2, 106, 107, 111, 112, 114-21, 154-5

Union of Islamic Courts (UIC, Somalia) 131, 139, 140, 142-4, 145
United Fruit Company 79-80, 94

violence
  apartheid 107, 108-9
  post-colonial 5-6, 156-7
  systemic 155
  against women 73-4

Wang Ku (character in *When We Were Orphans*) 31-2, 34
Watson, Dr (character in Sherlock Holmes stories) 18
Westenra, Lucy (character in *Dracula*) 96

When We Were Orphans (Kazuo Ishiguro, 2000) 14-39
  and crime fiction genre 9, 10, 11, 14, 15-16, 18, 21, 25, 26, 31, 32-3, 34, 36, 39, 152, 153, 154, 155, 159, 160
  and Englishness 15, 24, 26, 32, 33, 34
  and fear 26, 29, 31
  and identity 162, 169-70
  and memory 22-3
  and neocolonialism 161
  and opium trade 14, 25-6, 30, 31, 32, 33
  and orphanhood 26-7
  and Sino-Japanese War (1937-1945) 14, 20-2, 26, 27-8, 35, 36
  see also Akira; Banks, Christopher; Banks, Jennifer; Hemmings, Sarah; Kung, *Inspector*; Medhurst, Cecil; Philip, *Uncle*; Wang Ku
Williamson, Craig 109
worldliness 160-1
Wu Ling (character in the *The Lost Mine*) 30

Yellow Snake *see* Philip, *Uncle*
Yengeni, Tony 113, 116, 118
Young Thing (character in *Crossbones*) 144
Yusur (character in *Crossbones*) 132, 141